Praise for *Programming Collective Intelligence*

"I review a few books each year, and naturally, I read a fair number during the course of my work. And I have to admit that I have never had quite as much fun reading a preprint of a book as I have in reading this. Bravo! I cannot think of a better way for a developer to first learn these algorithms and methods, nor can I think of a better way for me (an old AI dog) to reinvigorate my knowledge of the details."

— Dan Russell, Uber Tech Lead, Google

"Toby's book does a great job of breaking down the complex subject matter of machine-learning algorithms into practical, easy-to-understand examples that can be used directly to analyze social interaction across the Web today. If I had this book two years ago, it would have saved me precious time going down some fruitless paths."

— Tim Wolters, CTO, Collective Intellect

"*Programming Collective Intelligence* is a stellar achievement in providing a comprehensive collection of computational methods for relating vast amounts of data. Specifically, it applies these techniques in context of the Internet, finding value in otherwise isolated data islands. If you develop for the Internet, this book is a must-have."

— Paul Tyma, Senior Software Engineer, Google

Programming Collective Intelligence

Other resources from O'Reilly

Related titles
Web 2.0 Report
Learning Python
Mastering Algorithms with C

AI for Game Developers
Mastering Algorithms with Perl

oreilly.com
oreilly.com is more than a complete catalog of O'Reilly books. You'll also find links to news, events, articles, weblogs, sample chapters, and code examples.

oreillynet.com is the essential portal for developers interested in open and emerging technologies, including new platforms, programming languages, and operating systems.

Conferences
O'Reilly brings diverse innovators together to nurture the ideas that spark revolutionary industries. We specialize in documenting the latest tools and systems, translating the innovator's knowledge into useful skills for those in the trenches. Visit *conferences.oreilly.com* for our upcoming events.

Safari Bookshelf (*safari.oreilly.com*) is the premier online reference library for programmers and IT professionals. Conduct searches across more than 1,000 books. Subscribers can zero in on answers to time-critical questions in a matter of seconds. Read the books on your Bookshelf from cover to cover or simply flip to the page you need. Try it today for free.

Programming Collective Intelligence
Building Smart Web 2.0 Applications

Toby Segaran

O'REILLY®

Beijing · Cambridge · Farnham · Köln · Paris · Sebastopol · Taipei · Tokyo

Programming Collective Intelligence
by Toby Segaran

Published by O'Reilly Media, Inc., 1005 Gravenstein Highway North, Sebastopol, CA 95472.

O'Reilly books may be purchased for educational, business, or sales promotional use. Online editions are also available for most titles (*safari.oreilly.com*). For more information, contact our corporate/institutional sales department: (800) 998-9938 or *corporate@oreilly.com*.

Editor: Mary Treseler O'Brien
Production Editor: Sarah Schneider
Copyeditor: Amy Thomson
Proofreader: Sarah Schneider

Indexer: Julie Hawks
Cover Designer: Karen Montgomery
Interior Designer: David Futato
Illustrators: Robert Romano and Jessamyn Read

Printing History:

August 2007:   First Edition.

 This book uses RepKover™, a durable and flexible lay-flat binding.

ISBN: 978-0-596-52932-1
[M]   [5/08]

Table of Contents

Foreword

When *Time* magazine picked "You" as the Person of the Year for 2006, it cemented the idea that Web 2.0 is about "user-generated content"—and that Wikipedia, YouTube, and MySpace are the heart of the Web 2.0 revolution. The true story is far more complex than that. The content that users contribute explicitly to Web 2.0 sites is the small fraction that is visible above the surface. Eighty percent of what matters is below, in the dark matter of implicitly contributed data.

In many ways, the defining moment of the Web 2.0 revolution was Google's invention of PageRank, the realization that every link on the World Wide Web was freighted with hidden meaning: a link is a vote about the importance of a site. Understanding those votes, and the relative importance of the sites that were voting, gave better search results than merely studying the web pages themselves. It was the breakthrough that launched Google on its path to becoming the most important tech company of the new century. PageRank is now one of hundreds of implicit factors that Google uses in deciding which search results to feature.

No one would characterize Google as a "user-generated content" company, yet it is clearly at the very heart of Web 2.0. That's why I prefer the phrase "harnessing collective intelligence" as the touchstone of the revolution. A link is user-generated content, but PageRank is a technique for extracting intelligence from that content. So are Flickr's "interestingness" algorithm, Amazon's "people who bought this product also bought..." feature, Last.fm's algorithms for "similar artist radio," eBay's reputation system, and Google's AdSense.

I defined Web 2.0 as "the design of systems that harness network effects to get better the more people use them." Getting users to participate is the first step. Learning from those users and shaping your site based on what they do and pay attention to is the second step.

In *Programming Collective Intelligence*, Toby Segaran teaches algorithms and techniques for extracting meaning from data, including user data. This is the programmer's toolbox for Web 2.0. It's no longer enough to know how to build a database-backed web site. If you want to succeed, you need to know how to mine the data that users are adding, both explicitly and as a side effect of their activity on your site.

There's been a lot written about Web 2.0 since we first coined the term in 2004, but in many ways, Toby's book is the first practical guide to programming Web 2.0 applications.

—Tim O'Reilly

Preface

The increasing number of people contributing to the Internet, either deliberately or incidentally, has created a huge set of data that gives us millions of potential insights into user experience, marketing, personal tastes, and human behavior in general. This book provides an introduction to the emerging field of *collective intelligence*. It covers ways to get hold of interesting datasets from many web sites you've probably heard of, ideas on how to collect data from users of your own applications, and many different ways to analyze and understand the data once you've found it.

This book's goal is to take you beyond simple database-backed applications and teach you how to write smarter programs to take advantage of the information you and others collect every day.

Prerequisites

The code examples in this book are written in Python, and familiarity with Python programming will help, but I provide explanations of all the algorithms so that programmers of other languages can follow. The Python code will be particularly easy to follow for those who know high-level languages like Ruby or Perl. This book is not intended as a guide for learning programming, so it's important that you've done enough coding to be familiar with the basic concepts. If you have a good understanding of recursion and some basic functional programming, you'll find the material even easier.

This book does not assume you have any prior knowledge of data analysis, machine learning, or statistics. I've tried to explain mathematical concepts in as simple a manner as possible, but having some knowledge of trigonometry and basic statistics will be help you understand the algorithms.

Style of Examples

The code examples in each section are written in a tutorial style, which encourages you to build the applications in stages and get a good appreciation for how the algorithms work. In most cases, after creating a new function or method, you'll use it in an interactive session to understand how it works. The algorithms are mostly simple variants that can be extended in many ways. By working through the examples and testing them interactively, you'll get insights into ways that you might improve them for your own applications.

Why Python?

Although the algorithms are described in words with explanations of the formulae involved, it's much more useful (and probably easier to follow) to have actual code for the algorithms and example problems. All the example code in this book is written in Python, an excellent, high-level language. I chose Python because it is:

Concise

    Code written in dynamically typed languages such as Python tends to be shorter than code written in other mainstream languages. This means there's less typing for you when working through the examples, but it also means that it's easier to fit the algorithm in your head and really understand what it's doing.

Easy to read

    Python has at times been referred to as "executable pseudocode." While this is clearly an exaggeration, it makes the point that most experienced programmers can read Python code and understand what it is supposed to do. Some of the less obvious constructs in Python are explained in the "Python Tips" section below.

Easily extensible

    Python comes standard with many libraries, including those for mathematical functions, XML (Extensible Markup Language) parsing, and downloading web pages. The nonstandard libraries used in the book, such as the RSS (Really Simple Syndication) parser and the SQLite interface, are free and easy to download, install, and use.

Interactive

    When working through an example, it's useful to try out the functions as you write them without writing another program just for testing. Python can run programs directly from the command line, and it also has an interactive prompt that lets you type in function calls, create objects, and test packages interactively.

Multiparadigm

    Python supports object-oriented, procedural, and functional styles of programming. Machine-learning algorithms vary greatly, and the clearest way to implement one may use a different paradigm than another. Sometimes it's useful to pass around functions as parameters and other times to capture state in an object. Python supports both approaches.

Multiplatform and free

Python has a single reference implementation for all the major platforms and is free for all of them. The code described in this book will work on Windows, Linux, and Macintosh.

Python Tips

For beginners interested in learning about programming in Python, I recommend reading *Learning Python* by Mark Lutz and David Ascher (O'Reilly), which gives an excellent overview. Programmers of other languages should find the Python code relatively easy to follow, although be aware that throughout this book I use some of Python's idiosyncratic syntax because it lets me more directly express the algorithm or fundamental concepts. Here's a quick overview for those of you who aren't Python programmers:

List and dictionary constructors

Python has a good set of primitive types and two that are used heavily throughout this book are *list* and *dictionary*. A list is an ordered list of any type of value, and it is constructed with square brackets:

```
number_list=[1,2,3,4]
string_list=['a', 'b', 'c', 'd']
mixed_list=['a', 3, 'c', 8]
```

A dictionary is an unordered set of key/value pairs, similar to a hash map in other languages. It is constructed with curly braces:

```
ages={'John':24,'Sarah':28,'Mike':31}
```

The elements of lists and dictionaries can be accessed using square brackets after the list name:

```
string_list[2]    # returns 'b'
ages['Sarah']     # returns 28
```

Significant Whitespace

Unlike most languages, Python actually uses the indentation of the code to define code blocks. Consider this snippet:

```
if x==1:
  print 'x is 1'
  print 'Still in if block'
print 'outside if block'
```

The interpreter knows that the first two print statements are executed when x is 1 because the code is indented. Indentation can be any number of spaces, as long as it is consistent. This book uses two spaces for indentation. When entering the code you'll need to be careful to copy the indentation correctly.

List comprehensions

A *list comprehension* is a convenient way of converting one list to another by filtering and applying functions to it. A list comprehension is written as:

```
[expression for variable in list]
```

or:

```
[expression for variable in list if condition]
```

For example, the following code:

```
l1=[1,2,3,4,5,6,7,8,9]
print [v*10 for v in l1 if v1>4]
```

would print this list:

```
[50,60,70,80,90]
```

List comprehensions are used frequently in this book because they are an extremely concise way to apply a function to an entire list or to remove bad items. The other manner in which they are often used is with the dict constructor:

```
l1=[1,2,3,4,5,6,7,8,9]
timesten=dict([(v,v*10) for v in l1])
```

This code will create a dictionary with the original list being the keys and each item multiplied by 10 as the value:

```
{1:10,2:20,3:30,4:40,5:50,6:60,7:70,8:80,9:90}
```

Open APIs

The algorithms for synthesizing collective intelligence require data from many users. In addition to machine-learning algorithms, this book discusses a number of Open Web APIs (application programming interfaces). These are ways that companies allow you to freely access data from their web sites by means of a specified protocol; you can then write programs that download and process the data. This data usually consists of contributions from the site's users, which can be mined for new insights. In some cases, there is a Python library available to access these APIs; if not, it's pretty straightforward to create your own interface to access the data using Python's built-in libraries for downloading data and parsing XML.

Here are some of the web sites with open APIs that you'll see in this book:

del.icio.us

A social bookmarking application whose open API lets you download links by tag or from a specific user.

Kayak

A travel site with an API for conducting searches for flights and hotels from within your own programs.

eBay

An online auction site with an API that allows you to query items that are currently for sale.

Hot or Not

A rating and dating site with an API to search for people and get their ratings and demographic information.

Akismet

An API for collaborative spam filtering.

A huge number of potential applications can be built by processing data from a single source, by combining data from multiple sources, and even by combining external information with input from your own users. The ability to harness data created by people in a variety of ways on different sites is a principle element of creating collective intelligence. A good starting point for finding more web sites with open APIs is ProgrammableWeb (*http://www.programmableweb.com*).

Overview of the Chapters

Every algorithm in the book is motivated by a realistic problem that can, I hope, be easily understood by all readers. I have tried to avoid problems that require a great deal of domain knowledge, and I have focused on problems that, while complex, are easy for most people to relate to.

Chapter 1, *Introduction to Collective Intelligence*

Explains the concepts behind machine learning, how it is applied in many different fields, and how it can be used to draw new conclusions from data gathered from many different people.

Chapter 2, *Making Recommendations*

Introduces the *collaborative filtering* techniques used by many online retailers to recommend products or media. The chapter includes a section on recommending links to people from a social bookmarking site, and building a move recommendation system from the MovieLens dataset.

Chapter 3, *Discovering Groups*

Builds on some of the ideas in Chapter 2 and introduces two different methods of *clustering*, which automatically detect groups of similar items in a large dataset. This chapter demonstrates the use of clustering to find groups on a set of popular weblogs and on people's desires from a social networking web site.

Chapter 4, *Searching and Ranking*

Describes the various parts of a search engine including the crawler, indexer, and query engine. It covers the *PageRank* algorithm for scoring pages based on inbound links and shows you how to create a *neural network* that learns which keywords are associated with different results.

Chapter 5, *Optimization*

Introduces algorithms for *optimization*, which are designed to search millions of possible solutions to a problem and choose the best one. The wide variety of uses for these algorithms is demonstrated with examples that find the best flights for a group of people traveling to the same location, find the best way of matching students to dorms, and lay out a network with the minimum number of crossed lines.

Chapter 6, *Document Filtering*

Demonstrates *Bayesian filtering*, which is used in many free and commercial spam filters for automatically classifying documents based on the type of words and other features that appear in the document. This is applied to a set of RSS search results to demonstrate automatic classification of the entries.

Chapter 7, *Modeling with Decision Trees*

Introduces *decision trees* as a method not only of making predictions, but also of modeling the way the decisions are made. The first decision tree is built with hypothetical data from server logs and is used to predict whether or not a user is likely to become a premium subscriber. The other examples use data from real web sites to model real estate prices and "hotness."

Chapter 8, *Building Price Models*

Approaches the problem of predicting numerical values rather than classifications using *k-nearest neighbors* techniques, and applies the optimization algorithms from Chapter 5. These methods are used in conjunction with the eBay API to build a system for predicting eventual auction prices for items based on a set of properties.

Chapter 9, *Advanced Classification: Kernel Methods and SVMs*

Shows how *support-vector machines* can be used to match people in online dating sites or when searching for professional contacts. Support-vector machines are a fairly advanced technique and this chapter compares them to other methods.

Chapter 10, *Finding Independent Features*

Introduces a relatively new technique called *non-negative matrix factorization*, which is used to find the independent features in a dataset. In many datasets the items are constructed as a composite of different features that we don't know in advance; the idea here is to detect these features. This technique is demonstrated on a set of news articles, where the stories themselves are used to detect themes, one or more of which may apply to a given story.

Chapter 11, *Evolving Intelligence*

Introduces *genetic programming*, a very sophisticated set of techniques that goes beyond optimization and actually builds algorithms using evolutionary ideas to solve a particular problem. This is demonstrated by a simple game in which the computer is initially a poor player that improves its skill by improving its own code the more the game is played.

Chapter 12, *Algorithm Summary*

Reviews all the machine-learning and statistical algorithms described in the book and compares them to a set of artificial problems. This will help you understand how they work and visualize the way that each of them divides data.

Appendix A, *Third-Party Libraries*

Gives information on third-party libraries used in the book, such as where to find them and how to install them.

Appendix B, *Mathematical Formulas*

Contains formulae, descriptions, and code for many of the mathematical concepts introduced throughout the book.

Exercises at the end of each chapter give ideas of ways to extend the algorithms and make them more powerful.

Conventions

The following typographical conventions are used in this book:

Plain text

Indicates menu titles, menu options, menu buttons, and keyboard accelerators (such as Alt and Ctrl).

Italic

Indicates new terms, URLs, email addresses, filenames, file extensions, pathnames, directories, and Unix utilities.

Constant width

Indicates commands, options, switches, variables, attributes, keys, functions, types, classes, namespaces, methods, modules, properties, parameters, values, objects, events, event handlers, XML tags, HTML tags, macros, the contents of files, or the output from commands.

Constant width bold

Shows commands or other text that should be typed literally by the user.

Constant width italic

Shows text that should be replaced with user-supplied values.

 This icon signifies a tip, suggestion, or general note.

Using Code Examples

This book is here to help you get your job done. In general, you may use the code in this book in your programs and documentation. You do not need to contact us for permission unless you're reproducing a significant portion of the code. For example, writing a program that uses several chunks of code from this book does not require permission. Selling or distributing a CD-ROM of examples from O'Reilly books *does* require permission. Answering a question by citing this book and quoting example code does not require permission. Incorporating a significant amount of example code from this book into your product's documentation *does* require permission.

We appreciate, but do not require, attribution. An attribution usually includes the title, author, publisher, and ISBN. For example: "*Programming Collective Intelligence* by Toby Segaran. Copyright 2007 Toby Segaran, 978-0-596-52932-1."

If you feel your use of code examples falls outside fair use or the permission given above, feel free to contact us at *permissions@oreilly.com*.

How to Contact Us

Please address comments and questions concerning this book to the publisher:

O'Reilly Media, Inc.
1005 Gravenstein Highway North
Sebastopol, CA 95472
800-998-9938 (in the United States or Canada)
707-829-0515 (international or local)
707-829-0104 (fax)

We have a web page for this book where we list errata, examples, and any additional information. You can access this page at:

http://www.oreilly.com/catalog/9780596529321

To comment or ask technical questions about this book, send email to:

bookquestions@oreilly.com

For more information about our books, conferences, Resource Centers, and the O'Reilly Network, see our web site at:

http://www.oreilly.com

Safari® Books Online

 When you see a Safari® Books Online icon on the cover of your favorite technology book, that means the book is available online through the O'Reilly Network Safari Bookshelf.

Safari offers a solution that's better than e-books. It's a virtual library that lets you easily search thousands of top tech books, cut and paste code samples, download chapters, and find quick answers when you need the most accurate, current information. Try it for free at *http://safari.oreilly.com*.

Acknowledgments

I'd like to express my gratitude to everyone at O'Reilly involved in the development and production of this book. First, I'd like to thank Nat Torkington for telling me that the idea had merit and was worth pitching, Mike Hendrickson and Brian Jepson for listening to my pitch and getting me excited to write the book, and especially Mary O'Brien who took over as editor from Brian and could always assuage my fears that the project was too much for me.

On the production team, I want to thank Marlowe Shaeffer, Rob Romano, Jessamyn Read, Amy Thomson, and Sarah Schneider for turning my illustrations and writing into something you might actually want to look at.

Thanks to everyone who took part in the review of the book, specifically Paul Tyma, Matthew Russell, Jeff Hammerbacher, Terry Camerlengo, Andreas Weigend, Daniel Russell, and Tim Wolters.

Thanks to my parents.

Finally, I owe so much gratitude to several of my friends who helped me brainstorm ideas for the book and who were always understanding when I had no time for them: Andrea Matthews, Jeff Beene, Laura Miyakawa, Neil Stroup, and Brooke Blumenstein. Writing this book would have been much harder without your support and I certainly would have missed out on some of the more entertaining examples.

## CHAPTER 1

Introduction to Collective Intelligence

Netflix is an online DVD rental company that lets people choose movies to be sent to their homes, and makes recommendations based on the movies that customers have previously rented. In late 2006 it announced a prize of $1 million to the first person to improve the accuracy of its recommendation system by 10 percent, along with progress prizes of $50,000 to the current leader each year for as long as the contest runs. Thousands of teams from all over the world entered and, as of April 2007, the leading team has managed to score an improvement of 7 percent. By using data about which movies each customer enjoyed, Netflix is able to recommend movies to other customers that they may never have even heard of and keep them coming back for more. Any way to improve its recommendation system is worth a lot of money to Netflix.

The search engine Google was started in 1998, at a time when there were already several big search engines, and many assumed that a new player would never be able to take on the giants. The founders of Google, however, took a completely new approach to ranking search results by using the links on millions of web sites to decide which pages were most relevant. Google's search results were so much better than those of the other players that by 2004 it handled 85 percent of searches on the Web. Its founders are now among the top 10 richest people in the world.

What do these two companies have in common? They both drew new conclusions and created new business opportunities by using sophisticated algorithms to combine data collected from many different people. The ability to collect information and the computational power to interpret it has enabled great collaboration opportunities and a better understanding of users and customers. This sort of work is happening all over the place—dating sites want to help people find their best match more quickly, companies that predict changes in airplane ticket prices are cropping up, and just about everyone wants to understand their customers better in order to create more targeted advertising.

These are just a few examples in the exciting field of collective intelligence, and the proliferation of new services means there are new opportunities appearing every day. I believe that understanding machine learning and statistical methods will become ever more important in a wide variety of fields, but particularly in interpreting and organizing the vast amount of information that is being created by people all over the world.

What Is Collective Intelligence?

People have used the phrase *collective intelligence* for decades, and it has become increasingly popular and more important with the advent of new communications technologies. Although the expression may bring to mind ideas of group consciousness or supernatural phenomena, when technologists use this phrase they usually mean the combining of behavior, preferences, or ideas of a group of people to create novel insights.

Collective intelligence was, of course, possible before the Internet. You don't need the Web to collect data from disparate groups of people, combine it, and analyze it. One of the most basic forms of this is a survey or census. Collecting answers from a large group of people lets you draw statistical conclusions about the group that no individual member would have known by themselves. Building new conclusions from independent contributors is really what collective intelligence is all about.

A well-known example is financial markets, where a price is not set by one individual or by a coordinated effort, but by the trading behavior of many independent people all acting in what they believe is their own best interest. Although it seems counterintuitive at first, *futures markets*, in which many participants trade contracts based on their beliefs about future prices, are considered to be better at predicting prices than experts who independently make projections. This is because these markets combine the knowledge, experience, and insight of thousands of people to create a projection rather than relying on a single person's persepective.

Although methods for collective intelligence existed before the Internet, the ability to collect information from thousands or even millions of people on the Web has opened up many new possibilities. At all times, people are using the Internet for making purchases, doing research, seeking out entertainment, and building their own web sites. All of this behavior can be monitored and used to derive information without ever having to interrupt the user's intentions by asking him questions. There are a huge number of ways this information can be processed and interpreted. Here are a couple of key examples that show the contrasting approaches:

- *Wikipedia* is an online encyclopedia created entirely from user contributions. Any page can be created or edited by anyone, and there are a small number of administrators who monitor repeated abuses. Wikipedia has more entries than any other encyclopedia, and despite some manipulation by malicious users, it is generally believed to be accurate on most subjects. This is an example of collective intelligence because each article is maintained by a large group of people and the result is an encyclopedia far larger than any single coordinated group has been able to create. The Wikipedia software does not do anything particularly intelligent with user contributions—it simply tracks the changes and displays the latest version.

- *Google*, mentioned earlier, is the world's most popular Internet search engine, and was the first search engine to rate web pages based on how many other pages link to them. This method of rating takes information about what thousands of people have said about a particular web page and uses that information to rank the results in a search. This is a very different example of collective intelligence. Where Wikipedia explicitly invites users of the site to contribute, Google extracts the important information from what web-content creators do on their own sites and uses it to generate scores for its users.

While Wikipedia is a great resource and an impressive example of collective intelligence, it owes its existence much more to the user base that contributes information than it does to clever algorithms in the software. This book focuses on the other end of the spectrum, covering algorithms like Google's PageRank, which take user data and perform calculations to create new information that can enhance the user experience. Some data is collected explicitly, perhaps by asking people to rate things, and some is collected casually, for example by watching what people buy. In both cases, the important thing is not just to collect and display the information, but to process it in an intelligent way and generate new information.

This book will show you ways to collect data through open APIs, and it will cover a variety of machine-learning algorithms and statistical methods. This combination will allow you to set up collective intelligence methods on data collected from your own applications, and also to collect and experiment with data from other places.

What Is Machine Learning?

Machine learning is a subfield of artificial intelligence (AI) concerned with algorithms that allow computers to *learn*. What this means, in most cases, is that an algorithm is given a set of data and infers information about the properties of the data—and that information allows it to make predictions about other data that it might see in the future. This is possible because almost all nonrandom data contains patterns, and these patterns allow the machine to generalize. In order to generalize, it trains a *model* with what it determines are the important aspects of the data.

To understand how models come to be, consider a simple example in the otherwise complex field of email filtering. Suppose you receive a lot of spam that contains the words "online pharmacy." As a human being, you are well equipped to recognize patterns, and you quickly determine that any message with the words "online pharmacy" is spam and should be moved directly to the trash. This is a generalization—you have, in fact, created a mental model of what is spam. After you report several of these messages as spam, a machine-learning algorithm designed to filter spam should be able to make the same generalization.

There are many different machine-learning algorithms, all with different strengths and suited to different types of problems. Some, such as decision trees, are transparent, so that an observer can totally understand the reasoning process undertaken by the machine. Others, such as neural networks, are *black box*, meaning that they produce an answer, but it's often very difficult to reproduce the reasoning behind it.

Many machine-learning algorithms rely heavily on mathematics and statistics. According to the definition I gave earlier, you could even say that simple correlation analysis and regression are both basic forms of machine learning. This book does not assume that the reader has a lot of knowledge of statistics, so I have tried to explain the statistics used in as straightforward a manner as possible.

Limits of Machine Learning

Machine learning is not without its weaknesses. The algorithms vary in their ability to generalize over large sets of patterns, and a pattern that is unlike any seen by the algorithm before is quite likely to be misinterpreted. While humans have a vast amount of cultural knowledge and experience to draw upon, as well as a remarkable ability to recognize similar situations when making decisions about new information, machine-learning methods can only generalize based on the data that has already been seen, and even then in a very limited manner.

The spam-filtering method you'll see in this book is based on the appearance of words or phrases without any regard to what they mean or to sentence structures. Although it's theoretically possible to build an algorithm that would take grammar into account, this is rarely done in practice because the effort required would be disproportionately large compared to the improvement in the algorithm. Understanding the meaning of words or their relevance to a person's life would require far more information than spam filters, in their current incarnation, can access.

In addition, although they vary in their propensity for doing so, all machine-learning methods suffer from the possibility of overgeneralizing. As with most things in life, strong generalizations based on a few examples are rarely entirely accurate. It's certainly possible that you could receive an important email message from a friend that contains the words "online pharmacy." In this case, you would tell the algorithm that the message is not spam, and it might infer that messages from that particular friend are acceptable. The nature of many machine-learning algorithms is that they can continue to learn as new information arrives.

Real-Life Examples

There are many sites on the Internet currently collecting data from many different people and using machine learning and statistical methods to benefit from it. Google is likely the largest effort—it not only uses web links to rank pages, but it constantly gathers information on when advertisements are clicked by different users, which allows Google to target the advertising more effectively. In Chapter 4 you'll learn about search engines and the PageRank algorithm, an important part of Google's ranking system.

Other examples include web sites with recommendation systems. Sites like Amazon and Netflix use information about the things people buy or rent to determine which people or items are similar to one another, and then make recommendations based on purchase history. Other sites like Pandora and Last.fm use your ratings of different bands and songs to create custom radio stations with music they think you will enjoy. Chapter 2 covers ways to build recommendation systems.

Prediction markets are also a form of collective intelligence. One of the most well known of these is the Hollywood Stock Exchange (*http://hsx.com*), where people trade stocks on movies and movie stars. You can buy or sell a stock at the current price knowing that its ultimate value will be one millionth of the movie's actual opening box office number. Because the price is set by trading behavior, the value is not chosen by any one individual but by the behavior of the group, and the current price can be seen as the whole group's prediction of box office numbers for the movie. The predictions made by the Hollywood Stock Exchange are routinely better than those made by individual experts.

Some dating sites, such as eHarmony, use information collected from participants to determine who would be a good match. Although these companies tend to keep their methods for matching people secret, it is quite likely that any successful approach would involve a constant reevaluation based on whether the chosen matches were successful or not.

Other Uses for Learning Algorithms

The methods described in this book are not new, and although the examples focus on Internet-based collective intelligence problems, knowledge of machine-learning algorithms can be helpful for software developers in many other fields. They are particularly useful in areas that deal with large datasets that can be searched for interesting patterns, for example:

Biotechnology
> Advances in sequencing and screening technology have created massive datasets of many different kinds, such as DNA sequences, protein structures, compound

screens, and RNA expression. Machine-learning techniques are applied extensively to all of these kinds of data in an effort to find patterns that can increase understanding of biological processes.

Financial fraud detection

Credit card companies are constantly searching for new ways to detect if transactions are fraudulent. To this end, they have employed such techniques as neural networks and inductive logic to verify transactions and catch improper usage.

Machine vision

Interpreting images from a video camera for military or surveillance purposes is an active area of research. Many machine-learning techniques are used to try to automatically detect intruders, identify vehicles, or recognize faces. Particularly interesting is the use of unsupervised techniques like *independent component analysis*, which finds interesting features in large datasets.

Product marketing

For a very long time, understanding demographics and trends was more of an art form than a science. Recently, the increased ability to collect data from consumers has opened up opportunities for machine-learning techniques such as clustering to better understand the natural divisions that exist in markets and to make better predictions about future trends.

Supply chain optimization

Large organizations can save millions of dollars by having their supply chains run effectively and accurately predict demand for products in different areas. The number of ways in which a supply chain can be constructed is massive, as is the number of factors that can potentially affect demand. Optimization and learning techniques are frequently used to analyze these datasets.

Stock market analysis

Ever since there has been a stock market, people have tried to use mathematics to make more money. As participants have become ever more sophisticated, it has become necessary to analyze larger sets of data and use advanced techniques to detect patterns.

National security

A huge amount of information is collected by government agencies around the world, and the analysis of this data requires computers to detect patterns and associate them with potential threats.

These are just a few examples of where machine learning is now used heavily. Since the trend is toward the creation of more information, it is likely that more fields will come to rely on machine learning and statistical techniques as the amount of information stretches beyond people's ability to manage in the old ways.

Given how much new information is being made available every day, there are clearly many more possibilities. Once you learn about a few machine-learning algorithms, you'll start seeing places to apply them just about everywhere.

## CHAPTER 2

Making Recommendations

To begin the tour of collective intelligence, I'm going to show you ways to use the preferences of a group of people to make recommendations to other people. There are many applications for this type of information, such as making product recommendations for online shopping, suggesting interesting web sites, or helping people find music and movies. This chapter shows you how to build a system for finding people who share tastes and for making automatic recommendations based on things that other people like.

You've probably come across recommendation engines before when using an online shopping site like Amazon. Amazon tracks the purchasing habits of all its shoppers, and when you log onto the site, it uses this information to suggest products you might like. Amazon can even suggest movies you might like, even if you've only bought books from it before. Some online concert ticket agencies will look at the history of shows you've seen before and alert you to upcoming shows that might be of interest. Sites like *reddit.com* let you vote on links to other web sites and then use your votes to suggest other links you might find interesting.

From these examples, you can see that preferences can be collected in many different ways. Sometimes the data are items that people have purchased, and opinions about these items might be represented as yes/no votes or as ratings from one to five. In this chapter, we'll look at different ways of representing these cases so that they'll all work with the same set of algorithms, and we'll create working examples with movie critic scores and social bookmarking.

Collaborative Filtering

You know that the low-tech way to get recommendations for products, movies, or entertaining web sites is to ask your friends. You also know that some of your friends have better "taste" than others, something you've learned over time by observing whether they usually like the same things as you. As more and more options become available, it becomes less practical to decide what you want by asking a small group of people, since they may not be aware of all the options. This is why a set of techniques called *collaborative filtering* was developed.

A collaborative filtering algorithm usually works by searching a large group of people and finding a smaller set with tastes similar to yours. It looks at other things they like and combines them to create a ranked list of suggestions. There are several different ways of deciding which people are similar and combining their choices to make a list; this chapter will cover a few of these.

The term *collaborative filtering* was first used by David Goldberg at Xerox PARC in 1992 in a paper called "Using collaborative filtering to weave an information tapestry." He designed a system called *Tapestry* that allowed people to annotate documents as either interesting or uninteresting and used this information to filter documents for other people.

There are now hundreds of web sites that employ some sort of collaborative filtering algorithm for movies, music, books, dating, shopping, other web sites, podcasts, articles, and even jokes.

Collecting Preferences

The first thing you need is a way to represent different people and their preferences. In Python, a very simple way to do this is to use a *nested dictionary*. If you'd like to work through the example in this section, create a file called *recommendations.py*, and insert the following code to create the dataset:

```
# A dictionary of movie critics and their ratings of a small
# set of movies
critics={'Lisa Rose': {'Lady in the Water': 2.5, 'Snakes on a Plane': 3.5,
 'Just My Luck': 3.0, 'Superman Returns': 3.5, 'You, Me and Dupree': 2.5,
 'The Night Listener': 3.0},
 'Gene Seymour': {'Lady in the Water': 3.0, 'Snakes on a Plane': 3.5,
 'Just My Luck': 1.5, 'Superman Returns': 5.0, 'The Night Listener': 3.0,
 'You, Me and Dupree': 3.5},
 'Michael Phillips': {'Lady in the Water': 2.5, 'Snakes on a Plane': 3.0,
 'Superman Returns': 3.5, 'The Night Listener': 4.0},
 'Claudia Puig': {'Snakes on a Plane': 3.5, 'Just My Luck': 3.0,
 'The Night Listener': 4.5, 'Superman Returns': 4.0,
 'You, Me and Dupree': 2.5},
 'Mick LaSalle': {'Lady in the Water': 3.0, 'Snakes on a Plane': 4.0,
 'Just My Luck': 2.0, 'Superman Returns': 3.0, 'The Night Listener': 3.0,
 'You, Me and Dupree': 2.0},
 'Jack Matthews': {'Lady in the Water': 3.0, 'Snakes on a Plane': 4.0,
 'The Night Listener': 3.0, 'Superman Returns': 5.0, 'You, Me and Dupree': 3.5},
 'Toby': {'Snakes on a Plane':4.5,'You, Me and Dupree':1.0,'Superman Returns':4.0}}
```

You will be working with Python interactively in this chapter, so you should save *recommendations.py* somewhere where the Python interactive interpreter can find it. This could be in the *python/Lib* directory, but the easiest way to do it is to start the Python interpreter in the same directory in which you saved the file.

This dictionary uses a ranking from 1 to 5 as a way to express how much each of these movie critics (and I) liked a given movie. No matter how preferences are expressed, you need a way to map them onto numerical values. If you were building a shopping site, you might use a value of 1 to indicate that someone had bought an item in the past and a value of 0 to indicate that they had not. For a site where people vote on news stories, values of −1, 0, and 1 could be used to represent "disliked," "didn't vote," and "liked," as shown in Table 2-1.

Table 2-1. Possible mappings of user actions to numerical scores

Concert tickets		Online shopping		Site recommender	
Bought	1	Bought	2	Liked	1
Didn't buy	0	Browsed	1	No vote	0
		Didn't buy	0	Disliked	−1

Using a dictionary is convenient for experimenting with the algorithms and for illustrative purposes. It's easy to search and modify the dictionary. Start your Python interpreter and try a few commands:

```
c:\code\collective\chapter2> python
Python 2.4.1 (#65, Mar 30 2005, 09:13:57) [MSC v.1310 32 bit (Intel)] on win32
Type "help", "copyright", "credits" or "license" for more information.
>>>
>> from recommendations import critics
>> critics['Lisa Rose']['Lady in the Water']
2.5
>> critics['Toby']['Snakes on a Plane']=4.5
>> critics['Toby']
{'Snakes on a Plane':4.5,'You, Me and Dupree':1.0}
```

Although you can fit a large number of preferences in memory in a dictionary, for very large datasets you'll probably want to store preferences in a database.

Finding Similar Users

After collecting data about the things people like, you need a way to determine how similar people are in their tastes. You do this by comparing each person with every other person and calculating a *similarity score*. There are a few ways to do this, and in this section I'll show you two systems for calculating similarity scores: *Euclidean distance* and *Pearson correlation*.

Euclidean Distance Score

One very simple way to calculate a similarity score is to use a Euclidean distance score, which takes the items that people have ranked in common and uses them as axes for a chart. You can then plot the people on the chart and see how close together they are, as shown in Figure 2-1.

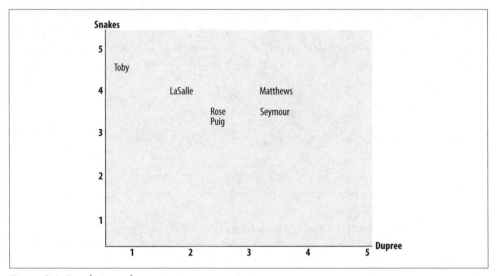

Figure 2-1. People in preference space

This figure shows the people charted in *preference space*. Toby has been plotted at 4.5 on the Snakes axis and at 1.0 on the Dupree axis. The closer two people are in the preference space, the more similar their preferences are. Because the chart is two-dimensional, you can only look at two rankings at a time, but the principle is the same for bigger sets of rankings.

To calculate the distance between Toby and LaSalle in the chart, take the difference in each axis, square them and add them together, then take the square root of the sum. In Python, you can use the pow(n,2) function to square a number and take the square root with the sqrt function:

```
>> from math import sqrt
>> sqrt(pow(5-4,2)+pow(4-1,2))
3.1622776601683795
```

This formula calculates the distance, which will be smaller for people who are more similar. However, you need a function that gives higher values for people who are similar. This can be done by adding 1 to the function (so you don't get a division-by-zero error) and inverting it:

```
>> 1/(1+sqrt(pow(5-4,2)+pow(4-1,2)))
0.2402530733520421
```

This new function always returns a value between 0 and 1, where a value of 1 means that two people have identical preferences. You can put everything together to create a function for calculating similarity. Add the following code to *recommendations.py*:

```
from math import sqrt

# Returns a distance-based similarity score for person1 and person2
def sim_distance(prefs,person1,person2):
  # Get the list of shared_items
  si={}
  for item in prefs[person1]:
    if item in prefs[person2]:
      si[item]=1

  # if they have no ratings in common, return 0
  if len(si)==0: return 0

  # Add up the squares of all the differences
  sum_of_squares=sum([pow(prefs[person1][item]-prefs[person2][item],2)
                      for item in prefs[person1] if item in prefs[person2]])

  return 1/(1+*sqr*t(sum_of_squares))
```

This function can be called with two names to get a similarity score. In your Python interpreter, run the following:

```
>>> reload(recommendations)
>>> recommendations.sim_distance(recommendations.critics,
...    'Lisa Rose','Gene Seymour')
0.148148148148
```

This gives you a similarity score between Lisa Rose and Gene Seymour. Try it with other names to see if you can find people who have more or less in common.

Pearson Correlation Score

A slightly more sophisticated way to determine the similarity between people's interests is to use a Pearson correlation coefficient. The correlation coefficient is a measure of how well two sets of data fit on a straight line. The formula for this is more complicated than the Euclidean distance score, but it tends to give better results in situations where the data isn't well normalized—for example, if critics' movie rankings are routinely more harsh than average.

To visualize this method, you can plot the ratings of two of the critics on a chart, as shown in Figure 2-2. *Superman* was rated 3 by Mick LaSalle and 5 by Gene Seymour, so it is placed at (3,5) on the chart.

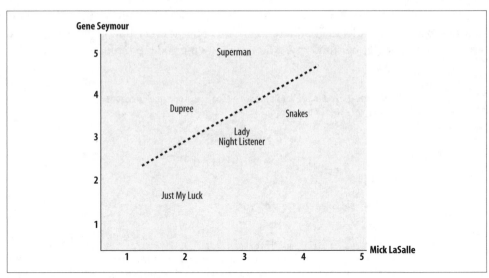

Figure 2-2. Comparing two movie critics on a scatter plot

You can also see a straight line on the chart. This is called the *best-fit line* because it comes as close to all the items on the chart as possible. If the two critics had identical ratings for every movie, this line would be diagonal and would touch every item in the chart, giving a perfect correlation score of 1. In the case illustrated, the critics disagree on a few movies, so the correlation score is about 0.4. Figure 2-3 shows an example of a much higher correlation, one of about 0.75.

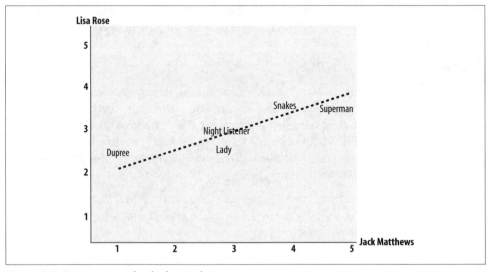

Figure 2-3. Two critics with a high correlation score

One interesting aspect of using the Pearson score, which you can see in the figure, is that it corrects for *grade inflation*. In this figure, Jack Matthews tends to give higher scores than Lisa Rose, but the line still fits because they have relatively similar preferences. If one critic is inclined to give higher scores than the other, there can still be perfect correlation if the difference between their scores is consistent. The Euclidean distance score described earlier will say that two critics are dissimilar because one is consistently harsher than the other, even if their tastes are very similar. Depending on your particular application, this behavior may or may not be what you want.

The code for the Pearson correlation score first finds the items rated by both critics. It then calculates the sums and the sum of the squares of the ratings for the two critics, and calculates the sum of the products of their ratings. Finally, it uses these results to calculate the Pearson correlation coefficient, shown in bold in the code below. Unlike the distance metric, this formula is not very intuitive, but it does tell you how much the variables change together divided by the product of how much they vary individually.

To use this formula, create a new function with the same signature as the sim_distance function in *recommendations.py*:

```
# Returns the Pearson correlation coefficient for p1 and p2
def sim_pearson(prefs,p1,p2):
  # Get the list of mutually rated items
  si={}
  for item in prefs[p1]:
    if item in prefs[p2]: si[item]=1

  # Find the number of elements
  n=len(si)

  # if they are no ratings in common, return 0
  if n==0: return 0

  # Add up all the preferences
  sum1=sum([prefs[p1][it] for it in si])
  sum2=sum([prefs[p2][it] for it in si])

  # Sum up the squares
  sum1Sq=sum([pow(prefs[p1][it],2) for it in si])
  sum2Sq=sum([pow(prefs[p2][it],2) for it in si])

  # Sum up the products
  pSum=sum([prefs[p1][it]*prefs[p2][it] for it in si])

  # Calculate Pearson score
  num=pSum-(sum1*sum2/n)
  den=sqrt((sum1Sq-pow(sum1,2)/n)*(sum2Sq-pow(sum2,2)/n))
  if den==0: return 0

  r=num/den

  return r
```

This function will return a value between −1 and 1. A value of 1 means that the two people have exactly the same ratings for every item. Unlike with the distance metric, you don't need to change this value to get it to the right scale. Now you can try getting the correlation score for Figure 2-3:

```
>>> reload(recommendations)
>>> print recommendations.sim_pearson(recommendations.critics,
...  'Lisa Rose','Gene Seymour')
0.396059017191
```

Which Similarity Metric Should You Use?

I've introduced functions for two different metrics here, but there are actually many more ways to measure similarity between two sets of data. The best one to use will depend on your application, and it is worth trying Pearson, Euclidean distance, or others to see which you think gives better results.

The functions in the rest of this chapter have an optional *similarity* parameter, which points to a function to make it easier to experiment: specify sim_pearson or sim_vector to choose which similarity parameter to use. There are many other functions such as the *Jaccard coefficient* or *Manhattan distance* that you can use as your similarity function, as long as they have the same signature and return a float where a higher value means more similar.

You can read about other metrics for comparing items at *http://en.wikipedia.org/wiki/Metric_%28mathematics%29#Examples*.

Ranking the Critics

Now that you have functions for comparing two people, you can create a function that scores everyone against a given person and finds the closest matches. In this case, I'm interested in learning which movie critics have tastes simliar to mine so that I know whose advice I should take when deciding on a movie. Add this function to *recommendations.py* to get an ordered list of people with similar tastes to the specified person:

```
# Returns the best matches for person from the prefs dictionary.
# Number of results and similarity function are optional params.
def topMatches(prefs,person,n=5,similarity=sim_pearson):
  scores=[(similarity(prefs,person,other),other)
                 for other in prefs if other!=person]

  # Sort the list so the highest scores appear at the top
  scores.sort()
  scores.reverse()
  return scores[0:n]
```

This function uses a Python *list comprehension* to compare me to every other user in the dictionary using one of the previously defined distance metrics. Then it returns the first *n* items of the sorted results.

Calling this function with my own name gives me a list of movie critics and their similarity scores:

```
>> reload(recommendations)
>> recommendations.topMatches(recommendations.critics,'Toby',n=3)
[(0.99124070716192991, 'Lisa Rose'), (0.92447345164190486, 'Mick LaSalle'),
 (0.89340514744156474, 'Claudia Puig')]
```

From this I know that I should be reading reviews by Lisa Rose, as her tastes tend to be similar to mine. If you've seen any of these movies, you can try adding yourself to the dictionary with your preferences and see who your favorite critic should be.

Recommending Items

Finding a good critic to read is great, but what I really want is a movie recommendation right now. I could just look at the person who has tastes most similar to mine and look for a movie he likes that I haven't seen yet, but that would be too permissive. Such an approach could accidentally turn up reviewers who haven't reviewed some of the movies that I might like. It could also return a reviewer who strangely liked a movie that got bad reviews from all the other critics returned by topMatches.

To solve these issues, you need to score the items by producing a weighted score that ranks the critics. Take the votes of all the other critics and multiply how similar they are to me by the score they gave each movie. Table 2-2 shows how this process works.

Table 2-2. Creating recommendations for Toby

Critic	Similarity	Night	S.xNight	Lady	S.xLady	Luck	S.xLuck
Rose	0.99	3.0	2.97	2.5	2.48	3.0	2.97
Seymour	0.38	3.0	1.14	3.0	1.14	1.5	0.57
Puig	0.89	4.5	4.02			3.0	2.68
LaSalle	0.92	3.0	2.77	3.0	2.77	2.0	1.85
Matthews	0.66	3.0	1.99	3.0	1.99		
Total			12.89		8.38		8.07
Sim. Sum			3.84		2.95		3.18
Total/Sim. Sum			3.35		2.83		2.53

This table shows correlation scores for each critic and the ratings they gave the three movies (*The Night Listener*, *Lady in the Water*, and *Just My Luck*) that I haven't rated. The columns beginning with S.x give the similarity multiplied by the rating, so a person who is similar to me will contribute more to the overall score than a person who is different from me. The Total row shows the sum of all these numbers.

You could just use the totals to calculate the rankings, but then a movie reviewed by more people would have a big advantage. To correct for this, you need to divide by the sum of all the similarities for critics that reviewed that movie (the Sim. Sum row in the table). Because *The Night Listener* was reviewed by everyone, its total is divided by the sum of all the similarities. *Lady in the Water*, however, was not reviewed by Puig, so the movie's score is divided by the sum of all the other similarities. The last row shows the results of this division.

The code for this is pretty straightforward, and it works with either the Euclidean distance or the Pearson correlation score. Add it to *recommendations.py*:

```python
# Gets recommendations for a person by using a weighted average
# of every other user's rankings
def getRecommendations(prefs,person,similarity=sim_pearson):
  totals={}
  simSums={}
  for other in prefs:
    # don't compare me to myself
    if other==person: continue
    sim=similarity(prefs,person,other)

    # ignore scores of zero or lower
    if sim<=0: continue
    for item in prefs[other]:

      # only score movies I haven't seen yet
      if item not in prefs[person] or prefs[person][item]==0:
        # Similarity * Score
        totals.setdefault(item,0)
        totals[item]+=prefs[other][item]*sim
        # Sum of similarities
        simSums.setdefault(item,0)
        simSums[item]+=sim

  # Create the normalized list
  rankings=[(total/simSums[item],item) for item,total in totals.items()]

  # Return the sorted list
  rankings.sort()
  rankings.reverse()
  return rankings
```

This code loops through every other person in the prefs dictionary. In each case, it calculates how similar they are to the person specified. It then loops through every item for which they've given a score. The line in bold shows how the final score for an item is calculated—the score for each item is multiplied by the similarity and these products are all added together. At the end, the scores are normalized by dividing each of them by the similarity sum, and the sorted results are returned.

Now you can find out what movies I should watch next:

```
>>> reload(recommendations)
>>> recommendations.getRecommendations(recommendations.critics,'Toby')
[(3.3477895267131013, 'The Night Listener'), (2.8325499182641614, 'Lady in the
Water'), (2.5309807037655645, 'Just My Luck')]
>>> recommendations.getRecommendations(recommendations.critics,'Toby',
...     similarity=recommendations.sim_distance)
[(3.5002478401415877, 'The Night Listener'), (2.7561242939959363, 'Lady in the
Water'), (2.4619884860743739, 'Just My Luck')]
```

Not only do you get a ranked list of movies, but you also get a guess at what my rating for each movie would be. This report lets me decide if I want to watch a movie at all, or if I'd rather do something else entirely. Depending on your application, you may decide not to give a recommendation if there's nothing that would meet a given user's standards. You'll find that the results are only affected very slightly by the choice of similarity metric.

You've now built a complete recommendation system, which will work with any type of product or link. All you have to do is set up a dictionary of people, items, and scores, and you can use this to create recommendations for any person. Later in this chapter you'll see how you can use the del.icio.us API to get real data for recommending web sites to people.

Matching Products

Now you know how to find similar people and recommend products for a given person, but what if you want to see which products are similar to each other? You may have encountered this on shopping web sites, particularly when the site hasn't collected a lot of information about you. A section of Amazon's web page for the book *Programming Python* is shown in Figure 2-4.

```
Customers who bought this item also bought
    Learning Python, Second Edition by Mark Lutz
    Python Cookbook by Alex Martelli
    Python in a Nutshell by Alex Martelli
    Python Essential Reference (2nd Edition) by David Beazley
    Foundations of Python Network Programming (Foundations) by John Goerzen
  ▸ Explore similar items : Books (42)
```

Figure 2-4. Amazon shows products that are similar to Programming Python

In this case, you can determine similarity by looking at who liked a particular item and seeing the other things they liked. This is actually the same method we used earlier to determine similarity between people—you just need to swap the people and the items. So you can use the same methods you wrote earlier if you transform the dictionary from:

```
{'Lisa Rose': {'Lady in the Water': 2.5, 'Snakes on a Plane': 3.5},
 'Gene Seymour': {'Lady in the Water': 3.0, 'Snakes on a Plane': 3.5}}
```

to:

```
{'Lady in the Water':{'Lisa Rose':2.5,'Gene Seymour':3.0},
 'Snakes on a Plane':{'Lisa Rose':3.5,'Gene Seymour':3.5}} etc..
```

Add a function to *recommendations.py* to do this transformation:

```
def transformPrefs(prefs):
  result={}
  for person in prefs:
    for item in prefs[person]:
      result.setdefault(item,{})

      # Flip item and person
      result[item][person]=prefs[person][item]
  return result
```

And now call the topMatches function used earlier to find the set of movies most similar to *Superman Returns*:

```
>> reload(recommendations)
>> movies=recommendations.transformPrefs(recommendations.critics)
>> recommendations.topMatches(movies,'Superman Returns')
[(0.657, 'You, Me and Dupree'), (0.487, 'Lady in the Water'), (0.111, 'Snakes on a
Plane'), (-0.179, 'The Night Listener'), (-0.422, 'Just My Luck')]
```

Notice that in this example there are actually some negative correlation scores, which indicate that those who like *Superman Returns* tend to dislike *Just My Luck*, as shown in Figure 2-5.

To twist things around even more, you can get recommended critics for a movie. Maybe you're trying to decide whom to invite to a premiere?

```
>> recommendations.getRecommendations(movies,'Just My Luck')
[(4.0, 'Michael Phillips'), (3.0, 'Jack Matthews')]
```

It's not always clear that flipping people and items will lead to useful results, but in many cases it will allow you to make interesting comparisons. An online retailer might collect purchase histories for the purpose of recommending products to individuals. Reversing the products with the people, as you've done here, would allow them to search for people who might buy certain products. This might be very useful in planning a marketing effort for a big clearance of certain items. Another potential use is making sure that new links on a link-recommendation site are seen by the people who are most likely to enjoy them.

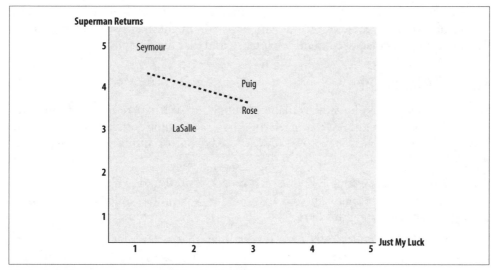

Figure 2-5. Superman Returns and Just My Luck have a negative correlation

Building a del.icio.us Link Recommender

This section shows you how to retrieve data from one of the most popular online bookmarking sites, and how to use that data to find similar users and recommend links they haven't seen before. This site, which you can access at *http://del.icio.us*, allows people to set up an account and post links that interest them for later reference. You can visit the site and look at links that other people have posted, and also browse "popular" links that have been posted by many different people. A sample page from del.icio.us is shown in Figure 2-6.

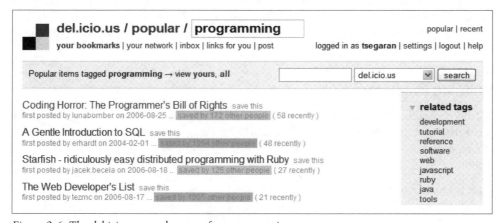

Figure 2-6. The del.icio.us popular page for programming

Unlike some link-sharing sites, del.icio.us doesn't (at the time of writing) include any way to find similar people or recommend links you might like. Fortunately, you can use the techniques discussed in this chapter to add that functionality yourself.

The del.icio.us API

Data from del.icio.us is made available through an API that returns data in XML format. To make things even easier for you, there is a Python API that you can download from *http://code.google.com/p/pydelicious/source* or *http://oreilly.com/catalog/9780596529321*.

To work through the example in this section, you'll need to download the latest version of this library and put it in your Python library path. (See Appendix A for more information on installing this library.)

This library has several simple calls to get links that people have submitted. For example, to get a list of recent popular posts about programming, you can use the get_popular call:

```
>> import pydelicious
>> pydelicious.get_popular(tag='programming')
[{'count': '', 'extended': '', 'hash': '', 'description': u'How To Write
Unmaintainable Code', 'tags': '', 'href': u'http://thc.segfault.net/root/phun/
unmaintain.html', 'user': u'dorsia', 'dt': u'2006-08-19T09:48:56Z'}, {'count': '',
'extended': '', 'hash': '', 'description': u'Threading in C#', 'tags': '', 'href':
u'http://www.albahari.com/threading/', 'user': u'mmihale', 'dt': u'2006-05-17T18:09:
24Z'},
...etc...
```

You can see that it returns a list of dictionaries, each one containing a URL, description, and the user who posted it. Since you are working from live data, your results will look different from the examples. There are two other calls you'll be using, get_urlposts, which returns all the posts for a given URL, and get_userposts, which returns all the posts for a given user. The data for these calls is returned in the same way.

Building the Dataset

It's not possible to download the full set of all user posts from del.icio.us, so you'll need to choose a subset of them. You could do this any way you like, but to make the example show interesting results, it would be good to find people who post frequently and have some similar posts.

One way to do this is to get a list of users who recently posted a popular link with a specified tag. Create a new file called *deliciousrec.py* and enter the following code:

```
from pydelicious import get_popular,get_userposts,get_urlposts

def initializeUserDict(tag,count=5):
  user_dict={}
```

```
# get the top count' popular posts
for p1 in get_popular(tag=tag)[0:count]:
  # find all users who posted this
  for p2 in get_urlposts(p1['href']):
    user=p2['user']
    user_dict[user]={}
return user_dict
```

This will give you a dictionary with some users, each referencing an empty dictionary waiting to be filled with links. The API only returns the last 30 people to post the link, so the function gathers users from the first 5 links to build a larger set.

Unlike the movie critic dataset, there are only two possible ratings in this case: 0 if the user did not post this link, and 1 if he did. Using the API, you can now create a function to fill in ratings for all the users. Add this code to *deliciousrec.py*:

```
def fillItems(user_dict):
  all_items={}
  # Find links posted by all users
  for user in user_dict:
    for i in range(3):
      try:
        posts=get_userposts(user)
        break
      except:
        print "Failed user "+user+", retrying"
        time.sleep(4)
    for post in posts:
      url=post['href']
      user_dict[user][url]=1.0
      all_items[url]=1

  # Fill in missing items with 0
  for ratings in user_dict.values():
    for item in all_items:
      if item not in ratings:
        ratings[item]=0.0
```

This can be used to build a dataset similar to the critics dictionary you created by hand at the beginning of this chapter:

```
>> from deliciousrec import *
>> delusers=initializeUserDict('programming')
>> delusers ['tsegaran']={} # Add yourself to the dictionary if you use delicious
>> fillItems(delusers)
```

The third line adds the user tsegaran to the list. You can replace tsegaran with your own username if you use del.icio.us.

The call to fillItems may take several minutes to run, as it is making a few hundred requests to the site. Sometimes the API blocks requests that are repeated too rapidly. In this case, the code pauses and retries the user up to three times.

Recommending Neighbors and Links

Now that you've built a dataset, you can apply the same functions that you used before on the movie critic dataset. To select a user at random and find other users who have tastes similar to his, enter this code in your Python session:

```
>> import random
>> user=delusers.keys( )[random.randint(0,len(delusers)-1)]
>> user
u'veza'
>> recommendations.topMatches(delusers,user)
[(0.083, u'kuzz99'), (0.083, u'arturoochoa'), (0.083, u'NickSmith'), (0.083,
u'MichaelDahl'), (0.050, u'zinggoat')]
```

You can also get recommendations for links for this user by calling getRecommendations. This will return all the items in order, so it's better to restrict it to the top 10:

```
>> recommendations.getRecommendations(delusers,user)[0:10]
[(0.278, u'http://www.devlisting.com/'),
(0.276, u'http://www.howtoforge.com/linux_ldap_authentication'),
(0.191, u'http://yarivsblog.com/articles/2006/08/09/secret-weapons-for-startups'),
(0.191, u'http://www.dadgum.com/james/performance.html'),
(0.191, u'http://www.codinghorror.com/blog/archives/000666.html')]
```

Of course, as demonstrated earlier, the preferences list can be transposed, allowing you to frame your searches in terms of links rather than people. To find a set of links similar to one that you found particularly interesting, you can try:

```
>> url=recommendations.getRecommendations(delusers,user)[0][1]
>> recommendations.topMatches(recommendations.transformPrefs(delusers),url)
[(0.312, u'http://www.fonttester.com/'),
(0.312, u'http://www.cssremix.com/'),
(0.266, u'http://www.logoorange.com/color/color-codes-chart.php'),
(0.254, u'http://yotophoto.com/'),
(0.254, u'http://www.wpdfd.com/editorial/basics/index.html')]
```

That's it! You've successfully added a recommendation engine to del.icio.us. There's a lot more that could be done here. Since del.icio.us supports searching by tags, you can look for tags that are similar to each other. You can even search for people trying to manipulate the "popular" pages by posting the same links with multiple accounts.

Item-Based Filtering

The way the recommendation engine has been implemented so far requires the use of all the rankings from every user in order to create a dataset. This will probably work well for a few thousand people or items, but a very large site like Amazon has millions of customers and products—comparing a user with every other user and then comparing every product each user has rated can be very slow. Also, a site that sells millions of products may have very little overlap between people, which can make it difficult to decide which people are similar.

The technique we have used thus far is called *user-based collaborative filtering*. An alternative is known as *item-based collaborative filtering*. In cases with very large datasets, item-based collaborative filtering can give better results, and it allows many of the calculations to be performed in advance so that a user needing recommendations can get them more quickly.

The procedure for item-based filtering draws a lot on what we have already discussed. The general technique is to precompute the most similar items for each item. Then, when you wish to make recommendations to a user, you look at his top-rated items and create a weighted list of the items most similar to those. The important difference here is that, although the first step requires you to examine all the data, *comparisons between items will not change as often as comparisons between users*. This means you do not have to continuously calculate each item's most similar items—you can do it at low-traffic times or on a computer separate from your main application.

Building the Item Comparison Dataset

To compare items, the first thing you'll need to do is write a function to build the complete dataset of similar items. Again, this does not have to be done every time a recommendation is needed—instead, you build the dataset once and reuse it each time you need it.

To generate the dataset, add the following function to *recommendations.py*:

```
def calculateSimilarItems(prefs,n=10):
  # Create a dictionary of items showing which other items they
  # are most similar to.
  result={}

  # Invert the preference matrix to be item-centric
  itemPrefs=transformPrefs(prefs)
  c=0
  for item in itemPrefs:
    # Status updates for large datasets
    c+=1
    if c%100==0: print "%d / %d" % (c,len(itemPrefs))
    # Find the most similar items to this one
    scores=topMatches(itemPrefs,item,n=n,similarity=sim_distance)
    result[item]=scores
  return result
```

This function first inverts the score dictionary using the `transformPrefs` function defined earlier, giving a list of items along with how they were rated by each user. It then loops over every item and passes the transformed dictionary to the `topMatches` function to get the most similar items along with their similarity scores. Finally, it creates and returns a dictionary of items along with a list of their most similar items.

In your Python session, build the item similarity dataset and see what it looks like:

```
>>> reload(recommendations)
>>> itemsim=recommendations.calculateSimilarItems(recommendations.critics)
>>> itemsim
{'Lady in the Water': [(0.40000000000000002, 'You, Me and Dupree'),
                       (0.2857142857142857, 'The Night Listener'),...
 'Snakes on a Plane': [(0.22222222222222221, 'Lady in the Water'),
                       (0.18181818181818182, 'The Night Listener'),...
etc.
```

Remember, this function only has to be run frequently enough to keep the item similarities up to date. You will need to do this more often early on when the user base and number of ratings is small, but as the user base grows, the similarity scores between items will usually become more stable.

Getting Recommendations

Now you're ready to give recommendations using the item similarity dictionary without going through the whole dataset. You're going to get all the items that the user has ranked, find the similar items, and weight them according to how similar they are. The items dictionary can easily be used to get the similarities.

Table 2-3 shows the process of finding recommendations using the item-based approach. Unlike Table 2-2, the critics are not involved at all, and instead there is a grid of movies I've rated versus movies I haven't rated.

Table 2-3. Item-based recommendations for Toby

Movie	Rating	Night	R.xNight	Lady	R.xLady	Luck	R.xLuck
Snakes	4.5	0.182	0.818	0.222	0.999	0.105	0.474
Superman	4.0	0.103	0.412	0.091	0.363	0.065	0.258
Dupree	1.0	0.148	0.148	0.4	0.4	0.182	0.182
Total		0.433	1.378	0.713	1.764	0.352	0.914
Normalized			3.183		2.598		2.473

Each row has a movie that I have already seen, along with my personal rating for it. For every movie that I haven't seen, there's a column that shows how similar it is to the movies I have seen—for example, the similarity score between *Superman* and *The Night Listener* is 0.103. The columns starting with R.x show my rating of the movie multiplied by the similarity—since I rated *Superman* 4.0, the value next to Night in the Superman row is $4.0 \times 0.103 = 0.412$.

The total row shows the total of the similarity scores and the total of the R.x columns for each movie. To predict what my rating would be for each movie, just divide the total for the R.x column by the total for the similarity column. My predicted rating for *The Night Listener* is thus $1.378/0.433 = 3.183$.

You can use this functionality by adding one last function to *recommendations.py*:

```
def getRecommendedItems(prefs,itemMatch,user):
  userRatings=prefs[user]
  scores={}
  totalSim={}

  # Loop over items rated by this user
  for (item,rating) in userRatings.items():

    # Loop over items similar to this one
    for (similarity,item2) in itemMatch[item]:

      # Ignore if this user has already rated this item
      if item2 in userRatings: continue

      # Weighted sum of rating times similarity
      scores.setdefault(item2,0)
      scores[item2]+=similarity*rating

      # Sum of all the similarities
      totalSim.setdefault(item2,0)
      totalSim[item2]+=similarity

  # Divide each total score by total weighting to get an average
  rankings=[(score/totalSim[item],item) for item,score in scores.items()]

  # Return the rankings from highest to lowest
  rankings.sort()
  rankings.reverse()
  return rankings
```

You can try this function with the similarity dataset you built earlier to get the new recommendations for Toby:

```
>> reload(recommendations)
>> recommendations.getRecommendedItems(recommendations.critics,itemsim,'Toby')
[(3.182, 'The Night Listener'),
 (2.598, 'Just My Luck'),
 (2.473, 'Lady in the Water')]
```

The Night Listener still comes in first by a significant margin, and *Just My Luck* and *Lady in the Water* have changed places although they are still close together. More importantly, the call to getRecommendedItems did not have to calculate the similarities scores for all the other critics because the item similarity dataset was built in advance.

Using the MovieLens Dataset

For the final example, let's look at a real dataset of movie ratings called *MovieLens*. MovieLens was developed by the GroupLens project at the University of Minnesota. You can download the dataset from *http://www.grouplens.org/node/12*. There are two datasets here. Download the 100,000 dataset in either *tar.gz* format or *zip* format, depending on your platform.

The archive contains several files, but the ones of interest are *u.item*, which contains a list of movie IDs and titles, and *u.data*, which contains actual ratings in this format:

```
196   242   3   881250949
186   302   3   891717742
22    377   1   878887116
244   51    2   880606923
166   346   1   886397596
298   474   4   884182806
```

Each line has a user ID, a movie ID, the rating given to the movie by the user, and a timestamp. You can get the movie titles, but the user data is anonymous, so you'll just be working with user IDs in this section. The set contains ratings of 1,682 movies by 943 users, each of whom rated at least 20 movies.

Create a new method called `loadMovieLens` in *recommendations.py* to load this dataset:

```python
def loadMovieLens(path='/data/movielens'):

  # Get movie titles
  movies={}
  for line in open(path+'/u.item'):
    (id,title)=line.split('|')[0:2]
    movies[id]=title

  # Load data
  prefs={}
  for line in open(path+'/u.data'):
    (user,movieid,rating,ts)=line.split('\t')
    prefs.setdefault(user,{})
    prefs[user][movies[movieid]]=float(rating)
  return prefs
```

In your Python session, load the data and look at some ratings for any arbitrary user:

```
>>> reload(recommendations)
>>> prefs=recommendations.loadMovieLens()
>>> prefs['87']
{'Birdcage, The (1996)': 4.0, 'E.T. the Extra-Terrestrial (1982)': 3.0,
 'Bananas (1971)': 5.0, 'Sting, The (1973)': 5.0, 'Bad Boys (1995)': 4.0,
 'In the Line of Fire (1993)': 5.0, 'Star Trek: The Wrath of Khan (1982)': 5.0,
 'Speechless (1994)': 4.0, etc...
```

Now you can get user-based recommendations:

```
>>> recommendations.getRecommendations(prefs,'87')[0:30]
[(5.0, 'They Made Me a Criminal (1939)'), (5.0, 'Star Kid (1997)'),
 (5.0, 'Santa with Muscles (1996)'), (5.0, 'Saint of Fort Washington (1993)'),
 etc...]
```

Depending on the speed of your computer, you may notice a pause when getting recommendations this way. This is because you're working with a much larger dataset now. The more users you have, the longer user-based recommendations will take. Now try doing item-based recommendations instead:

```
>>> itemsim=recommendations.calculateSimilarItems(prefs,n=50)
100 / 1664
200 / 1664
etc...
>>> recommendations.getRecommendedItems(prefs,itemsim,'87')[0:30]
[(5.0, "What's Eating Gilbert Grape (1993)"), (5.0, 'Vertigo (1958)'),
 (5.0, 'Usual Suspects, The (1995)'), (5.0, 'Toy Story (1995)'),etc...]
```

Although building the item similarity dictionary takes a long time, recommendations are almost instantaneous after it's built. Furthermore, the time it takes to get recommendations will not increase as the number of users increases.

This is a great dataset to experiment with to see how different scoring methods affect the outcomes, and to understand how item-based and user-based filtering perform differently. The GroupLens web site has a few other datasets to play with, including books, jokes, and more movies.

User-Based or Item-Based Filtering?

Item-based filtering is significantly faster than user-based when getting a list of recommendations for a large dataset, but it does have the additional overhead of maintaining the item similarity table. Also, there is a difference in accuracy that depends on how "sparse" the dataset is. In the movie example, since every critic has rated nearly every movie, the dataset is dense (not sparse). On the other hand, it would be unlikely to find two people with the same set of del.icio.us bookmarks—most bookmarks are saved by a small group of people, leading to a sparse dataset. Item-based filtering usually outperforms user-based filtering in sparse datasets, and the two perform about equally in dense datasets.

 To learn more about the difference in performance between these algorithms, check out a paper called "Item-based Collaborative Filtering Recommendation Algorithms" by Sarwar et al. at *http://citeseer.ist.psu.edu/sarwar01itembased.html*.

Having said that, user-based filtering is simpler to implement and doesn't have the extra steps, so it is often more appropriate with smaller in-memory datasets that change very frequently. Finally, in some applications, showing people which other users have preferences similar to their own has its own value—maybe not something you would want to do on a shopping site, but possibly on a link-sharing or music recommendation site.

You've now learned how to calculate similarity scores and how to use these to compare people and items. This chapter covered two different recommendation algorithms, user-based and item-based, along with ways to persist people's preferences and use the del.icio.us API to build a link recommendation system. In Chapter 3, you'll see how to build on some of the ideas from this chapter by finding groups of similar people using unsupervised clustering algorithms. Chapter 9 will look at alternative ways to match people when you already know the sort of people they like.

Exercises

1. *Tanimoto score*. Find out what a Tanimoto similarity score is. In what cases could this be used as the similarity metric instead of Euclidean distance or Pearson coefficient? Create a new similarity function using the Tanimoto score.

2. *Tag similarity*. Using the del.icio.us API, create a dataset of tags and items. Use this to calculate similarity between tags and see if you can find any that are almost identical. Find some items that could have been tagged "programming" but were not.

3. *User-based efficiency*. The user-based filtering algorithm is inefficient because it compares a user to all other users every time a recommendation is needed. Write a function to precompute user similarities, and alter the recommendation code to use only the top five other users to get recommendations.

4. *Item-based bookmark filtering*. Download a set of data from del.icio.us and add it to the database. Create an item-item table and use this to make item-based recommendations for various users. How do these compare to the user-based recommendations?

5. *Audioscrobbler*. Take a look at *http://www.audioscrobbler.net*, a dataset containing music preferences for a large set of users. Use their web services API to get a set of data for making and building a music recommendation system.

## CHAPTER 3

Discovering Groups

Chapter 2 discussed ways to find things that are closely related, so, for example, you could find someone who shares your taste in movies. This chapter expands on those ideas and introduces *data clustering*, a method for discovering and visualizing groups of things, people, or ideas that are all closely related. In this chapter, you'll learn: how to prepare data from a variety of sources; two different clustering algorithms; more on distance metrics; simple graphical visualization code for viewing the generated groups; and finally, a method for projecting very complicated datasets into two dimensions.

Clustering is used frequently in data-intensive applications. Retailers who track customer purchases can use this information to automatically detect groups of customers with similar buying patterns, in addition to regular demographic information. People of similar age and income may have vastly different styles of dress, but with the use of clustering, "fashion islands" can be discovered and used to develop a retail or marketing strategy. Clustering is also heavily used in computational biology to find groups of genes that exhibit similar behavior, which might indicate that they respond to a treatment in the same way or are part of the same biological pathway.

Since this book is about collective intelligence, the examples in this chapter come from sources in which many people contribute different information. The first example will look at blogs, the topics they discuss, and their particular word usage to show that blogs can be grouped according to their text and that words can be grouped by their usage. The second example will look at a community site where people list things they own and things they would like to own, and we will use this information to show how people's desires can be grouped into clusters.

Supervised versus Unsupervised Learning

Techniques that use example inputs and outputs to learn how to make predictions are known as *supervised learning methods*. We'll explore many supervised learning methods in this book, including neural networks, decision trees, support-vector machines, and Bayesian filtering. Applications using these methods "learn" by examining a set of inputs and expected outputs. When we want to extract information using one of these methods, we enter a set of inputs and expect the application to produce an output based on what it has learned so far.

Clustering is an example of *unsupervised learning*. Unlike a neural network or a decision tree, unsupervised learning algorithms are not trained with examples of correct answers. Their purpose is to find structure within a set of data where no one piece of data is the answer. In the fashion example given earlier, the clusters don't tell the retailers what an individual is likely to buy, nor do they make predictions about which fashion island a new person fits into. The goal of clustering algorithms is to take the data and find the distinct groups that exist within it. Other examples of unsupervised learning include *non-negative matrix factorization*, which will be discussed in Chapter 10, and *self-organizing maps*.

Word Vectors

The normal way of preparing data for clustering is to determine a common set of numerical attributes that can be used to compare the items. This is very similar to what was shown in Chapter 2, when critics' rankings were compared over a common set of movies, and when the presence or absence of a bookmark was translated to a 1 or a 0 for del.icio.us users.

Pigeonholing the Bloggers

This chapter will work through a couple of example datasets. In the first dataset, the items that will be clustered are a set of 120 of the top blogs, and the data they'll be clustered on is the number of times a particular set of words appears in each blog's feed. A small subset of what this looks like is shown in Table 3-1.

Table 3-1. Subset of blog word frequencies

	"china"	"kids"	"music"	"yahoo"
Gothamist	0	3	3	0
GigaOM	6	0	0	2
Quick Online Tips	0	2	2	22

By clustering blogs based on word frequencies, it might be possible to determine if there are groups of blogs that frequently write about similar subjects or write in similar styles. Such a result could be very useful in searching, cataloging, and discovering the huge number of blogs that are currently online.

To generate this dataset, you'll be downloading the feeds from a set of blogs, extracting the text from the entries, and creating a table of word frequencies. If you'd like to skip the steps for creating the dataset, you can download it from *http://kiwitobes.com/clusters/blogdata.txt*.

Counting the Words in a Feed

Almost all blogs can be read online or via their *RSS feeds*. An RSS feed is a simple XML document that contains information about the blog and all the entries. The first step in generating word counts for each blog is to parse these feeds. Fortunately, there is an excellent module for doing this called Universal Feed Parser, which you can download from *http://www.feedparser.org*.

This module makes it easy to get the title, links, and entries from any RSS or Atom feed. The next step is to create a function that will extract all the words from a feed. Create a new file called *generatefeedvector.py* and insert the following code:

```
import feedparser
import re

# Returns title and dictionary of word counts for an RSS feed
def getwordcounts(url):
  # Parse the feed
  d=feedparser.parse(url)
  wc={}

  # Loop over all the entries
  for e in d.entries:
    if 'summary' in e: summary=e.summary
    else: summary=e.description

    # Extract a list of words
    words=getwords(e.title+' '+summary)
    for word in words:
      wc.setdefault(word,0)
      wc[word]+=1
  return d.feed.title,wc
```

RSS and Atom feeds always have a title and a list of entries. Each entry usually has either a `summary` or `description` tag that contains the actual text of the entries. The getwordcounts function passes this summary to getwords, which strips out all of the HTML and splits the words by nonalphabetical characters, returning them as a list. Add getwords to *generatefeedvector.py*:

```
def getwords(html):
  # Remove all the HTML tags
  txt=re.compile(r'<[^>]+>').sub('',html)

  # Split words by all non-alpha characters
  words=re.compile(r'[^A-Z^a-z]+').split(txt)

  # Convert to lowercase
  return [word.lower() for word in words if word!='']
```

Now you'll need a list of feeds to work from. If you like, you can generate a list of feed URLs for a set of blogs yourself, or you can use a prebuilt list of 100 RSS URLs. This list was created by taking the feeds for all of the most highly referenced blogs and removing those that did not contain the full text of their entries or were mostly images. You can download the list at *http://kiwitobes.com/clusters/feedlist.txt*.

This is a plain text file with a URL on each line. If you have your own blog or some particular favorites and you would like to see how they compare to some of the most popular blogs out there, you can add them to this file.

The code for looping over the feeds and generating the dataset will be the main code in *generatefeedvector.py* (that is, not in a function). The first part of the code loops over every line in *feedlist.txt* and generates the word counts for each blog, as well as the number of blogs each word appeared in (apcount). Add this code to the end of *generatefeedvector.py*:

```
apcount={}
wordcounts={}
for feedurl in file('feedlist.txt'):
  title,wc=getwordcounts(feedurl)
  wordcounts[title]=wc
  for word,count in wc.items():
    apcount.setdefault(word,0)
    if count>1:
      apcount[word]+=1
```

The next step is to generate the list of words that will actually be used in the counts for each blog. Since words like "the" will appear in almost all of them, and others like "flim-flam" might only appear in one, you can reduce the total number of words included by selecting only those words that are within maximum and minimum percentages. In this case, you can start with 10 percent as the lower bound and 50 percent as the upper bound, but it's worth experimenting with these numbers if you find too many common words or too many strange words appearing:

```
wordlist=[]
for w,bc in apcount.items():
  frac=float(bc)/len(feedlist)
  if frac>0.1 and frac<0.5: wordlist.append(w)
```

The final step is to use the list of words and the list of blogs to create a text file containing a big matrix of all the word counts for each of the blogs:

```
out=file('blogdata.txt','w')
out.write('Blog')
for word in wordlist: out.write('\t%s' % word)
out.write('\n')
for blog,wc in wordcounts.items():
  out.write(blog)
  for word in wordlist:
    if word in wc: out.write('\t%d' % wc[word])
    else: out.write('\t0')
  out.write('\n')
```

To generate the word count file, run *generatefeedvector.py* from the command line:

```
c:\code\blogcluster>python generatefeedvector.py
```

Downloading all those feeds may take a few minutes, but this will eventually generate an output file called *blogdata.txt*. Open this file to verify that it contains a tab-separated table with columns of words and rows of blogs. This file format will be used by the functions in this chapter, so that later you can create a different dataset or even save a properly formatted spreadsheet as a tab-separated text file on which to use these clustering algorithms.

Hierarchical Clustering

Hierarchical clustering builds up a hierarchy of groups by continuously merging the two most similar groups. Each of these groups starts as a single item, in this case an individual blog. In each iteration this method calculates the distances between every pair of groups, and the closest ones are merged together to form a new group. This is repeated until there is only one group. Figure 3-1 shows this process.

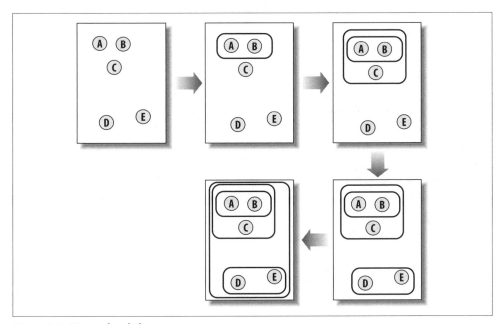

Figure 3-1. Hierarchical clustering in action

In the figure, the similarity of the items is represented by their relative locations—the closer two items are, the more similar they are. At first, the groups are just individual items. In the second step, you can see that A and B, the two items closest together, have merged to form a new group whose location is halfway between the two. In the third step, this new group is merged with C. Since D and E are now the two closest items, they form a new group. The final step unifies the two remaining groups.

After hierarchical clustering is completed, you usually view the results in a type of graph called a *dendrogram*, which displays the nodes arranged into their hierarchy. The dendrogram for the example above is shown in Figure 3-2.

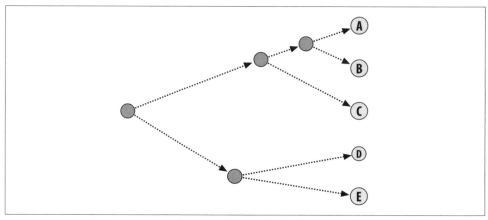

Figure 3-2. A dendrogram is a visualization of hierarchical clustering

This dendrogram not only uses connections to show which items ended up in each cluster, it also uses the distance to show how far apart the items were. The AB cluster is a lot closer to the individual A and B items than the DE cluster is to the individual D and E items. Rendering the graph this way can help you determine how similar the items within a cluster are, which could be interpreted as the *tightness* of the cluster.

This section will show you how to cluster the blogs dataset to generate a hierarchy of blogs, which, if successful, will group them thematically. First, you'll need a method to load in the data file. Create a file called *clusters.py* and add this function to it:

```
def readfile(filename):
  lines=[line for line in file(filename)]

  # First line is the column titles
  colnames=lines[0].strip().split('\t')[1:]
  rownames=[]
  data=[]
  for line in lines[1:]:
    p=line.strip().split('\t')
    # First column in each row is the rowname
    rownames.append(p[0])
    # The data for this row is the remainder of the row
    data.append([float(x) for x in p[1:]])
  return rownames,colnames,data
```

This function reads the top row into the list of column names and reads the leftmost column into a list of row names, then puts all the data into a big list where every item in the list is the data for that row. The count for any cell can be referenced by its row and column in data, which also corresponds to the indices of the rownames and colnames lists.

The next step is to define *closeness*. We discussed this in Chapter 2, using Euclidean distance and Pearson correlation as examples of ways to determine how similar two movie critics are. In the present example, some blogs contain more entries or much longer entries than others, and will thus contain more words overall. The Pearson correlation will correct for this, since it really tries to determine how well two sets of data fit onto a straight line. The Pearson correlation code for this module will take two lists of numbers and return their correlation score:

```
from math import sqrt
def pearson(v1,v2):
  # Simple sums
  sum1=sum(v1)
  sum2=sum(v2)

  # Sums of the squares
  sum1Sq=sum([pow(v,2) for v in v1])
  sum2Sq=sum([pow(v,2) for v in v2])

  # Sum of the products
  pSum=sum([v1[i]*v2[i] for i in range(len(v1))])

  # Calculate r (Pearson score)
  num=pSum-(sum1*sum2/len(v1))
  den=sqrt((sum1Sq-pow(sum1,2)/len(v1))*(sum2Sq-pow(sum2,2)/len(v1)))
  if den==0: return 0

  return 1.0-num/den
```

Remember that the Pearson correlation is 1.0 when two items match perfectly, and is close to 0.0 when there's no relationship at all. The final line of the code returns 1.0 minus the Pearson correlation to create a smaller distance between items that are more similar.

Each cluster in a hierarchical clustering algorithm is either a point in the tree with two branches, or an endpoint associated with an actual row from the dataset (in this case, a blog). Each cluster also contains data about its location, which is either the row data for the endpoints or the merged data from its two branches for other node types. You can create a class called `bicluster` that has all of these properties, which you'll use to represent the hierarchical tree. Create the cluster type as a class in *cluster.py*:

```
class bicluster:
  def __init__(self,vec,left=None,right=None,distance=0.0,id=None):
    self.left=left
    self.right=right
    self.vec=vec
    self.id=id
    self.distance=distance
```

The algorithm for hierarchical clustering begins by creating a group of clusters that are just the original items. The main loop of the function searches for the two best matches by trying every possible pair and calculating their correlation. The best pair of clusters is merged into a single cluster. The data for this new cluster is the average of the data for the two old clusters. This process is repeated until only one cluster remains. It can be very time consuming to do all these calculations, so it's a good idea to store the correlation results for each pair, since they will have to be calculated again and again until one of the items in the pair is merged into another cluster.

Add the hcluster algorithm to *clusters.py*:

```
def hcluster(rows,distance=pearson):
  distances={}
  currentclustid=-1

  # Clusters are initially just the rows
  clust=[bicluster(rows[i],id=i) for i in range(len(rows))]

  while len(clust)>1:
    lowestpair=(0,1)
    closest=distance(clust[0].vec,clust[1].vec)

    # loop through every pair looking for the smallest distance
    for i in range(len(clust)):
      for j in range(i+1,len(clust)):
        # distances is the cache of distance calculations
        if (clust[i].id,clust[j].id) not in distances:
          distances[(clust[i].id,clust[j].id)]=distance(clust[i].vec,clust[j].vec)

        d=distances[(clust[i].id,clust[j].id)]

        if d<closest:
          closest=d
          lowestpair=(i,j)

    # calculate the average of the two clusters
    mergevec=[
    (clust[lowestpair[0]].vec[i]+clust[lowestpair[1]].vec[i])/2.0
    for i in range(len(clust[0].vec))]

    # create the new cluster
    newcluster=bicluster(mergevec,left=clust[lowestpair[0]],
                         right=clust[lowestpair[1]],
                         distance=closest,id=currentclustid)

    # cluster ids that weren't in the original set are negative
    currentclustid-=1
    del clust[lowestpair[1]]
    del clust[lowestpair[0]]
    clust.append(newcluster)

  return clust[0]
```

Because each cluster references the two clusters that were merged to create it, the final cluster returned by this function can be searched recursively to recreate all the clusters and their end nodes.

To run the hierarchical clustering, start up a Python session, load in the file, and call hcluster on the data:

```
$ python
>> import clusters
>> blognames,words,data=clusters.readfile('blogdata.txt')
>> clust=clusters.hcluster(data)
```

This may take a few minutes to run. Storing the distances increases the speed significantly, but it's still necessary for the algorithm to calculate the correlation between every pair of blogs. This process can be made faster by using an external library to calculate the distances. To view your results, you can create a simple function that traverses the clustering tree recursively and prints it like a filesystem hierarchy. Add the function printclust to *clusters.py*:

```
def printclust(clust,labels=None,n=0):
  # indent to make a hierarchy layout
  for i in range(n): print ' ',
  if clust.id<0:
    # negative id means that this is branch
    print '-'
  else:
    # positive id means that this is an endpoint
    if labels==None: print clust.id
    else: print labels[clust.id]

  # now print the right and left branches
  if clust.left!=None: printclust(clust.left,labels=labels,n=n+1)
  if clust.right!=None: printclust(clust.right,labels=labels,n=n+1)
```

The output from this doesn't look very fancy and it's a little hard to read with a large dataset like the blog list, but it does give a good overall sense of whether clustering is working. In the next section, we'll look at creating a graphical version that is much easier to read and is drawn to scale to show the overall spread of each cluster.

In your Python session, call this function on the clusters you just built:

```
>> reload(clusters)
>> clusters.printclust(clust,labels=blognames)
```

The output listing will contain all 100 blogs and will thus be quite long. Here's an example of a cluster that I found when running this dataset:

```
John Battelle's Searchblog
-
  Search Engine Watch Blog
  -
    Read/WriteWeb
    -
      Official Google Blog
      -
        Search Engine Roundtable
        -
          Google Operating System
          Google Blogoscoped
```

The original items in the set are shown. The dashes represent a cluster of two or more merged items. Here you see a great example of finding a group; it's also interesting to see that there is such a large chunk of search-related blogs in the most popular feeds. Looking through, you also should be able to spot clusters of political blogs, technology blogs, and blogs about blogging.

You'll also probably notice some anomalies. These writers may not have written on the same themes, but the clustering algorithm says that their word frequencies are correlated. This might be a reflection of their writing style or could simply be a coincidence based on the day that the data was downloaded.

Drawing the Dendrogram

You can interpret the clusters more clearly by viewing them as a dendrogram. Hierarchical clustering results are usually viewed this way, since dendrograms pack a lot of information into a relatively small space. Since the dendrograms will be graphical and saved as JPGs, you'll need to download the Python Imaging Library (PIL), which is available at *http://pythonware.com*.

This library comes with an installer for Windows and source distributions for other platforms. More information on downloading and installing the PIL is available in Appendix A. The PIL makes it very easy to generate images with text and lines, which is all you'll really need to construct a dendrogram. Add the import statement to the beginning of *clusters.py*:

```
from PIL import Image,ImageDraw
```

The first step is to use a function that returns the total height of a given cluster. When determining the overall height of the image, and where to put the various nodes, it's necessary to know their total heights. If this cluster is an endpoint (i.e., it has no branches), then its height is 1; otherwise, its height is the sum of the heights of its branches. This is easily defined as a recursive function, which you can add to *clusters.py*:

```
def getheight(clust):
  # Is this an endpoint? Then the height is just 1
  if clust.left==None and clust.right==None: return 1

  # Otherwise the height is the same of the heights of
  # each branch
  return getheight(clust.left)+getheight(clust.right)
```

The other thing you need to know is the total error of the root node. Since the length of the lines will be scaled to how much error is in each node, you'll be generating a scaling factor based on how much total error there is. The error depth of a node is just the maximum possible error from each of its branches:

```
def getdepth(clust):
  # The distance of an endpoint is 0.0
  if clust.left==None and clust.right==None: return 0
```

```
# The distance of a branch is the greater of its two sides
# plus its own distance
return max(getdepth(clust.left),getdepth(clust.right))+clust.distance
```

The drawdendrogram function creates a new image allowing 20 pixels in height and a fixed width for each final cluster. The scaling factor is determined by dividing the fixed width by the total depth. The function creates a draw object for this image and then calls drawnode on the root node, telling it that its location should be halfway down the left side of the image.

```
def drawdendrogram(clust,labels,jpeg='clusters.jpg'):
  # height and width
  h=getheight(clust)*20
  w=1200
  depth=getdepth(clust)

  # width is fixed, so scale distances accordingly
  scaling=float(w-150)/depth

  # Create a new image with a white background
  img=Image.new('RGB',(w,h),(255,255,255))
  draw=ImageDraw.Draw(img)

  draw.line((0,h/2,10,h/2),fill=(255,0,0))

  # Draw the first node
  drawnode(draw,clust,10,(h/2),scaling,labels)
  img.save(jpeg,'JPEG')
```

The important function here is drawnode, which takes a cluster and its location. It takes the heights of the child nodes, calculates where they should be, and draws lines to them—one long vertical line and two horizontal lines. The lengths of the horizontal lines are determined by how much error is in the cluster. Longer lines show that the two clusters that were merged to create the cluster weren't all that similar, while shorter lines show that they were almost identical. Add the drawnode function to *clusters.py*:

```
def drawnode(draw,clust,x,y,scaling,labels):
  if clust.id<0:
    h1=getheight(clust.left)*20
    h2=getheight(clust.right)*20
    top=y-(h1+h2)/2
    bottom=y+(h1+h2)/2
    # Line length
    ll=clust.distance*scaling
    # Vertical line from this cluster to children
    draw.line((x,top+h1/2,x,bottom-h2/2),fill=(255,0,0))

    # Horizontal line to left item
    draw.line((x,top+h1/2,x+ll,top+h1/2),fill=(255,0,0))

    # Horizontal line to right item
    draw.line((x,bottom-h2/2,x+ll,bottom-h2/2),fill=(255,0,0))
```

```
    # Call the function to draw the left and right nodes
    drawnode(draw,clust.left,x+ll,top+h1/2,scaling,labels)
    drawnode(draw,clust.right,x+ll,bottom-h2/2,scaling,labels)
  else:
    # If this is an endpoint, draw the item label
    draw.text((x+5,y-7),labels[clust.id],(0,0,0))
```

To generate the image, go to your Python session and enter:

```
>> reload(clusters)
>> clusters.drawdendrogram(clust,blognames,jpeg='blogclust.jpg')
```

This will generate a file called *blogclust.jpg* with the dendrogram. The dendrogram should look similar to the one shown in Figure 3-3. If you like, you can change the height and width settings to make it easier to print or less cluttered.

Column Clustering

It's often necessary to cluster on both the rows and the columns. In a marketing study, it can be interesting to group people to find demographics and products, or perhaps to determine shelf locations of items that are commonly bought together. In the blog dataset, the columns represent words, and it's potentially interesting to see which words are commonly used together.

The easiest way to do this using the functions you've written thus far is to rotate the entire dataset so that the columns (the words) become rows, each with a list of numbers indicating how many times that particular word appears in each of the blogs. Add this function to *clusters.py*:

```
def rotatematrix(data):
  newdata=[]
  for i in range(len(data[0])):
    newrow=[data[j][i] for j in range(len(data))]
    newdata.append(newrow)
  return newdata
```

You can now rotate the matrix and run the same operations for clustering and drawing the dendrogram. As there are many more words than blogs, this will take longer than running the blog clustering. Remember that since the matrix has been rotated, the words rather than the blogs are now the labels.

```
>> reload(clusters)
>> rdata=clusters.rotatematrix(data)
>> wordclust=clusters.hcluster(rdata)
>> clusters.drawdendrogram(wordclust,labels=words,jpeg='wordclust.jpg')
```

One important thing to realize about clustering is that if you have many more items than variables, the likelihood of nonsensical clusters increases. There are many more words than there are blogs, so you'll notice more reasonable patterns in the blog clustering than in the word clustering. However, some interesting clusters definitely emerge, as shown in Figure 3-4.

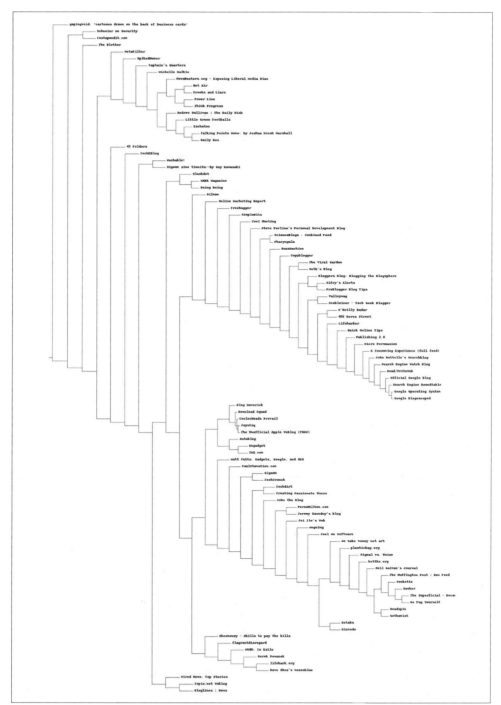

Figure 3-3. Dendrogram showing blog clusters

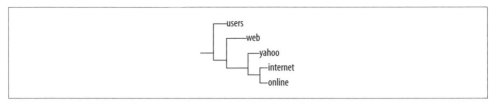

Figure 3-4. Word cluster showing online-service-related words

The cluster obviously shows that a set of words is often used together in blogs to discuss online services or Internet-related topics. It's possible to find clusters elsewhere that reflect usage patterns, such as "fact," "us," "say," "very," and "think," which indicate that a blog writes in an opinionated style.

K-Means Clustering

Hierarchical clustering gives a nice tree as a result, but it has a couple of disadvantages. The tree view doesn't really break the data into distinct groups without additional work, and the algorithm is extremely computationally intensive. Because the relationship between every pair of items must be calculated and then recalculated when items are merged, the algorithm will run slowly on very large datasets.

An alternative method of clustering is *K-means* clustering. This type of algorithm is quite different from hierarchical clustering because it is told in advance how many distinct clusters to generate. The algorithm will determine the size of the clusters based on the structure of the data.

K-means clustering begins with *k* randomly placed *centroids* (points in space that represent the center of the cluster), and assigns every item to the nearest one. After the assignment, the centroids are moved to the average location of all the nodes assigned to them, and the assignments are redone. This process repeats until the assignments stop changing. Figure 3-5 shows this process in action for five items and two clusters.

In the first frame, the two centroids (shown as dark circles) are placed randomly. Frame 2 shows that each of the items is assigned to the nearest centroid—in this case, A and B are assigned to the top centroid and C, D, and E are assigned to the bottom centroid. In the third frame, each centroid has been moved to the average location of the items that were assigned to it. When the assignments are calculated again, it turns out that C is now closer to the top centroid, while D and E remain closest to the bottom one. Thus, the final result is reached with A, B, and C in one cluster, and D and E in the other.

The function for doing K-means clustering takes the same data rows as input as does the hierarchical clustering algorithm, along with the number of clusters (k) that the caller would like returned. Add this code to *clusters.py*:

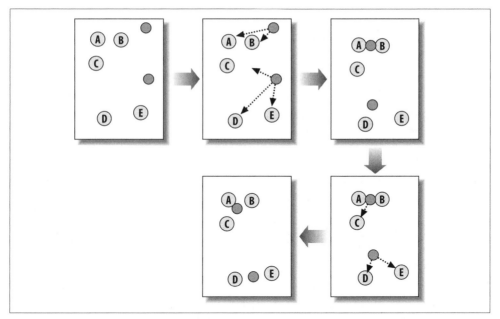

Figure 3-5. K-means clustering with two clusters

```
import random

def kcluster(rows,distance=pearson,k=4):
  # Determine the minimum and maximum values for each point
  ranges=[(min([row[i] for row in rows]),max([row[i] for row in rows]))
  for i in range(len(rows[0]))]

  # Create k randomly placed centroids
  clusters=[[random.random( )*(ranges[i][1]-ranges[i][0])+ranges[i][0]
  for i in range(len(rows[0]))] for j in range(k)]

  lastmatches=None
  for t in range(100):
    print 'Iteration %d' % t
    bestmatches=[[] for i in range(k)]

    # Find which centroid is the closest for each row
    for j in range(len(rows)):
      row=rows[j]
      bestmatch=0
      for i in range(k):
        d=distance(clusters[i],row)
        if d<distance(clusters[bestmatch],row): bestmatch=i
      bestmatches[bestmatch].append(j)

    # If the results are the same as last time, this is complete
    if bestmatches==lastmatches: break
    lastmatches=bestmatches
```

```
# Move the centroids to the average of their members
for i in range(k):
  avgs=[0.0]*len(rows[0])
  if len(bestmatches[i])>0:
    for rowid in bestmatches[i]:
      for m in range(len(rows[rowid])):
        avgs[m]+=rows[rowid][m]
    for j in range(len(avgs)):
      avgs[j]/=len(bestmatches[i])
    clusters[i]=avgs

return bestmatches
```

This code randomly creates a set of clusters within the ranges of each of the variables. With every iteration, the rows are each assigned to one of the centroids, and the centroid data is updated to the average of all its assignees. When the assignments are the same as they were the previous time, the process ends and the k lists, each representing a cluster, are returned. The number of iterations it takes to produce the final result is quite small compared to hierarchical clustering.

Because this function uses random centroids to start with, the order of the results returned will almost always be different. It's also possible for the contents of the clusters to be different depending on the initial locations of the centroids.

You can try this function on the blog dataset. It should run quite a bit faster than the hierarchical clustering:

```
>> reload(clusters)
>> kclust=clusters.kcluster(data,k=10)
Iteration 0
...
>> [rownames[r] for r in k[0]]
['The Viral Garden', 'Copyblogger', 'Creating Passionate Users', 'Oilman',
'ProBlogger Blog Tips', "Seth's Blog"]
>> [rownames[r] for r in k[1]]
etc..
```

kclust now contains an list of IDs for each cluster. Try the clustering with different values of k and see how it affects the results.

Clusters of Preferences

One of the best things about the growing interest in social networking sites is that big sets of data are becoming available, all contributed voluntarily by people. One such site is called Zebo (*http://www.zebo.com*), which encourages people to create accounts and make lists of things that they own and things that they would like to own. From an advertiser's or social critic's perspective, this is very interesting information, as it can allow them to determine the way that expressed preferences naturally group together.

Getting and Preparing the Data

This section will go through the process of creating a dataset from the Zebo web site. It involves downloading many pages from the site and parsing them to extract what each user says they want. If you would like to skip this section, you can download a precreated dataset from *http://kiwitobes.com/clusters/zebo.txt*.

Beautiful Soup

Beautiful Soup is an excellent library for parsing a web page and building a structured representation. It allows you to access any element of the page by type, ID, or any of its properties, and get a string representation of its contents. Beautiful Soup is also very tolerant of web pages with broken HTML, which is useful when generating datasets from web sites.

You can download Beautiful Soup from *http://crummy.com/software/BeautifulSoup*. It comes as a single Python file, which you can put in your Python library path or in the path where you'll be working and starting the Python interpreter.

Once you've installed Beautiful Soup, you can see it in action in your interpreter:

```
>> import urllib2
>> from BeautifulSoup import BeautifulSoup
>> c=urllib2.urlopen('http://kiwitobes.com/wiki/Programming_language.html')
>> soup=BeautifulSoup(c.read())
>> links=soup('a')
>> links[10]
<a href="/wiki/Algorithm.html" title="Algorithm">algorithms</a>
>> links[10]['href']
u'/wiki/Algorithm.html'
```

To construct a *soup*, which is Beautiful Soup's way of representing a web page, just initialize it with the contents of the page. You can call the soup with a tag type, such as a, and it will return a list of objects with that type. Each of these is also addressable, allowing you to drill down into properties and other objects beneath them in the hierarchy.

Scraping the Zebo Results

The structure of the search page on Zebo is fairly complex, but it's easy to determine which parts of the page are the lists of items because they all have the class bgverdanasmall. You can take advantage of this to extract the important data from the page. Create a new file called *downloadzebodata.py* and insert the following code:

```
from BeautifulSoup import BeautifulSoup
import urllib2
import re
chare=re.compile(r'[!-\.&]')
itemowners={}
```

```
# Words to remove
dropwords=['a','new','some','more','my','own','the','many','other','another']

currentuser=0
for i in range(1,51):
  # URL for the want search page
  c=urllib2.urlopen(
  'http://member.zebo.com/Main?event_key=USERSEARCH&wiowiw=wiw&keyword=car&page=%d'
  % (i))
  soup=BeautifulSoup(c.read())
  for td in soup('td'):
    # Find table cells of bgverdanasmall class
    if ('class' in dict(td.attrs) and td['class']=='bgverdanasmall'):
      items=[re.sub(chare,'',a.contents[0].lower()).strip() for a in td('a')]
      for item in items:
        # Remove extra words
        txt=' '.join([t for t in item.split(' ') if t not in dropwords])
        if len(txt)<2: continue
        itemowners.setdefault(txt,{})
        itemowners[txt][currentuser]=1
      currentuser+=1
```

This code will download and parse the first 50 pages of the "want" search from Zebo. Since all the items are entered as free text, there's a significant amount of cleanup to be done, including removing words like "a" and "some," getting rid of punctuation, and making everything lowercase.

Once this is done, the code first has to create a list of items that more than five people want, then it must build a matrix with anonymized users as columns and items as rows, and finally, it has to write the matrix to a file. Add this to the end of *downloadzebodata.py*:

```
out=file('zebo.txt','w')
out.write('Item')
for user in range(0,currentuser): out.write('\tU%d' % user)
out.write('\n')
for item,owners in itemowners.items():
  if len(owners)>10:
    out.write(item)
    for user in range(0,currentuser):
      if user in owners: out.write('\t1')
      else: out.write('\t0')
    out.write('\n')
```

Run the following from the command line to generate a file called zebo.txt, with the same format as the blog dataset. The only difference is that instead of counts, there is a 1 if a person wants a particular item and a 0 if he doesn't:

```
c:\code\cluster>python downloadzebodata.py
```

Defining a Distance Metric

The Pearson correlation works well for the blog dataset where the values are actual word counts. However, this dataset just has 1s and 0s for presence or absence, and it would be more useful to define some measure of overlap between the people who want two items. For this, there is a measure called the *Tanimoto* coefficient, which is the ratio of the intersection set (only the items that are in both sets) to the union set (all the items in either set). This is easily defined for two vectors like this:

```
def tanamoto(v1,v2):
  c1,c2,shr=0,0,0

  for i in range(len(v1)):
    if v1[i]!=0: c1+=1 # in v1
    if v2[i]!=0: c2+=1 # in v2
    if v1[i]!=0 and v2[i]!=0: shr+=1 # in both

  return 1.0-(float(shr)/(c1+c2-shr))
```

This will return a value between 1.0 and 0.0. A value of 1.0 indicates that nobody who wants the first item wants the second one, and 0.0 means that exactly the same set of people want the two items.

Clustering Results

Because the data is in the same format as before, the same functions can be used to generate and draw the hierarchical clusters. This is easily defined for two vectors with this function; add it to *clusters.py*:

```
>> reload(clusters)
>> wants,people,data=clusters.readfile('zebo.txt')
>> clust=clusters.hcluster(data,distance=clusters.tanamoto)
>> clusters.drawdendrogram(clust,wants)
```

This will create a new file, *clusters.jpg*, with the clusters of desired possessions. The results with the downloadable dataset are shown in Figure 3-6. There's nothing earth-shattering here in terms of marketing information—the same people want an Xbox, a PlayStation Portable, and a PlayStation 3—but there are some clear groups that emerge, such as the very ambitious (boat, plane, island) and the soul-searchers (friends, love, happiness). It's also interesting to notice that people who want "money" merely want a "house," while those who want "lots of money" would prefer a "nice house."

By altering the initial search, changing the number of pages retrieved, or getting the data from an "I own" search rather than an "I want" search, you can probably find other interesting groups of items. You can also try transposing the matrix and grouping the users, which would be made more interesting by collecting their ages to see how age divides people.

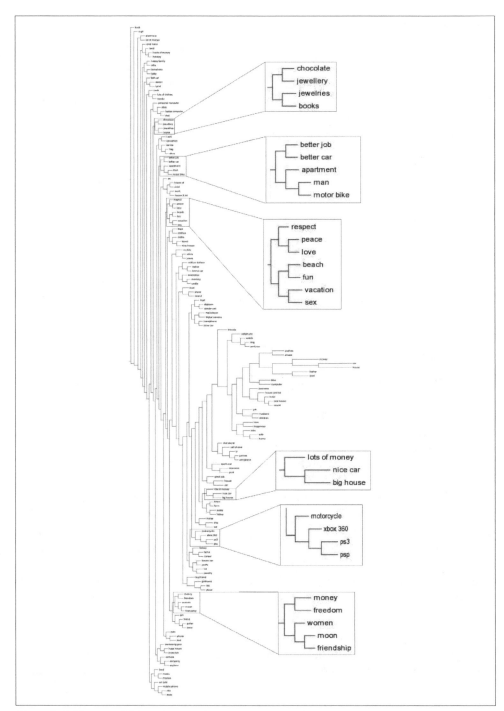

Figure 3-6. Clusters of things that people want

Viewing Data in Two Dimensions

The clustering algorithms in this chapter have been demonstrated using a stylized visualization of data in two dimensions, with the difference between the various items indicated by how far apart they are in the diagram. Since most real-life examples of items you would want to cluster have more than two numbers, you can't just take the data as-is and plot it in two dimensions. However, to understand the relationship between the various items, it would be very useful to see them charted on a page with closer distances indicating similarity.

This section will introduce a technique called *multidimensional scaling*, which will be used to find a two-dimensional representation of the dataset. The algorithm takes the difference between every pair of items and tries to make a chart in which the distances between the items match those differences. To do this, the algorithm first calculates the target distances between all the items. In the blog dataset, Pearson correlation was used to compare the items. An example of this is shown in Table 3-2.

Table 3-2. Sample distance matrix

	A	B	C	D
A	0.0	0.2	0.8	0.7
B	0.2	0.0	0.9	0.8
C	0.8	0.9	0.0	0.1
D	0.7	0.8	0.1	0.0

Next, all the items (blogs, in this case) are placed randomly on the two-dimensional chart, as shown in Figure 3-7.

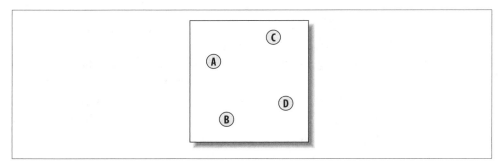

Figure 3-7. Starting locations of the 2D projection

The current distances between all the items are calculated using the actual distance (the sum of the differences of the squares), as shown in Figure 3-8.

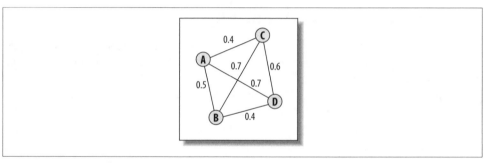

Figure 3-8. Distances between items

For every pair of items, the target distance is compared to the current distance and an error term is calculated. Every item is moved a small amount closer or further in proportion to the error between the two items. Figure 3-9 shows the forces acting on item A. The distance between A and B in the chart is 0.5, but the target distance is only 0.2, so A has to be moved closer to B. At the same time, A is also being pushed away by C and D because it is too close.

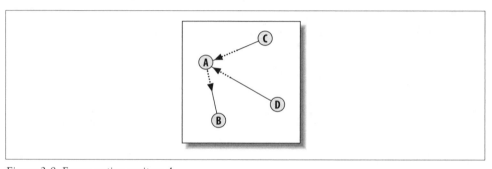

Figure 3-9. Forces acting on item A

Every node is moved according to the combination of all the other nodes pushing and pulling on it. Each time this happens, the difference between the current distances and the target distances gets a bit smaller. This procedure is repeated many times until the total amount of error cannot be reduced by moving the items any more.

The function for doing this takes the data vector and returns one with only two columns, the X and Y coordinates of the items on the two-dimensional chart. Add this function to *clusters.py*:

```
def scaledown(data,distance=pearson,rate=0.01):
  n=len(data)

  # The real distances between every pair of items
  realdist=[[distance(data[i],data[j]) for j in range(n)]
             for i in range(0,n)]

  outersum=0.0
```

```
# Randomly initialize the starting points of the locations in 2D
loc=[[random.random(),random.random()] for i in range(n)]
fakedist=[[0.0 for j in range(n)] for i in range(n)]

lasterror=None
for m in range(0,1000):
  # Find projected distances
  for i in range(n):
    for j in range(n):
      fakedist[i][j]=sqrt(sum([pow(loc[i][x]-loc[j][x],2)
                               for x in range(len(loc[i]))]))

  # Move points
  grad=[[0.0,0.0] for i in range(n)]

  totalerror=0
  for k in range(n):
    for j in range(n):
      if j==k: continue
      # The error is percent difference between the distances
      errorterm=(fakedist[j][k]-realdist[j][k])/realdist[j][k]

      # Each point needs to be moved away from or towards the other
      # point in proportion to how much error it has
      grad[k][0]+=((loc[k][0]-loc[j][0])/fakedist[j][k])*errorterm
      grad[k][1]+=((loc[k][1]-loc[j][1])/fakedist[j][k])*errorterm

      # Keep track of the total error
      totalerror+=abs(errorterm)
  print totalerror

  # If the answer got worse by moving the points, we are done
  if lasterror and lasterror<totalerror: break
  lasterror=totalerror

  # Move each of the points by the learning rate times the gradient
  for k in range(n):
    loc[k][0]-=rate*grad[k][0]
    loc[k][1]-=rate*grad[k][1]

return loc
```

To view this, you can use the PIL again to generate an image with all the labels of all the different items plotted at the new coordinates of that item.

```
def draw2d(data,labels,jpeg='mds2d.jpg'):
  img=Image.new('RGB',(2000,2000),(255,255,255))
  draw=ImageDraw.Draw(img)
  for i in range(len(data)):
    x=(data[i][0]+0.5)*1000
    y=(data[i][1]+0.5)*1000
    draw.text((x,y),labels[i],(0,0,0))
  img.save(jpeg,'JPEG')
```

To run this algorithm, call scaledown to get the two-dimensional dataset and then call draw2d to plot it:

```
>> reload(clusters)
>> blognames,words,data=clusters.readfile('blogdata.txt')
>> coords=clusters.scaledown(data)
...
>> clusters.draw2d(coords,blognames,jpeg='blogs2d.jpg')
```

Figure 3-10 shows the outcome of the multidimensional scaling algorithm. The clusters don't break out quite as well as they do on the dendrogram, but there's still clearly some topical grouping, such as the search-engine-related set near the top. These ended up very far away from the political and celebrity blogs. Had this representation been done in three dimensions, the clusters would be even better, but obviously this would be difficult to visualize on paper.

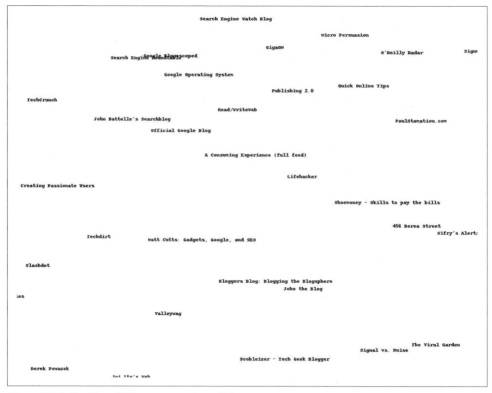

Figure 3-10. Portion of 2D representation of blog space

Other Things to Cluster

This chapter has looked at two datasets, but there are many other things that can be done. The del.icio.us dataset from Chapter 2 can also be clustered to find groups of users or bookmarks. In the same way that the blog feeds were transformed into word vectors, any set of pages that is download can be reduced to just the words.

These ideas can be extended to many different areas to find interesting things—message boards based on word usage, companies from Yahoo! Finance based on various statistics, or top reviewers on Amazon according to what they like. It would also be interesting to look at a large social network like MySpace and cluster people according to who their friends are, or possibly use other information they provide about themselves (favorite bands, foods, etc.).

The concept of imagining items in space depending on their parameters will be a recurring theme in this book. Using multidimensional scaling is an effective way to take a dataset and actually view it in a way that's easy to interpret. It's important to realize that some information is lost in the process of scaling, but the result should help you understand the algorithms better.

Exercises

1. Using the del.icio.us API from Chapter 2, create a dataset of bookmarks suitable for clustering. Run hierarchical and K-means clustering on it.

2. Modify the blog parsing code to cluster individual entries instead of entire blogs. Do entries from the same blog cluster together? What about entries from the same date?

3. Try using actual (Pythagorean) distance for blog clustering. How does this change the results?

4. Find out what Manhattan distance is. Create a function for it and see how it changes the results for the Zebo dataset.

5. Modify the K-means clustering function to return, along with the cluster results, the total distance between all the items and their respective centroids.

6. After completing Exercise 5, create a function that runs K-means clustering over different values of k. How does the total distance change as the number of clusters increases? At what point does the improvement from having more clusters become very small?

7. Multidimensional scaling in two dimensions is easy to print, but scaling can be done in any number of dimensions. Try changing the code to scale in one dimension (all the points on a line). Now try making it work for three dimensions.

## CHAPTER 4

Searching and Ranking

This chapter covers full-text search engines, which allow people to search a large set of documents for a list of words, and which rank results according to how relevant the documents are to those words. Algorithms for full-text searches are among the most important collective intelligence algorithms, and many fortunes have been made by new ideas in this field. It is widely believed that Google's rapid rise from an academic project to the world's most popular search engine was based largely on the PageRank algorithm, a variation that you'll learn about in this chapter.

Information retrieval is a huge field with a long history. This chapter will only be able to cover a few key concepts, but we'll go through the construction of a search engine that will index a set of documents and leave you with ideas on how to improve things further. Although the focus will be on algorithms for searching and ranking rather than on the infrastructure requirements for indexing large portions of the Web, the search engine you build should have no problem with collections of up to 100,000 pages. Throughout this chapter, you'll learn all the necessary steps to crawl, index, and search a set of pages, and even rank their results in many different ways.

What's in a Search Engine?

The first step in creating a search engine is to develop a way to collect the documents. In some cases, this will involve *crawling* (starting with a small set of documents and following links to others) and in other cases it will begin with a fixed collection of documents, perhaps from a corporate intranet.

After you collect the documents, they need to be indexed. This usually involves creating a big table of the documents and the locations of all the different words. Depending on the particular application, the documents themselves do not necessarily have to be stored in a database; the index simply has to store a reference (such as a file system path or URL) to their locations.

The final step is, of course, returning a ranked list of documents from a query. Retrieving every document with a given set of words is fairly straightforward once you have an index, but the real magic is in how the results are sorted. A huge number of metrics can be generated, and there is no shortage of ways you can tweak them to change the sort order. Just learning all the different metrics might make you wish that the big search engines would let you control more of them ("Why can't I tell Google that my words must be close together?"). This chapter will look at several metrics based on the content of the page, such as word frequency, and then cover metrics based on information external to the content of the page, such as the Page-Rank algorithm, which looks at how other pages link to the page in question.

Finally, you'll build a *neural network* for ranking queries. The neural network will learn to associate searches with results based on what links people click on after they get a list of search results. The neural network will use this information to change the ordering of the results to better reflect what people have clicked on in the past.

To work through the examples in this chapter, you'll need to create a Python module called *searchengine*, which has two classes: one for crawling and creating the database, and the other for doing full-text searches by querying the database. The examples will use *SQLite*, but they can easily be adapted to work with a traditional client-server database.

To start, create a new file called *searchengine.py* and add the following crawler class and method signatures, which you'll be filling in throughout this chapter:

```
class crawler:
  # Initialize the crawler with the name of database
  def __init__(self,dbname):
    pass

  def __del__(self):
    pass
  def dbcommit(self):
    pass

  # Auxilliary function for getting an entry id and adding
  # it if it's not present
  def getentryid(self,table,field,value,createnew=True):
    return None

  # Index an individual page
  def addtoindex(self,url,soup):
    print 'Indexing %s' % url

  # Extract the text from an HTML page (no tags)
  def gettextonly(self,soup):
    return None

  # Separate the words by any non-whitespace character
  def separatewords(self,text):
    return None
```

```
# Return true if this url is already indexed
def isindexed(self,url):
  return False

# Add a link between two pages
def addlinkref(self,urlFrom,urlTo,linkText):
  pass

# Starting with a list of pages, do a breadth
# first search to the given depth, indexing pages
# as we go
def crawl(self,pages,depth=2):
  pass

# Create the database tables
def createindextables(self):
  pass
```

A Simple Crawler

I'll assume for now that you don't have a big collection of HTML documents sitting on your hard drive waiting to be indexed, so I'll show you how to build a simple crawler. It will be seeded with a small set of pages to index and will then follow any links on that page to find other pages, whose links it will also follow. This process is called crawling or *spidering*.

To do this, your code will have to download the pages, pass them to the indexer (which you'll build in the next section), and then parse the pages to find all the links to the pages that have to be crawled next. Fortunately, there are a couple of libraries that can help with this process.

For the examples in this chapter, I have set up a copy of several thousand files from Wikipedia, which will remain static at *http://kiwitobes.com/wiki*.

You're free to run the crawler on any set of pages you like, but you can use this site if you want to compare your results to those in this chapter.

Using urllib2

urllib2 is a library bundled with Python that makes it easy to download pages—all you have to do is supply the URL. You'll use it in this section to download the pages that will be indexed. To see it in action, start up your Python interpreter and try this:

```
>> import urllib2
>> c=urllib2.urlopen('http://kiwitobes.com/wiki/Programming_language.html')
>> contents=c.read()
>> print contents[0:50]
'<!DOCTYPE html PUBLIC "-//W3C//DTD XHTML 1.0 Trans'
```

All you have to do to store a page's HTML code into a string is create a connection and read its contents.

Crawler Code

The crawler will use the Beautiful Soup API that was introduced in Chapter 3, an excellent library that builds a structured representation of web pages. It is very tolerant of web pages with broken HTML, which is useful when constructing a crawler because you never know what pages you might come across. For more information on downloading and installing Beautiful Soup, see Appendix A.

Using urllib2 and Beautiful Soup you can build a crawler that will take a list of URLs to index and crawl their links to find other pages to index. First, add these `import` statements to the top of *searchengine.py*:

```
import urllib2
from BeautifulSoup import *
from urlparse import urljoin

# Create a list of words to ignore
ignorewords=set(['the','of','to','and','a','in','is','it'])
```

Now you can fill in the code for the crawler function. It won't actually save anything it crawls yet, but it will print the URLs as it goes so you can see that it's working. You need to put this at the end of the file (so it's part of the crawler class):

```
def crawl(self,pages,depth=2):
  for i in range(depth):
    newpages=set( )
    for page in pages:
      try:
        c=urllib2.urlopen(page)
      except:
        print "Could not open %s" % page
        continue
      soup=BeautifulSoup(c.read( ))
      self.addtoindex(page,soup)

      links=soup('a')
      for link in links:
        if ('href' in dict(link.attrs)):
          url=urljoin(page,link['href'])
          if url.find("'")!=-1: continue
          url=url.split('#')[0]  # remove location portion
          if url[0:4]=='http' and not self.isindexed(url):
            newpages.add(url)
          linkText=self.gettextonly(link)
          self.addlinkref(page,url,linkText)

      self.dbcommit( )

    pages=newpages
```

This function loops through the list of pages, calling addtoindex on each one (right now this does nothing except print the URL, but you'll fill it in the next section). It then uses Beautiful Soup to get all the links on that page and adds their URLs to a set called newpages. At the end of the loop, newpages becomes pages, and the process repeats.

This function can be defined recursively so that each link calls the function again, but doing a breadth-first search allows for easier modification of the code later, either to keep crawling continuously or to save a list of unindexed pages for later crawling. It also avoids the risk of overflowing the stack.

You can test this function in the Python interpreter (there's no need to let it finish, so press Ctrl-C when you get bored):

```
>> import searchengine
>> pagelist=['http://kiwitobes.com/wiki/Perl.html']
>> crawler=searchengine.crawler('')
>> crawler.crawl(pagelist)
Indexing http://kiwitobes.com/wiki/Perl.html
Could not open http://kiwitobes.com/wiki/Module_%28programming%29.html
Indexing http://kiwitobes.com/wiki/Open_Directory_Project.html
Indexing http://kiwitobes.com/wiki/Common_Gateway_Interface.html
```

You may notice that some pages are repeated. There is a placeholder in the code for another function, isindexed, which will determine if a page has been indexed recently before adding it to newpages. This will let you run this function on any list of URLs at any time without worrying about doing unnecessary work.

Building the Index

The next step is to set up the database for the full-text index. As I mentioned earlier, the index is a list of all the different words, along with the documents in which they appear and their locations in the documents. In this example, you'll be looking at the actual text on the page and ignoring nontext elements. You'll also be indexing individual words with all the punctuation characters removed. The method for separating words is not perfect, but it will suffice for building a basic search engine.

Because covering different database software or setting up a database server is outside the scope of this book, this chapter will show you how to store the index using SQLite. SQLite is an embedded database that is very easy to set up and stores a whole database in one file. SQLite uses SQL for queries, so it shouldn't be too difficult to convert the sample code to use a different database. The Python implementation is called pysqlite, and you can download it from *http://initd.org/tracker/pysqlite*.

There is a Windows installer as well as instructions for installing it on other operating systems. Appendix A contains more information on getting and installing pysqlite.

Once you have SQLite installed, add this line to the start of *searchengine.py*:

```
from pysqlite2 import dbapi2 as sqlite
```

You'll also need to change the __init__, __del__, and dbcommit methods to open and close the database:

```
def __init__(self,dbname):
  self.con=sqlite.connect(dbname)

def __del__(self):
  self.con.close( )

def dbcommit(self):
  self.con.commit( )
```

Setting Up the Schema

Don't run the code just yet—you still need to prepare the database. The schema for the basic index is five tables. The first table (urllist) is the list of URLs that have been indexed. The second table (wordlist) is the list of words, and the third table (wordlocation) is a list of the locations of words in the documents. The remaining two tables specify links between documents. The link table stores two URL IDs, indicating a link from one table to another, and linkwords uses the wordid and linkid columns to store which words are actually used in that link. The schema is shown in Figure 4-1.

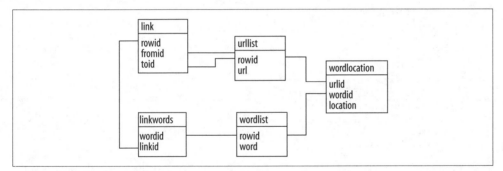

Figure 4-1. Schema for the search engine

All tables in SQLite have a field called rowid by default, so there's no need to explicitly specify an ID for these tables. To create a function for adding all the tables, add this code to the end of *searchengine.py* so that it's part of the crawler class:

```
def createindextables(self):
  self.con.execute('create table urllist(url)')
  self.con.execute('create table wordlist(word)')
  self.con.execute('create table wordlocation(urlid,wordid,location)')
  self.con.execute('create table link(fromid integer,toid integer)')
  self.con.execute('create table linkwords(wordid,linkid)')
  self.con.execute('create index wordidx on wordlist(word)')
  self.con.execute('create index urlidx on urllist(url)')
  self.con.execute('create index wordurlidx on wordlocation(wordid)')
```

```
self.con.execute('create index urltoidx on link(toid)')
self.con.execute('create index urlfromidx on link(fromid)')
self.dbcommit()
```

This function will create the schema for all the tables that you will be using, along with some indices to speed up searching. These indices are important, since the dataset can potentially get very large. Enter these commands in your Python session to create a database called *searchindex.db*:

```
>> reload(searchengine)
>> crawler=searchengine.crawler('searchindex.db')
>> crawler.createindextables()
```

Later you'll be adding an additional table to the schema for a scoring metric based on counting inbound links.

Finding the Words on a Page

The files that you're downloading from the Web are HTML and thus contain a lot of tags, properties, and other information that doesn't belong in the index. The first step is to extract all the parts of the page that are text. You can do this by searching the soup for text nodes and collecting all their content. Add this code to your gettextonly function:

```
def gettextonly(self,soup):
  v=soup.string
  if v==None:
    c=soup.contents
    resulttext=''
    for t in c:
      subtext=self.gettextonly(t)
      resulttext+=subtext+'\n'
    return resulttext
  else:
    return v.strip()
```

The function returns a long string containing all the text on the page. It does this by recursively traversing down the HTML document object model, looking for text nodes. Text that was in separate sections is separated into different paragraphs. It's important to preserve the order of the sections for some of the metrics you'll be calculating later.

Next is the separatewords function, which splits a string into a list of separate words so that they can be added to the index. It's not as easy as you might think to do this perfectly, and there has been a lot of research into improving the technique. However, for these examples it will suffice to consider anything that isn't a letter or a number to be a separator. You can do this using a regular expression. Replace the definition of separatewords with the following:

```
def separatewords(self,text):
  splitter=re.compile('\\W*')
  return [s.lower( ) for s in splitter.split(text) if s!='']
```

Because this function considers anything nonalphanumeric to be a separator, it will have no problem extracting English words, but it won't properly handle terms like "C++" (no trouble searching for "python," though). You can experiment with the regular expression to make it work better for different kinds of searches.

 Another possibility is to remove suffixes from the words using a *stemming* algorithm. These algorithms attempt to convert the words to their stems. For example, the word "indexing" becomes "index" so that people searching for the word "index" are also shown documents containing the word "indexing." To do this, stem the words while crawling documents and also stem the words in the search query. A full discussion of stemming is outside the scope of this chapter, but you can find a Python implementation of the well-known *Porter Stemmer* at *http://www.tartarus.org/~martin/PorterStemmer/index.html*.

Adding to the Index

You're ready to fill in the code for the addtoindex method. This method will call the two functions that were defined in the previous section to get a list of words on the page. Then it will add the page and all the words to the index, and will create links between them with their locations in the document. For this example, the location will be the index within the list of words.

Here is the code for addtoindex:

```
def addtoindex(self,url,soup):
  if self.isindexed(url): return
  print 'Indexing '+url

  # Get the individual words
  text=self.gettextonly(soup)
  words=self.separatewords(text)

  # Get the URL id
  urlid=self.getentryid('urllist','url',url)

  # Link each word to this url
  for i in range(len(words)):
    word=words[i]
    if word in ignorewords: continue
    wordid=self.getentryid('wordlist','word',word)
    self.con.execute("insert into wordlocation(urlid,wordid,location) \
      values (%d,%d,%d)" % (urlid,wordid,i))
```

You'll also need this to update the helper function getentryid. All this does is return the ID of an entry. If the entry doesn't exist, it is created and the ID is returned:

```
def getentryid(self,table,field,value,createnew=True):
  cur=self.con.execute(
  "select rowid from %s where %s='%s'" % (table,field,value))
  res=cur.fetchone()
  if res==None:
    cur=self.con.execute(
    "insert into %s (%s) values ('%s')" % (table,field,value))
    return cur.lastrowid
  else:
    return res[0]
```

Finally, you'll need to fill in the code for isindexed, which determines whether the page is already in the database, and if so, whether there are any words associated with it:

```
def isindexed(self,url):
  u=self.con.execute \
    ("select rowid from urllist where url='%s'" % url).fetchone()
  if u!=None:
    # Check if it has actually been crawled
    v=self.con.execute(
    'select * from wordlocation where urlid=%d' % u[0]).fetchone()
    if v!=None: return True
  return False
```

Now you can rerun the crawler and have it actually index the pages as it goes. You can do this in your interactive session:

```
>> reload(searchengine)
>> crawler=searchengine.crawler('searchindex.db')
>> pages= \
.. ['http://kiwitobes.com/wiki/Categorical_list_of_programming_languages.html']
>> crawler.crawl(pages)
```

The crawler will probably take a long time to run. Instead of waiting for it to finish, I recommend that you download a preloaded copy of *searchindex.db* from *http:// kiwitobes.com/db/searchindex.db* and save it in the directory with your Python code.

If you'd like to make sure that the crawl worked properly, you can try checking the entries for a word by querying the database:

```
>> [row for row in crawler.con.execute(
.. 'select rowid from wordlocation where wordid=1')]
[(1,), (46,), (330,), (232,), (406,), (271,), (192,),...
```

The list that is returned is the list of all the URL IDs containing "word," which means that you've successfully run a full-text search. This is a great start, but it will only work with one word at a time, and will just return the documents in the order in which they were loaded. The next section will show you how to expand this functionality by doing these searches with multiple words in the query.

Querying

You now have a working crawler and a big collection of documents indexed, and you're ready to set up the search part of the search engine. First, create a new class in *searchengine.py* that you'll use for searching:

```
class searcher:
  def __init__(self,dbname):
    self.con=sqlite.connect(dbname)

  def __del__(self):
    self.con.close()
```

The wordlocation table gives an easy way to link words to tables, so it is quite easy to see which pages contain a single word. However, a search engine is pretty limited unless it allows multiple-word searches. To do this, you'll need a query function that takes a query string, splits it into separate words, and constructs a SQL query to find only those URLs containing all the different words. Add this function to the definition for the searcher class:

```
def getmatchrows(self,q):
  # Strings to build the query
  fieldlist='w0.urlid'
  tablelist=''
  clauselist=''
  wordids=[]

  # Split the words by spaces
  words=q.split(' ')
  tablenumber=0

  for word in words:
    # Get the word ID
    wordrow=self.con.execute(
      "select rowid from wordlist where word='%s'" % word).fetchone()
    if wordrow!=None:
      wordid=wordrow[0]
      wordids.append(wordid)
      if tablenumber>0:
        tablelist+=','
        clauselist+=' and '
        clauselist+='w%d.urlid=w%d.urlid and ' % (tablenumber-1,tablenumber)
      fieldlist+=',w%d.location' % tablenumber
      tablelist+='wordlocation w%d' % tablenumber
      clauselist+='w%d.wordid=%d' % (tablenumber,wordid)
      tablenumber+=1

  # Create the query from the separate parts
  fullquery='select %s from %s where %s' % (fieldlist,tablelist,clauselist)
  cur=self.con.execute(fullquery)
  rows=[row for row in cur]

  return rows,wordids
```

This function looks a bit complicated, but it's just creating a reference to the wordlocation table for each word in the list and joining them all on their URL IDs (Figure 4-2).

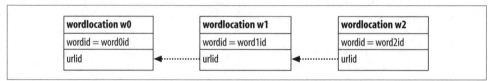

Figure 4-2. Table joins for getmatchrows

So a query for two words with the IDs 10 and 17 becomes:

```
select w0.urlid,w0.location,w1.location
from   wordlocation w0,wordlocation w1
where  w0.urlid=w1.urlid
and    w0.wordid=10
and    w1.wordid=17
```

Try calling this function with your first multiple-word search:

```
>> reload(searchengine)
>> e=searchengine.searcher('searchindex.db')
>> e.getmatchrows('functional programming')
([(1, 327, 23), (1, 327, 162), (1, 327, 243), (1, 327, 261),
   (1, 327, 269), (1, 327, 436), (1, 327, 953),..
```

You'll notice that each URL ID is returned many times with different combinations of word locations. The next few sections will cover some ways to rank the results. *Content-based ranking* uses several possible metrics with just the content of the page to determine the relevance of the query. *Inbound-link ranking* uses the link structure of the site to determine what's important. We will also explore a way to look at what people actually click on when they search in order to improve the rankings over time.

Content-Based Ranking

So far you've managed to retrieve pages that match the queries, but the order in which they are returned is simply the order in which they were crawled. In a large set of pages, you would be stuck sifting through a lot of irrelevant content for any mention of each of the query terms in order to find the pages that are really related to your search. To address this issue, you need ways to give pages a *score* for a given query, as well as the ability to return them with the highest scoring results first.

This section will look at several ways to calculate a score based only on the query and the content of the page. These scoring metrics include:

Word frequency
> The number of times the words in the query appear in the document can help determine how relevant the document is.

Document location

The main subject of a document will probably appear near the beginning of the document.

Word distance

If there are multiple words in the query, they should appear close together in the document.

The earliest search engines often worked with only these types of metrics and were able to give usable results. Later sections will cover ways to improve results with information external to the page, such as the number and quality of incoming links.

First, you'll need a new method that will take a query, get the rows, put them in a dictionary, and display them in a formatted list. Add these functions to your searcher class:

```
def getscoredlist(self,rows,wordids):
  totalscores=dict([(row[0],0) for row in rows])

  # This is where you'll later put the scoring functions
  weights=[]

  for (weight,scores) in weights:
    for url in totalscores:
      totalscores[url]+=weight*scores[url]

  return totalscores

def geturlname(self,id):
  return self.con.execute(
  "select url from urllist where rowid=%d" % id).fetchone()[0]

def query(self,q):
  rows,wordids=self.getmatchrows(q)
  scores=self.getscoredlist(rows,wordids)
  rankedscores=sorted([(score,url) for (url,score) in scores.items()],reverse=1)
  for (score,urlid) in rankedscores[0:10]:
    print '%f\t%s' % (score,self.geturlname(urlid))
```

Right now the query method doesn't apply any scoring to the results, but it does display the URLs along with a placeholder for their scores:

```
>> reload(searchengine)
>> e=searchengine.searcher('searchindex.db')
>> e.query('functional programming')
0.000000 http://kiwitobes.com/wiki/XSLT.html
0.000000 http://kiwitobes.com/wiki/XQuery.html
0.000000 http://kiwitobes.com/wiki/Unified_Modeling_Language.html
...
```

The important function here is getscoredlist, which you'll be filling in throughout this section. As you add scoring functions, you can add calls to the weights list (the line in bold) and start to get some real scores.

Normalization Function

All the scoring methods introduced here return dictionaries of the URL IDs and a numerical score. To complicate things, sometimes a larger score is better and sometimes a smaller score is better. In order to compare the results from different methods, you need a way to *normalize* them; that is, to get them all within the same range and direction.

The normalization function will take a dictionary of IDs and scores and return a new dictionary with the same IDs, but with scores between 0 and 1. Each score is scaled according to how close it is to the best result, which will always have a score of 1. All you have to do is pass the function a list of scores and indicate whether a lower or higher score is better:

```
def normalizescores(self,scores,smallIsBetter=0):
  vsmall=0.00001 # Avoid division by zero errors
  if smallIsBetter:
    minscore=min(scores.values())
    return dict([(u,float(minscore)/max(vsmall,l)) for (u,l) \
      in scores.items()])
  else:
    maxscore=max(scores.values())
    if maxscore==0: maxscore=vsmall
    return dict([(u,float(c)/maxscore) for (u,c) in scores.items()])
```

Each of the scoring functions calls this function to normalize its results and return a value between 0 and 1.

Word Frequency

The word frequency metric scores a page based on how many times the words in the query appear on that page. If I search for "python," I'd rather get a page about Python (or pythons) with many mentions of the word, and not a page about a musician who happens to mention near the end that he has a pet python.

The word frequency function looks like this. You can add it to your searcher class:

```
def frequencyscore(self,rows):
  counts=dict([(row[0],0) for row in rows])
  for row in rows: counts[row[0]]+=1
  return self.normalizescores(counts)
```

This function creates a dictionary with an entry for every unique URL ID in *rows*, and counts how many times each item appears. It then normalizes the scores (bigger is better, in this case) and returns the result.

To activate frequency scoring in your results, change the weights line in getscoredlist to read:

```
weights=[(1.0,self.frequencyscore(rows))]
```

Now you can try another search and see how well this works as a scoring metric:

```
>> reload(searchengine)
>> e=searchengine.searcher('searchindex.db')
>> e.query('functional programming')
1.000000 http://kiwitobes.com/wiki/Functional_programming.html
0.262476 http://kiwitobes.com/wiki/Categorical_list_of_programming_languages.html
0.062310 http://kiwitobes.com/wiki/Programming_language.html
0.043976 http://kiwitobes.com/wiki/Lisp_programming_language.html
0.036394 http://kiwitobes.com/wiki/Programming_paradigm.html
...
```

This returns the page on "Functional programming" in first place, followed by several other relevant pages. Notice that "Functional programming" scored four times better than the result directly below it. Most search engines don't report scores to end users, but these scores can be very useful for some applications. For instance, you might want to take the user directly to the top result if it exceeds a certain threshold, or display results in a font size proportional to the relevance of the result.

Document Location

Another simple metric for determining a page's relevance to a query is the search term's location in the page. Usually, if a page is relevant to the search term, it will appear closer to the top of the page, perhaps even in the title. To take advantage of this, the search engine can score results higher if the query term appears early in the document. Fortunately for us, when the pages were indexed earlier, the locations of the words were recorded, and the title of the page is first in the list.

Add this method to searcher:

```
def locationscore(self,rows):
    locations=dict([(row[0],1000000) for row in rows])
    for row in rows:
        loc=sum(row[1:])
        if loc<locations[row[0]]: locations[row[0]]=loc

    return self.normalizescores(locations,smallIsBetter=1)
```

Remember that the first item in each row element is the URL ID, followed by the locations of all the different search terms. Each ID can appear multiple times, once for every combination of locations. For each row, the method sums the locations of all the words and determines how this result compares to the best result for that URL so far. It then passes the final results to the normalize function. Note that smallIsBetter means that the URL with the lowest location sum gets a score of 1.0.

To see what the results look like using only the location score, change the weights line to this:

```
weights=[(1.0,self.locationscore(rows))]
```

Now try the query again in your interpreter:

```
>> reload(searchengine)
>> e=searchengine.searcher('searchindex.db')
>> e.query('functional programming')
```

You'll notice that "Functional programming" is still the winner, but the other top results are now examples of functional programming languages. The previous search returned results in which the words were mentioned several times, but these tended to be discussions about programming languages in general. With this search, however, the presence of the words in the opening sentence (e.g., "Haskell is a standardized pure functional programming language") gave them a much higher score.

It's important to realize that neither one of the metrics shown so far is better in every case. Both of these lists are valid depending on the searcher's intent, and different combinations of weights are required to give the best results for a particular set of documents and applications. You can try experimenting with different weights for the two metrics by changing your weights line to something like this:

```
weights=[(1.0,self.frequencyscore(rows)),
         (1.5,self.locationscore(rows))]
```

Experiment with different weights and queries and see how your results are affected.

Location is a more difficult metric to cheat than word frequency, since page authors can only put one word first in a document and repeating it doesn't make any difference to the results.

Word Distance

When a query contains multiple words, it is often useful to seek results in which the words in the query are close to each other in the page. Most of the time, when people make multiple-word queries, they are interested in a page that conceptually relates the different words. This is a little looser than the quoted-phrase searches supported by most search engines where the words must appear in the correct order with no additional words—in this case, the metric will tolerate a different order and additional words between the query words.

The distancescore function looks pretty similar to locationscore:

```
def distancescore(self,rows):
  # If there's only one word, everyone wins!
  if len(rows[0])<=2: return dict([(row[0],1.0) for row in rows])

  # Initialize the dictionary with large values
  mindistance=dict([(row[0],1000000) for row in rows])

  for row in rows:
    dist=sum([abs(row[i]-row[i-1]) for i in range(2,len(row))])
    if dist<mindistance[row[0]]: mindistance[row[0]]=dist
  return self.normalizescores(mindistance,smallIsBetter=1)
```

The main difference here is that when the function loops through the locations (on the line shown in bold), it takes the difference between each location and the previous location. Since every combination of distances is returned by the query, it is guaranteed to find the smallest total distance.

You can try the word distance metric by itself if you like, but it really works better when combined with other metrics. Try adding distancescore to the weights list and changing the numbers to see how it affects the results of different queries.

Using Inbound Links

The scoring metrics discussed so far have all been based on the content of the page. Although many search engines still work this way, the results can often be improved by considering information that others have provided about the page, specifically, who has linked to the page and what they have said about it. This is particularly useful when indexing pages of dubious value or pages that might have been created by spammers, as these are less likely to be linked than pages with real content.

The crawler that you built at the beginning of the chapter already captures all the important information about the links, so there's no need to change it. The links table has the URL IDs for the source and target of every link that it has encountered, and the linkwords table connects the words with the links.

Simple Count

The easiest thing to do with inbound links is to count them on each page and use the total number of links as a metric for the page. Academic papers are often rated in this way, with their importance tied to the number of other papers that reference them. The scoring function below creates a dictionary of counts by querying the link table for every unique URL ID in rows, and then it returns the normalized scores:

```
def inboundlinkscore(self,rows):
  uniqueurls=set([row[0] for row in rows])
  inboundcount=dict([(u,self.con.execute( \
    'select count(*) from link where toid=%d' % u).fetchone()[0]) \
      for u in uniqueurls])
  return self.normalizescores(inboundcount)
```

Obviously, using this metric by itself will simply return all the pages containing the search terms, ranked solely on how many inbound links they have. In the dataset, "Programming language" has many more inbound links than "Python," but you'd rather see "Python" first in the results if that's what you searched for. To combine relevance with ranking, you need to use the inbound-links metric in combination with one of the metrics shown earlier.

This algorithm also weights every inbound link equally, which, while nice and egalitarian, is open to manipulation because someone can easily set up several sites pointing to a page whose score they want to increase. It's also possible that people are more interested in results that have attracted the attention of very popular sites. Next, you'll see how to make links from popular pages worth more in calculating rankings.

The PageRank Algorithm

The PageRank algorithm was invented by the founders of Google, and variations on the idea are now used by all the large search engines. This algorithm assigns every page a score that indicates how important that page is. The importance of the page is calculated from the importance of all the other pages that link to it and from the number of links each of the other pages has.

 In theory, PageRank (named after one of its inventors, Larry Page) calculates the probability that someone randomly clicking on links will arrive at a certain page. The more inbound links the page has from other popular pages, the more likely it is that someone will end up there purely by chance. Of course, if the user keeps clicking forever, they'll eventually reach every page, but most people stop surfing after a while. To capture this, PageRank also uses a *damping factor* of 0.85, indicating that there is an 85 percent chance that a user will continue clicking on links at each page.

Figure 4-3 shows an example set of pages and links.

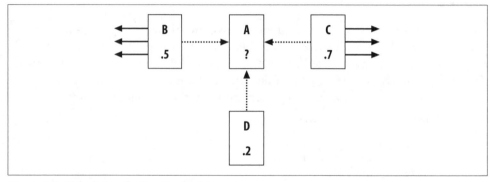

Figure 4-3. Calculating the PageRank of A

Pages B, C, and D all link to A, and they already have their PageRanks calculated. B also links to three other pages and C links to four other pages. D only links to A. To get A's PageRank, take the PageRank (PR) of each of the pages that links to A divided by the total number of links on that page, then multiply this by a damping factor of 0.85, and add a minimum value of 0.15. The calculation for PR(A) is:

```
PR(A) = 0.15 + 0.85 * ( PR(B)/links(B) + PR(C)/links(C) + PR(D)/links(D) )
      = 0.15 + 0.85 * ( 0.5/4 + 0.7/5 + 0.2/1 )
      = 0.15 + 0.85 * ( 0.125 + 0.14 + 0.2)
      = 0.15 + 0.85 * 0.465
      = 0.54525
```

You'll notice that D actually contributes more to A's PageRank than either B or C does, even though it has a lower PageRank of its own, because it links exclusively to A and is able to contribute its entire score.

Pretty easy, right? Well, there's a small catch—in this example, all the pages linking to A already had PageRanks. You can't calculate a page's score until you know the scores of all the pages that link there, and you can't calculate their scores without doing the same for all the pages that link to *them*. How is it possible to calculate PageRanks for a whole set of pages that don't already have PageRanks?

The solution is to set all the PageRanks to an initial arbitrary value (the code will use 1.0, but the actual value doesn't make any difference), and repeat the calculation over several iterations. After each iteration, the PageRank for each page gets closer to its true PageRank value. The number of iterations needed varies with the number of pages, but in the small set you're working with, 20 should be sufficient.

Because the PageRank is time-consuming to calculate and stays the same no matter what the query is, you'll be creating a function that precomputes the PageRank for every URL and stores it in a table. This function will recalculate all the PageRanks every time it is run. Add this function to the crawler class:

```python
def calculatepagerank(self,iterations=20):
  # clear out the current PageRank tables
  self.con.execute('drop table if exists pagerank')
  self.con.execute('create table pagerank(urlid primary key,score)')

  # initialize every url with a PageRank of 1
  self.con.execute('insert into pagerank select rowid, 1.0 from urllist')
  self.dbcommit()

  for i in range(iterations):
    print "Iteration %d" % (i)
    for (urlid,) in self.con.execute('select rowid from urllist'):
      pr=0.15

      # Loop through all the pages that link to this one
      for (linker,) in self.con.execute(
      'select distinct fromid from link where toid=%d' % urlid):
        # Get the PageRank of the linker
        linkingpr=self.con.execute(
        'select score from pagerank where urlid=%d' % linker).fetchone()[0]

        # Get the total number of links from the linker
        linkingcount=self.con.execute(
        'select count(*) from link where fromid=%d' % linker).fetchone()[0]
        pr+=0.85*(linkingpr/linkingcount)
      self.con.execute(
      'update pagerank set score=%f where urlid=%d' % (pr,urlid))
    self.dbcommit()
```

This function initially sets the PageRank of every page to 1.0. It then loops over every URL and gets the PageRank and the total number of links for every inbound link. The line in bold shows the formula being applied for each of the inbound links.

Running this function will take a few minutes, but you only need to do it when you update the index.

```
>> reload(searchengine)
>> crawler=searchengine.crawler('searchindex.db')
>> crawler.calculatepagerank()
Iteration 0
Iteration 1
...
```

If you're curious about which pages from the example dataset have the highest Page-Ranks, you can query the database directly:

```
>> cur=crawler.con.execute('select * from pagerank order by score desc')
>> for i in range(3): print cur.next()
(438, 2.5285160000000002)
(2, 1.1614640000000001)
(543, 1.064252)
>> e.geturlname(438)
u'http://kiwitobes.com/wiki/Main_Page.html'
```

"Main Page" has the highest PageRank, which is not surprising since every other page in Wikipedia links to it. Now that you have a table of PageRank scores, using them is just a matter of creating a function to retrieve them from the database and to normalize the scores. Add this method to the searcher class:

```
def pagerankscore(self,rows):
    pageranks=dict([(row[0],self.con.execute('select score from pagerank where
urlid=%d' % row[0]).fetchone()[0]) for row in rows])
    maxrank=max(pageranks.values())
    normalizedscores=dict([(u,float(l)/maxrank) for (u,l) in pageranks.items()])
    return normalizedscores
```

Once again, you should modify the `weights` list to include PageRank. For example, try:

```
weights=[(1.0,self.locationscore(rows)),
         (1.0,self.frequencyscore(rows)),
         (1.0,self.pagerankscore(rows))]
```

The results for your searches will take into account content and ranking scores. The results for "Functional programming" now look even better:

```
2.318146 http://kiwitobes.com/wiki/Functional_programming.html
1.074506 http://kiwitobes.com/wiki/Programming_language.html
0.517633 http://kiwitobes.com/wiki/Categorical_list_of_programming_languages.html
0.439568 http://kiwitobes.com/wiki/Programming_paradigm.html
0.426817 http://kiwitobes.com/wiki/Lisp_programming_language.html
```

The value of the PageRank score is a little harder to see with this closed, tightly controlled set of documents, which likely contains fewer useless pages or pages intended solely to get attention than you'd find on the Web. However, even in this case, it's clear that PageRank is a useful metric for returning higher-level, more general pages.

Using the Link Text

Another very powerful way to rank searches is to use the text of the links to a page to decide how relevant the page is. Many times you will get better information from what the links to a page say about it than from the linking page itself, as site developers tend to include a short description of whatever it is they are linking to.

The method for scoring the pages by their link text takes an additional argument, which is the list of word IDs produced when you perform a query. You can add this method to searcher:

```
def linktextscore(self,rows,wordids):
  linkscores=dict([(row[0],0) for row in rows])
  for wordid in wordids:
    cur=self.con.execute('select link.fromid,link.toid from linkwords,link where
wordid=%d and linkwords.linkid=link.rowid' % wordid)
    for (fromid,toid) in cur:
      if toid in linkscores:
        pr=self.con.execute('select score from pagerank where urlid=%d' % fromid).
fetchone( )[0]
        linkscores[toid]+=pr
  maxscore=max(linkscores.values( ))
  normalizedscores=dict([(u,float(l)/maxscore) for (u,l) in linkscores.items( )])
  return normalizedscores
```

This code loops through all the words in wordids looking for links containing these words. If the target of the link matches one of the search results, then the PageRank of the source of the link is added to the destination page's final score. A page with a lot of links from important pages that contain the query terms will get a very high score. Many of the pages in the results will have no links with the correct text, and will get a score of 0.

To enable link-text ranking, just add the following anywhere in your weights list:

```
(1.0,self.linktextscore(rows,wordids))
```

There is no standard set of weightings for these metrics that will work in all cases. Even the major search sites frequently change their methods of ranking results. The metrics you'll use and the weights you'll give them are highly dependent on the application you're trying to build.

Learning from Clicks

One of the major advantages of online applications is that they receive constant feedback in the form of user behavior. In the case of a search engine, each user will immediately provide information about how much he likes the results for a given search by clicking on one result and choosing not to click on the others. This section will look at a way to record when a user clicks on a result after a query, and how that record can be used to improve the rankings of the results.

To do this, you're going to build an *artificial neural network* that you'll train by giving it the words in the query, the search results presented to the user, and what the user decided to click. Once the network has been trained with many different queries, you can use it to change the ordering of the search results to better reflect what users actually clicked on in the past.

Design of a Click-Tracking Network

While there are many different kinds of neural networks, they all consist of a set of nodes (the *neurons*) and connections between them. The network you'll learn how to build is called a *multilayer perceptron* (MLP) network. This type of network consists of multiple layers of neurons, the first of which takes the input—in this case, the words entered by the user. The last layer gives the output, which in this example is a list of weightings for the different URLs that were returned.

There can be multiple middle layers, but the network in this example will just use a single one. This is called the *hidden layer* because the outside world never interacts with it directly, and it responds to combinations of inputs. In this case, a combination of inputs is a set of words, so you could also think of this as the *query layer*. Figure 4-4 shows the structure of the network. All the nodes in the input layer are connected to all the nodes in the hidden layer, and all the nodes in the hidden layer are connected to all the nodes in the output layer.

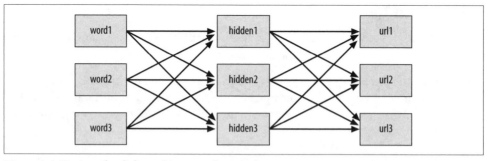

Figure 4-4. Design of a click-tracking neural network

To ask the neural network to get the best results for a query, the input nodes for the words in that query have their values set to 1. The outputs of those nodes are turned on and they attempt to activate the hidden layer. In turn, the nodes in the hidden layer that get a strong enough input will turn on their outputs and try to activate nodes in the output layer.

The nodes in the output layer then become active in various degrees, and their activity level can be used to determine how strongly a URL is associated with the words in the original query. Figure 4-5 shows a query for "world bank." The solid lines indicate strong connections, and the bold text indicates that a node has become very active.

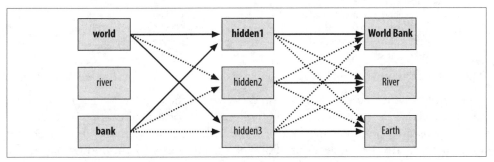

Figure 4-5. Neural network response to "world bank"

This, of course, depends on the connection strengths being correct. This is achieved by *training* the network every time someone performs a search and chooses one of the links out of the results. In the network pictured in Figure 4-5, a number of people had previously clicked the World Bank result after a search for "world bank," and this strengthened the associations between the words and the URL. This section will show you how the network is trained with an algorithm called backpropagation.

You might be wondering why you would need a sophisticated technique like a neural network instead of just remembering the query and counting how many times each result was clicked. The power of the neural network you're going to build is that it can make reasonable guesses about results for queries it has never seen before, based on their similarity to other queries. Also, neural networks are useful for a wide variety of applications and will be a great addition to your collective intelligence toolbox.

Setting Up the Database

Since the neural network will have to be trained over time as users perform queries, you'll need to store a representation of the network in the database. The database already has a table of words and URLs, so all that's needed is a table for the hidden layer (which will be called hiddennode) and two tables of connections (one from the word layer to the hidden layer, and one that links the hidden layer to the output layer).

Create a new file called *nn.py*, and create a new class in it called searchnet:

```
from math import tanh
from pysqlite2 import dbapi2 as sqlite

class searchnet:
    def __init__(self,dbname):
      self.con=sqlite.connect(dbname)

    def __del__(self):
      self.con.close()

    def maketables(self):
      self.con.execute('create table hiddennode(create_key)')
      self.con.execute('create table wordhidden(fromid,toid,strength)')
      self.con.execute('create table hiddenurl(fromid,toid,strength)')
      self.con.commit()
```

The tables currently have no indices, but you can add them later if speed is an issue.

You'll need to create a couple of methods to access the database. The first method, called getstrength, determines the current strength of a connection. Because new connections are only created when necessary, this method has to return a default value if there are no connections. For links from words to the hidden layer, the default value will be –0.2 so that, by default, extra words will have a slightly negative effect on the activation level of a hidden node. For links from the hidden layer to URLs, the method will return a default value of 0.

```
    def getstrength(self,fromid,toid,layer):
      if layer==0: table='wordhidden'
      else: table='hiddenurl'
      res=self.con.execute('select strength from %s where fromid=%d and toid=%d' %
(table,fromid,toid)).fetchone()
      if res==None:
          if layer==0: return -0.2
          if layer==1: return 0
      return res[0]
```

You'll also need a setstrength method to determine if a connection already exists, and to update or create the connection with the new strength. This will be used by the code that trains the network:

```
    def setstrength(self,fromid,toid,layer,strength):
      if layer==0: table='wordhidden'
      else: table='hiddenurl'
      res=self.con.execute('select rowid from %s where fromid=%d and toid=%d' %
(table,fromid,toid)).fetchone()
      if res==None:
        self.con.execute('insert into %s (fromid,toid,strength) values (%d,%d,%f)' %
(table,fromid,toid,strength))
      else:
        rowid=res[0]
        self.con.execute('update %s set strength=%f where rowid=%d' %
(table,strength,rowid))
```

Most of the time, when building a neural network, all the nodes in the network are created in advance. You could create a huge network up front with thousands of nodes in the hidden layer and all the connections already in place, but in this case, it will be faster and simpler to create new hidden nodes as they are needed.

This function will create a new node in the hidden layer every time it is passed a combination of words that it has never seen together before. The function then creates default-weighted links between the words and the hidden node, and between the query node and the URL results returned by this query.

```
def generatehiddennode(self,wordids,urls):
  if len(wordids)>3: return None
  # Check if we already created a node for this set of words
  createkey='_'.join(sorted([str(wi) for wi in wordids]))
  res=self.con.execute(
  "select rowid from hiddennode where create_key='%s'" % createkey).fetchone()

  # If not, create it
  if res==None:
    cur=self.con.execute(
    "insert into hiddennode (create_key) values ('%s')" % createkey)
    hiddenid=cur.lastrowid
    # Put in some default weights
    for wordid in wordids:
      self.setstrength(wordid,hiddenid,0,1.0/len(wordids))
    for urlid in urls:
      self.setstrength(hiddenid,urlid,1,0.1)
    self.con.commit()
```

In the Python interpreter, try creating a database and generating a hidden node with some example word and URL IDs:

```
>> import nn
>> mynet=nn.searchnet('nn.db')
>> mynet.maketables()
>> wWorld,wRiver,wBank =101,102,103
>> uWorldBank,uRiver,uEarth =201,202,203
>> mynet.generatehiddennode([wWorld,wBank],[uWorldBank,uRiver,uEarth])
>> for c in mynet.con.execute('select * from wordhidden'): print c
(101, 1, 0.5)
(103, 1, 0.5)
>> for c in mynet.con.execute('select * from hiddenurl'): print c
(1, 201, 0.1)
(1, 202, 0.1)
...
```

A new node has been created in the hidden layer, and links to the new node have been created with default values. The function will initially respond whenever "world" and "bank" are entered together, but these connections may weaken over time.

Feeding Forward

You're now ready to make functions that will take the words as inputs, activate the links in the network, and give a set of outputs for the URLs.

First, choose a function that indicates how much each node should respond to its input. The neural network described here will use the *hyperbolic tangent* (tanh) function, shown in Figure 4-6.

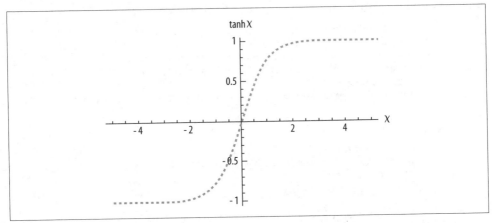

Figure 4-6. The tanh function

The x-axis is the total input to the node. As the input approaches 0, the output starts to climb quickly. With an input of 2, the output is almost at 1 and doesn't get much higher. This is a type of *sigmoid* function, all types of which have this S shape. Neural networks almost always use sigmoid functions to calculate the outputs of the neurons.

Before running the feedforward algorithm, the class will have to query the nodes and connections in the database, and build, in memory, the portion of the network that is relevant to a specific query. The first step is to create a function that finds all the nodes from the hidden layer that are relevant to a specific query—in this case, they must be connected to one of the words in the query or to one of the URLs in the results. Since the other nodes will not be used either to determine an outcome or to train the network, it's not necessary to include them:

```
def getallhiddenids(self,wordids,urlids):
  l1={}
  for wordid in wordids:
    cur=self.con.execute(
    'select toid from wordhidden where fromid=%d' % wordid)
    for row in cur: l1[row[0]]=1
  for urlid in urlids:
    cur=self.con.execute(
    'select fromid from hiddenurl where toid=%d' % urlid)
    for row in cur: l1[row[0]]=1
  return l1.keys()
```

You will also need a method for constructing the relevant network with all the current weights from the database. This function sets a lot of instance variables for this class—the list of words, query nodes and URLs, the output level of every node, and the weights of every link between nodes. The weights are taken from the database using the functions that were defined earlier.

```
def setupnetwork(self,wordids,urlids):
    # value lists
    self.wordids=wordids
    self.hiddenids=self.getallhiddenids(wordids,urlids)
    self.urlids=urlids

    # node outputs
    self.ai = [1.0]*len(self.wordids)
    self.ah = [1.0]*len(self.hiddenids)
    self.ao = [1.0]*len(self.urlids)

    # create weights matrix
    self.wi = [[self.getstrength(wordid,hiddenid,0)
                for hiddenid in self.hiddenids]
                for wordid in self.wordids]
    self.wo = [[self.getstrength(hiddenid,urlid,1)
                for urlid in self.urlids]
                for hiddenid in self.hiddenids]
```

You're finally ready to create the feedforward algorithm. This takes a list of inputs, pushes them through the network, and returns the output of all the nodes in the output layer. In this case, since you've only constructed a network with words in the query, the output from all the input nodes will always be 1:

```
def feedforward(self):
    # the only inputs are the query words
    for i in range(len(self.wordids)):
        self.ai[i] = 1.0

    # hidden activations
    for j in range(len(self.hiddenids)):
        sum = 0.0
        for i in range(len(self.wordids)):
            sum = sum + self.ai[i] * self.wi[i][j]
        self.ah[j] = tanh(sum)

    # output activations
    for k in range(len(self.urlids)):
        sum = 0.0
        for j in range(len(self.hiddenids)):
            sum = sum + self.ah[j] * self.wo[j][k]
        self.ao[k] = tanh(sum)

    return self.ao[:]
```

The feedforward algorithm works by looping over all the nodes in the hidden layer and adding together all the outputs from the input layer multiplied by the strengths of the links. The output of each node is the tanh function of the sum of all the inputs, which is passed on to the output layer. The output layer does the same thing, multiplying the outputs of the previous layer by their strengths, and applies the tanh function to produce the final output. It is easy to extend the network to have more layers by continually using the output of one layer as the input to the next layer.

Now you can write a short function that will set up the network and use feedforward to get the outputs for a set of words and URLs:

```
def getresult(self,wordids,urlids):
  self.setupnetwork(wordids,urlids)
  return self.feedforward( )
```

You can use Python to try this in the network:

```
>> reload(nn)
>> mynet=nn.searchnet('nn.db')
>> mynet.getresult([wWorld,wBank],[uWorldBank,uRiver,uEarth])
[0.76,0.76,0.76]
```

The numbers in the returned list correspond to the relevance of the input URLs. Not surprisingly, because it hasn't yet had any training, the neural network gives the same answer for every URL.

Training with Backpropagation

Here's where things get interesting. The network will take inputs and give outputs, but because it hasn't been taught what a good result looks like, the results are pretty useless. You're now going to train the network by showing it some actual examples of what people searched for, which results were returned, and what the users decided to click on.

For this to work, you need an algorithm that alters the weights of the links between the nodes to better reflect what the network is being told is the right answer. The weights have to be adjusted slowly because you can't assume that the each user will click on an answer that's appropriate for everyone. The algorithm you'll use is called *backpropagation* because it moves backward through the network adjusting the weights.

When training a network, you always know the desired output of each node in the output layer. In this case, it should be pushed toward 1 if the user clicked on that result, and pushed toward 0 if he did not. The only way to change the output of a node is to change the total input to that node.

To determine how much the total input should be changed, the training algorithm has to know the slope of the tanh function at its current level of output. In the middle of the function, when the output is 0.0, the slope is very steep, so changing the input by only a small amount gives a big change. As the outputs get closer to −1 or 1, changing the input has a smaller effect on the output. The slope of the function for any output value is specified by this function, which you can add to the start of *nn.py*:

```
def dtanh(y):
    return 1.0-y*y
```

Before running the backpropagation method, it's necessary to run feedforward so that the current output of every node will be stored in the instance variables. The backpropagation algorithm then performs the following steps.

For each node in the output layer:

1. Calculate the difference between the node's current output and what it should be.

2. Use the dtanh function to determine how much the node's total input has to change.

3. Change the strength of every incoming link in proportion to the link's current strength and the learning rate.

For each node in the hidden layer:

1. Change the output of the node by the sum of the strength of each output link multiplied by how much its target node has to change.

2. Use the dtanh function to determine how much the node's total input has to change.

3. Change the strength of every input link in proportion to the link's current strength and the learning rate.

The implementation of this algorithm actually calculates all the errors in advance and then adjusts the weights, because all the calculations rely on knowing the current weights rather than the updated weights. Here's the code for the algorithm, which you can add to the searchnet class:

```
def backPropagate(self, targets, N=0.5):
    # calculate errors for output
    output_deltas = [0.0] * len(self.urlids)
    for k in range(len(self.urlids)):
        error = targets[k]-self.ao[k]
        output_deltas[k] = dtanh(self.ao[k]) * error

    # calculate errors for hidden layer
    hidden_deltas = [0.0] * len(self.hiddenids)
    for j in range(len(self.hiddenids)):
        error = 0.0
        for k in range(len(self.urlids)):
            error = error + output_deltas[k]*self.wo[j][k]
        hidden_deltas[j] = dtanh(self.ah[j]) * error
```

```
# update output weights
for j in range(len(self.hiddenids)):
    for k in range(len(self.urlids)):
        change = output_deltas[k]*self.ah[j]
        self.wo[j][k] = self.wo[j][k] + N*change

# update input weights
for i in range(len(self.wordids)):
    for j in range(len(self.hiddenids)):
        change = hidden_deltas[j]*self.ai[i]
        self.wi[i][j] = self.wi[i][j] + N*change
```

Now all you need is a simple method that will set up the network, run feedforward, and run the backpropagation. This method takes the list of wordids, urlids, and a selected URL:

```
def trainquery(self,wordids,urlids,selectedurl):
    # generate a hidden node if necessary
    self.generatehiddennode(wordids,urlids)

    self.setupnetwork(wordids,urlids)
    self.feedforward()
    targets=[0.0]*len(urlids)
    targets[urlids.index(selectedurl)]=1.0
    error = self.backPropagate(targets)
    self.updatedatabase()
```

To save the results, you'll also need a method to update the database with the new weights, which are stored in the wi and wo instance variables:

```
def updatedatabase(self):
    # set them to database values
    for i in range(len(self.wordids)):
        for j in range(len(self.hiddenids)):
            self.setstrength(self.wordids[i],self. hiddenids[j],0,self.wi[i][j])
    for j in range(len(self.hiddenids)):
        for k in range(len(self.urlids)):
            self.setstrength(self.hiddenids[j],self.urlids[k],1,self.wo[j][k])
    self.con.commit()
```

Now you can do a simple test with the query you tried earlier to see how the network responds to training:

```
>> reload(nn)
>> mynet=nn.searchnet('nn.db')
>> mynet.trainquery([wWorld,wBank],[uWorldBank,uRiver,uEarth],uWorldBank)
>> mynet.getresult([wWorld,wBank],[uWorldBank,uRiver,uEarth])
[0.335,0.055,0.055]
```

The output for the World Bank URL increased and the output for the other URLs decreased after the network learned that a particular user made that selection. The more users make this selection, the bigger the difference will get.

Training Test

So far you've seen that training with one sample result increases the output for that result. Although that's useful, it doesn't really demonstrate what neural networks are capable of—that is, reasoning about inputs they've never seen before. Try this code in your interactive Python session:

```
>> allurls=[uWorldBank,uRiver,uEarth]
>> for i in range(30):
...     mynet.trainquery([wWorld,wBank],allurls,uWorldBank)
...     mynet.trainquery([wRiver,wBank],allurls,uRiver)
...     mynet.trainquery([wWorld],allurls,uEarth)
...
>> mynet.getresult([wWorld,wBank],allurls)
[0.861, 0.011, 0.016]
>> mynet.getresult([wRiver,wBank],allurls)
[-0.030, 0.883, 0.006]
>> mynet.getresult([wBank],allurls)
[0.865, 0.001, -0.85]
```

Even though the network has never seen a query for "bank" by itself before, it gives a reasonable guess. Not only that, it gives the World Bank URL a much better score than the River URL, even though in the training sample queries "bank" was associated just as often with "river" as it was with World Bank. The network has not only learned which URLs are related to which queries, it has also learned what the important words are in a particular query—something that could not have been achieved with a simple query-URL correlation.

Connecting to the Search Engine

The query method of the searcher class gets a list of URL IDs and word IDs in the course of creating and printing the results. You can have the method return these results by adding the following line to the end of the query in *searchengine.py*:

```
return wordids,[r[1] for r in rankedscores[0:10]]
```

These can be passed directly to the trainquery method of searchnet.

The method for capturing which of the results the user liked best is specific to the design of your application. It's possible that a web page could include an intermediate page that captures the click and calls trainquery before redirecting to the actual search, or you could even let users vote on the relevance of search results to help improve your algorithm.

The final step in building the artificial neural network is creating a new method in the searcher class to allow you to weight the results. This function looks pretty similar to the other weighting functions. The first thing you'll need to do is import the neural network class in *searchengine.py*:

```
import nn
mynet=nn.searchnet('nn.db')
```

And add this method to the searcher class:

```
def nnscore(self,rows,wordids):
  # Get unique URL IDs as an ordered list
  urlids=[urlid for urlid in set([row[0] for row in rows])]
  nnres=mynet.getresult(wordids,urlids)
  scores=dict([(urlids[i],nnres[i]) for i in range(len(urlids))])
  return self.normalizescores(scores)
```

Again, you can experiment by including this in your weights list with various weights. In practice, it's better to hold off on including it as part of your scoring until the network has been trained on a large number of different examples.

This chapter has covered a wide range of possibilities for developing a search engine, but it's still very limited compared to what's possible. The exercises will explore some further ideas. This chapter has not focused on performance—which would require work to index millions of pages—but what you've built will perform adequately on a set of 100,000 pages, enough for a news site or corporate intranet.

Exercises

1. *Word separation*. The separatewords method currently considers any nonalphanumeric character to be a separator, meaning it will not properly index entries like "C++," "$20," "Ph.D.," or "617-555-1212." What is a better way to separate words? Does using whitespace as a separator work? Write a better word separation function.

2. *Boolean operations*. Many search engines support Boolean queries, which allow users to construct searches like "python OR perl." An OR search can work by doing the queries separately and combining the results, but what about "python AND (program OR code)"? Modify the query methods to support some basic Boolean operations.

3. *Exact matches*. Search engines often support "exact match" queries, where the words in the page must match the words in the query in the same order with no additional words in between. Create a new version of getrows that only returns results that are exact matches. (Hint: you can use subtraction in SQL to get the difference between the word locations.)

4. *Long/short document search*. Sometimes the length of a page will be a determining factor in whether it is relevant to a particular search application or user. A user may be interested in finding a long article about a difficult subject or a quick reference page for a command-line tool. Write a weighting function that will give preference to longer or shorter documents depending on its parameters.

5. *Word frequency bias*. The "word count" metric is biased to favor longer documents, since a long document has more words and can therefore contain the target words more often. Write a new metric that calculates frequency as a percentage of the number of words in the document.

6. *Inbound link searching.* Your code can rank items based on the text of the inbound links, but they must already be results based on the content of the page. Sometimes the most relevant page doesn't contain the query text at all, but rather a lot of links with the text pointing to it—this is often the case with links to images. Modify the search code to also include results where an inbound link contains some of the search terms.

7. *Different training options.* The neural network is trained with a set of 0s for all the URLs that a user did not click, and a 1 for the URL that she did click. Alter the training function so that it works instead for an application where users get to rate results from 1 to 5.

8. *Additional layers.* Your neural network has only one hidden layer. Update the class to support an arbitrary number of hidden layers, which can be specified upon initialization.

CHAPTER 5
Optimization

This chapter will look at how to solve collaboration problems using a set of techniques called *stochastic optimization*. Optimization techniques are typically used in problems that have many possible solutions across many variables, and that have outcomes that can change greatly depending on the combinations of these variables. These optimization techniques have a wide variety of applications: we use them in physics to study molecular dynamics, in biology to predict protein structures, and in computer science to determine the worst possible running time of an algorithm. NASA even uses optimization techniques to design antennas that have the right operating characteristics, which look unlike anything a human designer would create.

Optimization finds the best solution to a problem by trying many different solutions and scoring them to determine their quality. Optimization is typically used in cases where there are too many possible solutions to try them all. The simplest but least effective method of searching for solutions is just trying a few thousand random guesses and seeing which one is best. More effective methods, which will be discussed in this chapter, involve intelligently modifying the solutions in a way that is likely to improve them.

The first example in this chapter concerns group travel planning. Anyone who has planned a trip for a group of people, or perhaps even for an individual, realizes that there are a lot of different inputs required, such as what everyone's flight schedule should be, how many cars should be rented, and which airport is easiest. Many outputs must also be considered, such as total cost, time spent waiting at airports, and time taken off work. Because the inputs can't be mapped to the outputs with a simple formula, the problem of finding the best solution lends itself to optimization.

The other examples in the chapter show the flexibility of optimization by considering two completely different problems: how to allocate limited resources based on people's preferences, and how to visualize a social network with minimal crossed lines. By the end of the chapter, you'll be able to spot other types of problems that can be solved using optimization.

Group Travel

Planning a trip for a group of people (the Glass family in this example) from different locations all arriving at the same place is always a challenge, and it makes for an interesting optimization problem. To begin, create a new file called *optimization.py* and insert the following code:

```
import time
import random
import math

people = [('Seymour','BOS'),
          ('Franny','DAL'),
          ('Zooey','CAK'),
          ('Walt','MIA'),
          ('Buddy','ORD'),
          ('Les','OMA')]

# LaGuardia airport in New York
destination='LGA'
```

The family members are from all over the country and wish to meet up in New York. They will all arrive on the same day and leave on the same day, and they would like to share transportation to and from the airport. There are dozens of flights per day to New York from any of the family members' locations, all leaving at different times. The flights also vary in price and in duration.

You can download a sample file of flight data from *http://kiwitobes.com/optimize/ schedule.txt*.

This file contains origin, destination, departure time, arrival time, and price for a set of flights in a comma-separated format:

```
LGA,MIA,20:27,23:42,169
MIA,LGA,19:53,22:21,173
LGA,BOS,6:39,8:09,86
BOS,LGA,6:17,8:26,89
LGA,BOS,8:23,10:28,149
```

Load this data into a dictionary with the origin and destination (dest) as the keys and a list of potential flight details as the values. Add this code to load the data into *optimization.py*:

```
flights={}
#
for line in file('schedule.txt'):
  origin,dest,depart,arrive,price=line.strip().split(',')
  flights.setdefault((origin,dest),[])

  # Add details to the list of possible flights
  flights[(origin,dest)].append((depart,arrive,int(price)))
```

It's also useful at this point to define a utility function, getminutes, which calculates how many minutes into the day a given time is. This makes it easy to calculate flight times and waiting times. Add this function to *optimization.py*:

```
def getminutes(t):
  x=time.strptime(t,'%H:%M')
  return x[3]*60+x[4]
```

The challenge now is to decide which flight each person in the family should take. Of course, keeping total price down is a goal, but there are many other possible factors that the optimal solution will take into account and try to minimize, such as total waiting time at the airport or total flight time. These other factors will be discussed in more detail shortly.

Representing Solutions

When approaching a problem like this, it's necessary to determine how a potential solution will be represented. The optimization functions you'll see later are generic enough to work on many different types of problems, so it's important to choose a simple representation that's not specific to the group travel problem. A very common representation is a list of numbers. In this case, each number can represent which flight a person chooses to take, where 0 is the first flight of the day, 1 is the second, and so on. Since each person needs an outbound flight and a return flight, the length of this list is twice the number of people.

For example, the list:

```
[1,4,3,2,7,3,6,3,2,4,5,3]
```

Represents a solution in which Seymour takes the second flight of the day from Boston to New York, and the fifth flight back to Boston on the day he returns. Franny takes the fourth flight from Dallas to New York, and the third flight back.

Because it will be difficult to interpret solutions from this list of numbers, you'll need a routine that prints all the flights that people decide to take in a nice table. Add this function to *optimization.py*:

```
def printschedule(r):
  for d in range(len(r)/2):
    name=people[d][0]
    origin=people[d][1]
    out=flights[(origin,destination)][r[d]]
    ret=flights[(destination,origin)][r[d+1]]
    print '%10s%10s %5s-%5s $%3s %5s-%5s $%3s' % (name,origin,
                                                  out[0],out[1],out[2],
                                                  ret[0],ret[1],ret[2])
```

This will print a line containing each person's name and origin, as well as the departure time, arrival time, and price for the outgoing and return flights. Try this function in your Python session:

```
>>> import optimization
>>> s=[1,4,3,2,7,3,6,3,2,4,5,3]
>>> optimization.printschedule(s)
   Seymour     Boston 12:34-15:02 $109 12:08-14:05 $142
    Franny     Dallas 12:19-15:25 $342  9:49-13:51 $229
     Zooey      Akron  9:15-12:14 $247 15:50-18:45 $243
      Walt      Miami 15:34-18:11 $326 14:08-16:09 $232
     Buddy    Chicago 14:22-16:32 $126 15:04-17:23 $189
       Les      Omaha 15:03-16:42 $135  6:19- 8:13 $239
```

Even disregarding price, this schedule has some problems. In particular, since the family members are traveling to and from the airport together, everyone has to arrive at the airport at 6 a.m. for Les's return flight, even though some of them don't leave until nearly 4 p.m. To determine the best combination, the program needs a way of weighting the various properties of different schedules and deciding which is the best.

The Cost Function

The *cost function* is the key to solving any problem using optimization, and it's usually the most difficult thing to determine. The goal of any optimization algorithm is to find a set of inputs—flights, in this case—that minimizes the cost function, so the cost function has to return a value that represents how bad a solution is. There is no particular scale for *badness*; the only requirement is that the function returns larger values for worse solutions.

Often it is difficult to determine what makes a solution good or bad across many variables. Consider a few of the things that can be measured in the group travel example:

Price
> The total price of all the plane tickets, or possibly a weighted average that takes financial situations into account.

Travel time
> The total time that everyone has to spend on a plane.

Waiting time
> Time spent at the airport waiting for the other members of the party to arrive.

Departure time
> Flights that leave too early in the morning may impose an additional cost by requiring travelers to miss out on sleep.

Car rental period
> If the party rents a car, they must return it earlier in the day than when they rented it, or be forced to pay for a whole extra day.

It's not too hard to think of even more aspects of a particular schedule that could make the experience more or less pleasant. Any time you're faced with finding the best solution to a complicated problem, you'll need to decide what the important factors are. Although this can be difficult, the big advantage is that once it's done, you can use the optimization algorithms in this chapter on almost any problem with minimal modification.

After choosing some variables that impose costs, you'll need to determine how to combine them into a single number. In this example, it's necessary to decide, for instance, how much money that time on the plane or time waiting in the airport is worth. You might decide that it's worth spending $1 for every minute saved on air travel (this translates into spending an extra $90 for a direct flight that saves an hour and a half), and $0.50 for every minute saved waiting in the airport. You could also add the cost of an extra day of car rental if everyone returns to the airport at a later time of the day than when they first rented the car.

There are a huge number of possibilities for the getcost function defined here. This function takes into account the total cost of the trip and the total time spent waiting at airports for the various members of the family. It also adds a penalty of $50 if the car is returned at a later time of the day than when it was rented. Add this function to *optimization.py*, and feel free to add additional costs or to tweak the relative importance of money and time:

```python
def schedulecost(sol):
    totalprice=0
    latestarrival=0
    earliestdep=24*60

    for d in range(len(sol)/2):
        # Get the inbound and outbound flights
        origin=people[d][1]
        outbound=flights[(origin,destination)][int(sol[d])]
        returnf=flights[(destination,origin)][int(sol[d+1])]

        # Total price is the price of all outbound and return flights
        totalprice+=outbound[2]
        totalprice+=returnf[2]

        # Track the latest arrival and earliest departure
        if latestarrival<getminutes(outbound[1]): latestarrival=getminutes(outbound[1])
        if earliestdep>getminutes(returnf[0]): earliestdep=getminutes(returnf[0])

    # Every person must wait at the airport until the latest person arrives.
    # They also must arrive at the same time and wait for their flights.
    totalwait=0
    for d in range(len(sol)/2):
        origin=people[d][1]
        outbound=flights[(origin,destination)][int(sol[d])]
        returnf=flights[(destination,origin)][int(sol[d+1])]
        totalwait+=latestarrival-getminutes(outbound[1])
        totalwait+=getminutes(returnf[0])-earliestdep
```

```
# Does this solution require an extra day of car rental? That'll be $50!
if latestarrival>earliestdep: totalprice+=50

return totalprice+totalwait
```

The logic in this function is quite simplistic, but it illustrates the point. It can be enhanced in several ways—right now, the total wait time assumes that all the family members will leave the airport together when the last person arrives, and will all go to the airport for the earliest departure. This can be modified so that anyone facing a two-hour or longer wait rents his own car instead, and the prices and waiting time can be adjusted accordingly.

You can try this function in your Python session:

```
>>> reload(optimization)
>>> optimization.schedulecost(s)
5285
```

Now that the cost function has been created, it should be clear that the goal is to minimize cost by choosing the correct set of numbers. In theory, you could try every possible combination, but in this example there are 16 flights, all with 9 possibilities, giving a total of 9^{16} (around 300 billion) combinations. Testing every combination would guarantee you'd get the best answer, but it would take a very long time on most computers.

Random Searching

Random searching isn't a very good optimization method, but it makes it easy to understand exactly what all the algorithms are trying to do, and it also serves as a baseline so you can see if the other algorithms are doing a good job.

The function takes a couple of parameters. Domain is a list of 2-tuples that specify the minimum and maximum values for each variable. The length of the solution is the same as the length of this list. In the current example, there are nine outbound flights and nine inbound flights for every person, so the domain in the list is (0,8) repeated twice for each person.

The second parameter, costf, is the cost function, which in this example will be schedulecost. This is passed as a parameter so that the function can be reused for other optimization problems. This function randomly generates 1,000 guesses and calls costf on them. It keeps track of the best guess (the one with the lowest cost) and returns it. Add it to *optimization.py*:

```
def randomoptimize(domain,costf):
  best=999999999
  bestr=None
  for i in range(1000):
    # Create a random solution
    r=[random.randint(domain[i][0],domain[i][1])
        for i in range(len(domain))]
```

```
    # Get the cost
    cost=costf(r)

    # Compare it to the best one so far
    if cost<best:
      best=cost
      bestr=r
  return r
```

Of course, 1,000 guesses is a very small fraction of the total number of possibilities. However, this example has many possibilities that are good (if not the best), so with a thousand tries, the function will likely come across a solution that isn't awful. Try it in your Python session:

```
>>> reload(optimization)
>>> domain=[(0,8)]*(len(optimization.people)*2)
>>> s=optimization.randomoptimize(domain,optimization.schedulecost)
>>> optimization.schedulecost(s)
3328
>>> optimization.printschedule(s)
   Seymour    Boston 12:34-15:02 $109 12:08-14:05 $142
    Franny    Dallas 12:19-15:25 $342  9:49-13:51 $229
     Zooey     Akron  9:15-12:14 $247 15:50-18:45 $243
      Walt     Miami 15:34-18:11 $326 14:08-16:09 $232
     Buddy   Chicago 14:22-16:32 $126 15:04-17:23 $189
       Les     Omaha 15:03-16:42 $135  6:19- 8:13 $239
```

Due to the random element, your results will be different from the results here. The results shown are not great, as they have Zooey waiting at the airport for six hours until Walt arrives, but they could definitely be worse. Try running this function several times to see if the cost changes very much, or try increasing the loop size to 10,000 to see if you find better results that way.

Hill Climbing

Randomly trying different solutions is very inefficient because it does not take advantage of the good solutions that have already been discovered. In our example, a schedule with a low overall cost is probably similar to other schedules that have a low cost. Because random optimization jumps around, it won't automatically look at similar schedules to locate the good ones that have already been found.

An alternate method of random searching is called *hill climbing*. Hill climbing starts with a random solution and looks at the set of neighboring solutions for those that are better (have a lower cost function). This is analogous to going down a hill, as shown in Figure 5-1.

Imagine you are the person shown in the figure, having been randomly dropped into this landscape. You want to reach the lowest point to find water. To do this, you might look in each direction and walk toward wherever the land slopes downward

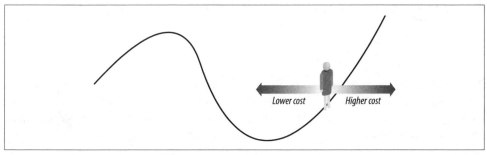

Figure 5-1. Seeking the lowest cost on a hill

most steeply. You would continue to walk in the most steeply sloping direction until you reached a point where the terrain was flat or began sloping uphill.

You can apply this hill climbing approach to the task of finding the best travel schedule for the Glass family. Start with a random schedule and find all the neighboring schedules. In this case, that means finding all the schedules that have one person on a slightly earlier or slightly later flight. The cost is calculated for each of the neighboring schedules, and the one with the lowest cost becomes the new solution. This process is repeated until none of the neighboring schedules improves the cost.

To implement this, add hillclimb to *optimization.py*:

```python
def hillclimb(domain,costf):
  # Create a random solution
  sol=[random.randint(domain[i][0],domain[i][1])
      for i in range(len(domain))]

  # Main loop
  while 1:

    # Create list of neighboring solutions
    neighbors=[]
    for j in range(len(domain)):

      # One away in each direction
      if sol[j]>domain[j][0]:
        neighbors.append(sol[0:j]+[sol[j]+1]+sol[j+1:])
      if sol[j]<domain[j][1]:
        neighbors.append(sol[0:j]+[sol[j]-1]+sol[j+1:])

    # See what the best solution amongst the neighbors is
    current=costf(sol)
    best=current
    for j in range(len(neighbors)):
      cost=costf(neighbors[j])
      if cost<best:
        best=cost
        sol=neighbors[j]
```

```
# If there's no improvement, then we've reached the top
if best==current:
    break

return sol
```

This function generates a random list of numbers within the given domain to create the initial solution. It finds all the neighbors for the current solution by looping over every element in the list and then creating two new lists with that element increased by one and decreased by one. The best of these neighbors becomes the new solution.

Try this function in your Python session to see how it compares to randomly searching for a solution:

```
>>> s=optimization.hillclimb(domain,optimization.schedulecost)
>>> optimization.schedulecost(s)
3063
>>> optimization.printschedule(s)
  Seymour     BOS 12:34-15:02 $109 10:33-12:03 $ 74
   Franny     DAL 10:30-14:57 $290 10:51-14:16 $256
    Zooey     CAK 10:53-13:36 $189 10:32-13:16 $139
     Walt     MIA 11:28-14:40 $248 12:37-15:05 $170
    Buddy     ORD 12:44-14:17 $134 10:33-13:11 $132
      Les     OMA 11:08-13:07 $175 18:25-20:34 $205
```

This function runs quickly and usually finds a better solution than randomly searching. There is, however, one major drawback to hill climbing. Look at Figure 5-2.

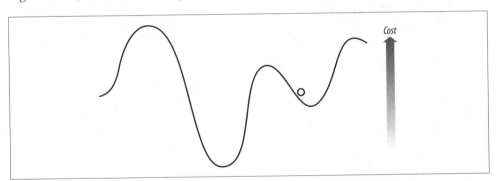

Figure 5-2. Stuck in a local minimum

From this figure it's clear that simply moving down the slope will not necessarily lead to the best solution overall. The final solution will be a *local minimum*, a solution better than those around it but not the best overall. The best overall is called the *global minimum*, which is what optimization algorithms are ultimately supposed to find. One approach to this dilemma is called *random-restart hill climbing*, where the hill climbing algorithm is run several times with random starting points in the hope that one of them will be close to the global minimum. The next two sections, "Simulated Annealing" and "Genetic Algorithms," show other ways to avoid getting stuck in a local minimum.

Simulated Annealing

Simulated annealing is an optimization method inspired by physics. Annealing is the process of heating up an alloy and then cooling it down slowly. Because the atoms are first made to jump around a lot and then gradually settle into a low energy state, the atoms can find a low energy configuration.

The algorithm version of annealing begins with a random solution to the problem. It uses a variable representing the temperature, which starts very high and gradually gets lower. In each iteration, one of the numbers in the solution is randomly chosen and changed in a certain direction. In our example, Seymour's return flight might be moved from the second of the day to the third. The cost is calculated before and after the change, and the costs are compared.

Here's the important part: if the new cost is lower, the new solution becomes the current solution, which is very much like the hill-climbing method. However, if the cost is *higher*, the new solution can still become the current solution with a certain probability. This is an attempt to avoid the local minimum problem shown in Figure 5-2.

In some cases, it's necessary to move to a worse solution before you can get to a better one. Simulated annealing works because it will always accept a move for the better, and because it is willing to accept a worse solution near the beginning of the process. As the process goes on, the algorithm becomes less and less likely to accept a worse solution, until at the end it will only accept a better solution. The probability of a higher-cost solution being accepted is given by this formula:

$$p=e^{((-highcost-lowcost)/temperature)}$$

Since the temperature (the willingness to accept a worse solution) starts very high, the exponent will always be close to 0, so the probability will almost be 1. As the temperature decreases, the difference between the high cost and the low cost becomes more important—a bigger difference leads to a lower probability, so the algorithm will favor only slightly worse solutions over much worse ones.

Create a new function in *optimization.py* called annealingoptimize, which implements this algorithm:

```
def annealingoptimize(domain,costf,T=10000.0,cool=0.95,step=1):
  # Initialize the values randomly
  vec=[float(random.randint(domain[i][0],domain[i][1]))
      for i in range(len(domain))]

  while T>0.1:
    # Choose one of the indices
    i=random.randint(0,len(domain)-1)

    # Choose a direction to change it
    dir=random.randint(-step,step)
```

```
# Create a new list with one of the values changed
vecb=vec[:]
vecb[i]+=dir
if vecb[i]<domain[i][0]: vecb[i]=domain[i][0]
elif vecb[i]>domain[i][1]: vecb[i]=domain[i][1]

# Calculate the current cost and the new cost
ea=costf(vec)
eb=costf(vecb)
p=pow(math.e,(-eb-ea)/T)

# Is it better, or does it make the probability
# cutoff?
if (eb<ea or random.random( )<p):
  vec=vecb

# Decrease the temperature
T=T*cool
return vec
```

To do annealing, this function first creates a random solution of the right length with all the values in the range specified by the domain parameter. The temperature and the cooling rate are optional parameters. In each iteration, i is set to a random index of the solution, and dir is set to a random number between −step and step. It calculates the current function cost and the cost if it were to change the value at i by dir.

The line of code in bold shows the probability calculation, which gets lower as T gets lower. If a random float between 0 and 1 is less than this value, or if the new solution is better, the function accepts the new solution. The function loops until the temperature has almost reached 0, each time multiplying it by the cooling rate.

Now you can try to optimize with simulated annealing in your Python session:

```
>>> reload(optimization)
>>> s=optimization.annealingoptimize(domain,optimization.schedulecost)
>>> optimization.schedulecost(s)
2278
>>> optimization.printschedule(s)
   Seymour     Boston 12:34-15:02 $109 10:33-12:03 $ 74
    Franny     Dallas 10:30-14:57 $290 10:51-14:16 $256
     Zooey      Akron 10:53-13:36 $189 10:32-13:16 $139
      Walt      Miami 11:28-14:40 $248 12:37-15:05 $170
     Buddy    Chicago 12:44-14:17 $134 10:33-13:11 $132
       Les      Omaha 11:08-13:07 $175 15:07-17:21 $129
```

This optimization did a good job of reducing the overall wait times while keeping the costs down. Obviously, your results will be different, and there is a chance that they will be worse. For any given problem, it's a good idea to experiment with different parameters for the initial temperature and the cooling rate. You can also vary the possible step size for the random movements.

Genetic Algorithms

Another set of techniques for optimization, also inspired by nature, is called *genetic algorithms*. These work by initially creating a set of random solutions known as the *population*. At each step of the optimization, the cost function for the entire population is calculated to get a ranked list of solutions. An example is shown in Table 5-1.

Table 5-1. Ranked list of solutions and costs

Solution	Cost
[7, 5, 2, 3, 1, 6, 1, 6, 7, 1, 0, 3]	4394
[7, 2, 2, 2, 3, 3, 2, 3, 5, 2, 0, 8]	4661
…	…
[0, 4, 0, 3, 8, 8, 4, 4, 8, 5, 6, 1]	7845
[5, 8, 0, 2, 8, 8, 8, 2, 1, 6, 6, 8]	8088

After the solutions are ranked, a new population—known as the next *generation*—is created. First, the top solutions in the current population are added to the new population as they are. This process is called *elitism*. The rest of the new population consists of completely new solutions that are created by modifying the best solutions.

There are two ways that solutions can be modified. The simpler of these is called *mutation*, which is usually a small, simple, random change to an existing solution. In this case, a mutation can be done simply by picking one of the numbers in the solution and increasing or decreasing it. A couple of examples are shown in Figure 5-3.

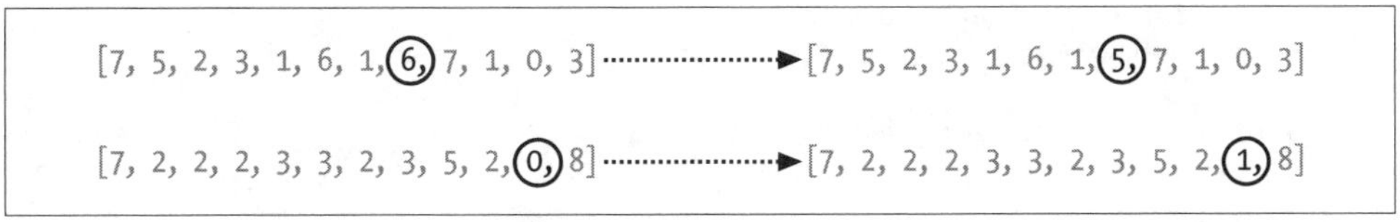

Figure 5-3. Examples of mutating a solution

The other way to modify solutions is called *crossover* or *breeding*. This method involves taking two of the best solutions and combining them in some way. In this case, a simple way to do crossover is to take a random number of elements from one solution and the rest of the elements from another solution, as illustrated in Figure 5-4.

A new population, usually the same size as the old one, is created by randomly mutating and breeding the best solutions. Then the process repeats—the new population is ranked and another population is created. This continues either for a fixed number of iterations or until there has been no improvement over several generations.

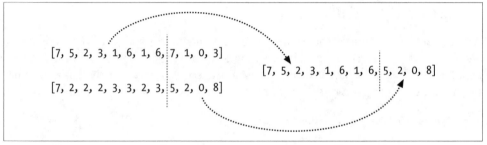

Figure 5-4. Example of crossover

Add geneticoptimize to *optimization.py*:

```
def geneticoptimize(domain,costf,popsize=50,step=1,
                    mutprod=0.2,elite=0.2,maxiter=100):
  # Mutation Operation
  def mutate(vec):
    i=random.randint(0,len(domain)-1)
    if random.random( )<0.5 and vec[i]>domain[i][0]:
      return vec[0:i]+[vec[i]-step]+vec[i+1:]
    elif vec[i]<domain[i][1]:
      return vec[0:i]+[vec[i]+step]+vec[i+1:]

  # Crossover Operation
  def crossover(r1,r2):
    i=random.randint(1,len(domain)-2)
    return r1[0:i]+r2[i:]

  # Build the initial population
  pop=[]
  for i in range(popsize):
    vec=[random.randint(domain[i][0],domain[i][1])
         for i in range(len(domain))]
    pop.append(vec)

  # How many winners from each generation?
  topelite=int(elite*popsize)

  # Main loop
  for i in range(maxiter):
    scores=[(costf(v),v) for v in pop]
    scores.sort( )
    ranked=[v for (s,v) in scores]

    # Start with the pure winners
    pop=ranked[0:topelite]

    # Add mutated and bred forms of the winners
    while len(pop)<popsize:
      if random.random( )<mutprob:
```

```
      # Mutation
      c=random.randint(0,topelite)
      pop.append(mutate(ranked[c]))
    else:

      # Crossover
      c1=random.randint(0,topelite)
      c2=random.randint(0,topelite)
      pop.append(crossover(ranked[c1],ranked[c2]))

  # Print current best score
  print scores[0][0]

  return scores[0][1]
```

This function takes several optional parameters:

popsize

> The size of the population

mutprob

> The probability that a new member of the population will be a mutation rather than a crossover

elite

> The fraction of the population that are considered good solutions and are allowed to pass into the next generation

maxiter

> The number of generations to run

Try optimizing the travel plans using the genetic algorithm in your Python session:

```
>>> s=optimization.geneticoptimize(domain,optimization.schedulecost)
3532
3503
...
2591
2591
2591
>>> optimization.printschedule(s)
  Seymour      BOS 12:34-15:02 $109 10:33-12:03 $ 74
   Franny      DAL 10:30-14:57 $290 10:51-14:16 $256
    Zooey      CAK 10:53-13:36 $189 10:32-13:16 $139
     Walt      MIA 11:28-14:40 $248 12:37-15:05 $170
    Buddy      ORD 12:44-14:17 $134 10:33-13:11 $132
      Les      OMA 11:08-13:07 $175 11:07-13:24 $171
```

In Chapter 11, you'll see an extension of genetic algorithms called *genetic programming*, where similar ideas are used to create entirely new programs.

The computer scientist John Holland is widely considered to be the father of genetic algorithms because of his 1975 book, *Adaptation in Natural and Artificial Systems* (University of Michigan Press). Yet the work goes back to biologists in the 1950s who were attempting to model evolution on computers. Since then, genetic algorithms and other optimization methods have been used for a huge variety of problems, including:

- Finding which concert hall shape gives the best acoustics
- Designing an optimal wing for a supersonic aircraft
- Suggesting the best library of chemicals to research as potential drugs
- Automatically designing a chip for voice recognition

Potential solutions to these problems can be turned into lists of numbers. This makes it easy to apply genetic algorithms or simulated annealing.

Whether a particular optimization method will work depends very much on the problem. Simulated annealing, genetic optimization, and most other optimization methods rely on the fact that, in most problems, the best solution is close to other good solutions. To see a case where optimization might not work, look at Figure 5-5.

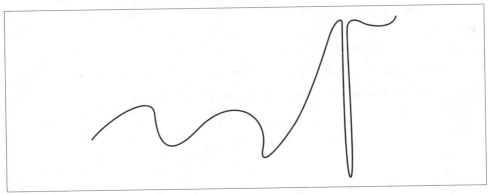

Figure 5-5. Poor problem for optimization

The cost is actually lowest at a very steep point on the far right of the figure. Any solution that is close by would probably be dismissed from consideration because of its high cost, and you would never find your way to the global minimum. Most algorithms would settle in one of the local minima on the left side of the figure.

The flight scheduling example works because moving a person from the second to the third flight of the day would probably change the overall cost by a smaller amount than moving that person to the eighth flight of the day would. If the flights were in random order, the optimization methods would work no better than a random search—in fact, there's no optimization method that will consistently work better than a random search in that case.

Real Flight Searches

Now that everything is working with the sample data, it's time to try getting real flight data to see if the same optimizations can be used. You'll be downloading data from Kayak, which provides an API for doing flight searches. The main difference between real flight data and the sample you've been working with is that in the real flight data, there are many more than nine flights per day between most major cities.

The Kayak API

Kayak, shown in Figure 5-6, is a popular *vertical search engine* for travel. Although there are lots of travel sites online, Kayak is useful for this example because it has a nice XML API that can be used to perform real travel searches from within a Python program. To use the API, you'll need to sign up for a developer key by going to *http://www.kayak.com/labs/api/search*.

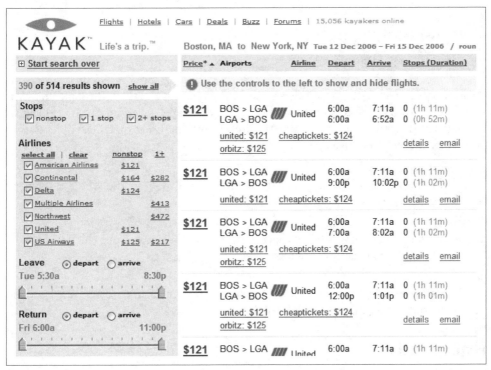

Figure 5-6. Screenshot of the Kayak travel search interface

The developer key is a long string of numbers and letters that you'll use to do flight searches in Kayak (it can also be used for hotel searches, but that won't be covered here). At the time of writing, there is not a specific Python API for Kayak like there is for del.icio.us, but the XML interface is very well explained. This chapter will show you how to create searches using the Python packages *urllib2* and *xml.dom.minidom*, both of which are included with the standard Python distribution.

The minidom Package

The *minidom* package is part of the standard Python distribution. It is a lightweight implementation of the Document Object Model (DOM) interface, a standard way of treating an XML document as a tree of objects. The package takes strings or open files containing XML and returns an object that you can use to easily extract information. For example, enter the following in a Python session:

```
>>> import xml.dom.minidom
>>> dom=xml.dom.minidom.parseString('<data><rec>Hello!</rec></data>')
>>> dom
<xml.dom.minidom.Document instance at 0x00980C38>
>>> r=dom.getElementsByTagName('rec')
>>> r
[<DOM Element: rec at 0xa42350>]
>>> r[0].firstChild
<DOM Text node "Hello!">
>>> r[0].firstChild.data
u'Hello!'
```

Because many web sites now offer a way to access information through an XML interface, learning how to use the Python XML packages is very useful for collective intelligence programming. Here are the important methods of DOM objects that you'll be using for the Kayak API:

getElementsByTagName(name)
: Returns a list of all DOM nodes by searching throughout the whole document for elements whose tag matches name.

firstChild
: Returns the first child node of this object. In the above example, the first child of r is the node representing the text "Hello."

data
: Returns the data associated with this object, which in most cases is a Unicode string of the text that the node contains.

Flight Searches

Begin by creating a new file called *kayak.py* and adding the following statements:

```
import time
import urllib2
import xml.dom.minidom

kayakkey='YOURKEYHERE'
```

The first thing you'll need is code to get a new Kayak session using your developer key. The function to do this sends a request to apisession with the token parameter set to your developer key. The XML returned by this URL will contain a tag sid, with a session ID inside it:

```
<sid>1-hX4lII_wS$8b06a07kHj</sid>
```

The function just has to parse the XML to extract the contents of the sid tag. Add this function to *kayak.py*:

```
def getkayaksession( ):
  # Construct the URL to start a session
  url='http://www.kayak.com/k/ident/apisession?token=%s&version=1' % kayakkey

  # Parse the resulting XML
  doc=xml.dom.minidom.parseString(urllib2.urlopen(url).read( ))

  # Find <sid>xxxxxxxx</sid>
  sid=doc.getElementsByTagName('sid')[0].firstChild.data
  return sid
```

The next step is to create a function to start the flight search. The URL for this search is very long because it contains all the parameters for the flight search. The important parameters for this search are sid (the session ID returned by getkayaksession), destination, and depart_date.

The resulting XML has a tag called searchid, which the function will extract in the same manner as getkayaksession. Since the search may take a long time, this call doesn't actually return any results—it just begins the search and returns an ID that can be used to poll for the results.

Add this function to *kayak.py*:

```
def flightsearch(sid,origin,destination,depart_date):

  # Construct search URL
  url='http://www.kayak.com/s/apisearch?basicmode=true&oneway=y&origin=%s' % origin
  url+='&destination=%s&depart_date=%s' % (destination,depart_date)
  url+='&return_date=none&depart_time=a&return_time=a'
  url+='&travelers=1&cabin=e&action=doFlights&apimode=1'
  url+='&_sid_=%s&version=1' % (sid)

  # Get the XML
  doc=xml.dom.minidom.parseString(urllib2.urlopen(url).read( ))

  # Extract the search ID
  searchid=doc.getElementsByTagName('searchid')[0].firstChild.data

  return searchid
```

Finally, you'll need a function that requests the results until there are no more. Kayak provides another URL, flight, which gives these results. In the returned XML, there is a tag called morepending, which contains the word "true" until the search is complete. The function has to request the page until morepending is no longer true, and then the functions gets the complete results.

Add this function to *kayak.py*:

```
def flightsearchresults(sid,searchid):

  # Removes leading $, commas and converts number to a float
  def parseprice(p):
    return float(p[1:].replace(',',''))

  # Polling loop
  while 1:
    time.sleep(2)

    # Construct URL for polling
    url='http://www.kayak.com/s/basic/flight?'
    url+='searchid=%s&c=5&apimode=1&_sid_=%s&version=1' % (searchid,sid)
    doc=xml.dom.minidom.parseString(urllib2.urlopen(url).read())

    # Look for morepending tag, and wait until it is no longer true
    morepending=doc.getElementsByTagName('morepending')[0].firstChild
    if morepending==None or morepending.data=='false': break

  # Now download the complete list
  url='http://www.kayak.com/s/basic/flight?'
  url+='searchid=%s&c=999&apimode=1&_sid_=%s&version=1' % (searchid,sid)
  doc=xml.dom.minidom.parseString(urllib2.urlopen(url).read())

  # Get the various elements as lists
  prices=doc.getElementsByTagName('price')
  departures=doc.getElementsByTagName('depart')
  arrivals=doc.getElementsByTagName('arrive')

  # Zip them together
  return zip([p.firstChild.data.split(' ')[1] for p in departures],
             [p.firstChild.data.split(' ')[1] for p in arrivals],
             [parseprice(p.firstChild.data) for p in prices])
```

Notice that at the end the function just gets all the price, depart, and arrive tags. There will be an equal number of them—one for each flight—so the zip function can be used to join them all together into tuples in a big list. The departure and arrival information is given as date and time separated by a space, so the function splits the string to get only the time. The function also converts the price to a float by passing it to parseprice.

You can try a real flight search in your Python session to make sure everything is working (remember to change the date to some time in the future):

```
>>> import kayak
>>> sid=kayak.getkayaksession()
>>> searchid=kayak.flightsearch(sid,'BOS','LGA','11/17/2006')
>>> f=kayak.flightsearchresults(sid,searchid)
>>> f[0:3]
[(u'07:00', u'08:25', 60.3),
 (u'08:30', u'09:49', 60.3),
 (u'06:35', u'07:54', 65.0)]
```

Flights are conveniently returned in order of price, and for flights that are the same price, in order of time. This works out well since, like before, it means that similar solutions are close together. The only requirement to integrate this with the rest of the code is to create a full schedule for all the different people in the Glass family with the same structure that was originally loaded in from the file. This is just a matter of looping over the people in the list and performing the flight search for their outbound and return flights. Add the createschedule function to *kayak.py*:

```
def createschedule(people,dest,dep,ret):
  # Get a session id for these searches
  sid=getkayaksession()
  flights={}

  for p in people:
    name,origin=p
    # Outbound flight
    searchid=flightsearch(sid,origin,dest,dep)
    flights[(origin,dest)]=flightsearchresults(sid,searchid)

    # Return flight
    searchid=flightsearch(sid,dest,origin,ret)
    flights[(dest,origin)]=flightsearchresults(sid,searchid)

  return flights
```

Now you can try to optimize the flights for the family using actual flight data. The Kayak searches can take a while, so limit the search to just the first two family members to start with. Enter this in your Python session:

```
>>> reload(kayak)
>>> f=kayak.createschedule(optimization.people[0:2],'LGA',
... '11/17/2006','11/19/2006')
>>> optimization.flights=f
>>> domain=[(0,30)]*len(f)
>>> optimization.geneticoptimize(domain,optimization.schedulecost)
770.0
703.0
...
>>> optimization.printschedule(s)
   Seymour       BOS 16:00-17:20 $85.0 19:00-20:28 $65.0
   Franny        DAL 08:00-17:25 $205.0 18:55-00:15 $133.0
```

Congratulations! You've just run an optimization on real live flight data. The search space is much bigger, so it's a good idea to experiment with the maximum velocity and learning rate.

There are many ways this can be expanded. You might combine it with a weather search to optimize for combinations of prices and warm temperatures at potential destinations, or with a hotel search to find destinations with a reasonable combination of flight and hotel prices. There are thousands of sites on the Internet that provide travel destination data that can be used as part of an optimization.

The Kayak API has a limit on searches per day, but it does return links to purchase any flight or hotel directly, which means you can easily incorporate the API into any application.

Optimizing for Preferences

You've seen one example of a problem that optimization can be used to solve, but there are many seemingly unrelated problems that can be attacked using the same methods. Remember, the primary requirements for solving with optimization are that the problem has a defined cost function and that similar solutions tend to yield similar results. Not every problem with these properties will be solvable with optimization, but there's a good chance that optimization will return some interesting results that you hadn't considered.

This section will consider a different problem, one that clearly lends itself to optimization. The general problem is how to allocate limited resources to people who have expressed preferences and make them all as happy as possible (or, depending on their dispositions, annoy them as little as possible).

Student Dorm Optimization

The example problem in this section is that of assigning students to dorms depending on their first and second choices. Although this is a very specific example, it's easy to generalize this case to other problems—the exact same code can be used to assign tables to players in an online card game, assign bugs to developers in a large coding project, or even to assign housework to household members. Once again, the purpose is to take information from individuals and combine it to produce the optimal result.

There are five dorms in our example, each with two spaces available and ten students vying for spots. Each student has first and second choices. Create a new file called *dorm.py* and add the list of dorms and the list of people, along with their top two choices:

```
import random
import math

# The dorms, each of which has two available spaces
dorms=['Zeus','Athena','Hercules','Bacchus','Pluto']

# People, along with their first and second choices
prefs=[('Toby', ('Bacchus', 'Hercules')),
       ('Steve', ('Zeus', 'Pluto')),
       ('Andrea', ('Athena', 'Zeus')),
       ('Sarah', ('Zeus', 'Pluto')),
       ('Dave', ('Athena', 'Bacchus')),
       ('Jeff', ('Hercules', 'Pluto')),
       ('Fred', ('Pluto', 'Athena')),
       ('Suzie', ('Bacchus', 'Hercules')),
       ('Laura', ('Bacchus', 'Hercules')),
       ('Neil', ('Hercules', 'Athena'))]
```

You can see immediately that every person can't have his top choice, since there are only two spots in Bacchus and three people want them. Putting any of these people in their second choice would mean there wouldn't be enough space in Hercules for the people who chose it.

This problem is deliberately small so it's easy to follow, but in real life, this problem might include hundreds or thousands of students competing for many more spots in a larger selection of dorms. Since this example only has about 100,000 possible solutions, it's possible to try them all and see which one is the best. But the number quickly grows to trillions of possibilities when there are four slots in each dorm.

The representation for solutions is a bit trickier for this problem than for the flight problem. You could, in theory, create a list of numbers, one for each student, where each number represents the dorm in which you've put the student. The problem is that this representation doesn't constrain the solution to only two students in each dorm. A list of all zeros would indicate that everyone had been placed in Zeus, which isn't a real solution at all.

One way to resolve this is to make the cost function return a very high value for invalid solutions, but this makes it very difficult for the optimization algorithm to find better solutions because it has no way to determine if it's close to other good or even valid solutions. In general, it's better not to waste processor cycles searching among invalid solutions.

A better way to approach the issue is to find a way to represent solutions so that every one is valid. A valid solution is not necessarily a good solution; it just means that there are exactly two students assigned to each dorm. One way to do this is to think of every dorm as having two slots, so that in the example there are ten slots in total. Each student, in order, is assigned to one of the open slots—the first person can be placed in any one of the ten, the second person can be placed in any of the nine remaining slots, and so on.

The domain for searching has to capture this restriction. Add this line to *dorm.py*:

```
# [(0,9),(0,8),(0,7),(0,6),...,(0,0)]
domain=[(0,(len(dorms)*2)-i-1) for i in range(0,len(dorms)*2)]
```

The code to print the solution illustrates how the slots work. This function first creates a list of slots, two for each dorm. It then loops over every number in the solution and finds the dorm number at that location in the slots list, which is the dorm that a student is assigned to. It prints the student and the dorm, and then it removes that slot from the list so no other student will be given that slot. After the final iteration, the slots list is empty and every student and dorm assignment has been printed. Add this function to *dorm.py*:

```
def printsolution(vec):
  slots=[]
  # Create two slots for each dorm
  for i in range(len(dorms): slots+=[i,i]

  # Loop over each students assignment
  for i in range(len(vec)):
    x=int(vec[i])

    # Choose the slot from the remaining ones
    dorm=dorms[slots[x]]
    # Show the student and assigned dorm
    print prefs[i][0],dorm
    # Remove this slot
    del slots[x]
```

In your Python session, you can import this and try printing a solution:

```
>>> import dorm
>>> dorm.printsolution([0,0,0,0,0,0,0,0,0,0])
Toby Zeus
Steve Zeus
Andrea Athena
Sarah Athena
Dave Hercules
Jeff Hercules
Fred Bacchus
Suzie Bacchus
Laura Pluto
Neil Pluto
```

If you change the numbers around to view different solutions, remember that each number must stay in the appropriate range. The first item in the list can be between 0 and 9, the second between 0 and 8, etc. If you set one of the numbers outside the appropriate range, the function will throw an exception. Since the optimization functions will keep the numbers in the ranges specified in the domain parameter, this won't be a problem when optimizing.

The Cost Function

The cost function works in a way that is similar to the print function. A list of slots is constructed and slots are removed as they are used up. The cost is calculated by comparing a student's current dorm assignment to his top two choices. The total cost will increase by 0 if the student is currently assigned to his top choice, by 1 if he is assigned to his second choice, and by 3 if he is not assigned to either of his choices:

```python
def dormcost(vec):
  cost=0
  # Create list a of slots
  slots=[0,0,1,1,2,2,3,3,4,4]

  # Loop over each student
  for i in range(len(vec)):
    x=int(vec[i])
    dorm=dorms[slots[x]]
    pref=prefs[i][1]
    # First choice costs 0, second choice costs 1
    if pref[0]==dorm: cost+=0
    elif pref[1]==dorm: cost+=1
    else: cost+=3
    # Not on the list costs 3

    # Remove selected slot
    del slots[x]

  return cost
```

A useful rule when creating a cost function is, if possible, to make the perfect solution (which in this example is everyone being assigned to their top choice) have a cost of zero. In this case, you've already determined that the perfect solution is impossible, but knowing that its cost is zero gives you an idea of how close you are to it. The other advantage of this rule is that you can tell an optimization algorithm to stop searching for better solutions if it ever finds a perfect solution.

Running the Optimization

With a solution representation, a cost function, and a function to print the results, you have enough to run the optimization functions that you defined earlier. Enter the following in your Python session:

```python
>>> reload(dorm)
>>> s=optimization.randomoptimize(dorm.domain,dorm.dormcost)
>>> dorm.dormcost(s)
18
>>> optimization.geneticoptimize(dorm.domain,dorm.dormcost)
13
10
...
4
>>> dorm.printsolution(s)
```

```
Toby Athena
Steve Pluto
Andrea Zeus
Sarah Pluto
Dave Hercules
Jeff Hercules
Fred Bacchus
Suzie Bacchus
Laura Athena
Neil Zeus
```

Again, you can tweak the parameters to see if you can make the genetic optimization find a good solution more quickly.

Network Visualization

The final example in this chapter shows another way in which optimization can be used on problems that are completely unrelated to one another. In this case, the problem is the visualization of networks. A network in this case is any set of things that are connected together. A good example in online applications is a social network like MySpace, Facebook, or LinkedIn, where people are connected because they are friends or have a professional relationship. Each member of the site chooses to whom they are connected, and collectively this creates a network of people. It is interesting to visualize such networks to determine their structure, perhaps in order to find the people who are connectors (those who know a lot of people or who serve as a link between otherwise self-contained cliques).

The Layout Problem

When drawing a network to visualize a big group of people and the links between them, one problem is deciding where each name (or icon) should be placed in the picture. For example, consider the network in Figure 5-7.

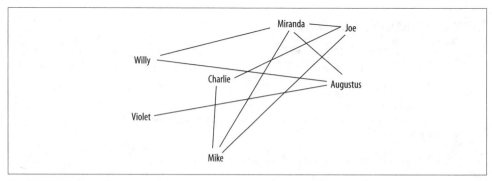

Figure 5-7. A confusing network layout

In this figure, you can see that Augustus is friends with Willy, Violet, and Miranda. But the layout of the network is a bit messy, and adding more people would make it very confusing. A much cleaner layout is shown in Figure 5-8.

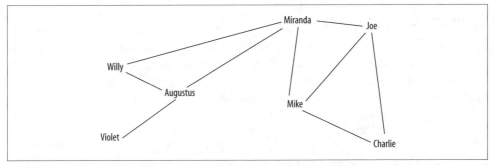

Figure 5-8. A clean network layout

This section will look at how optimization can be used to create better, less confusing visuals. To begin, create a new file called *socialnetwork.py* and add some facts about a subsection of the social network:

```
import math

people=['Charlie','Augustus','Veruca','Violet','Mike','Joe','Willy','Miranda']

links=[('Augustus', 'Willy'),
       ('Mike', 'Joe'),
       ('Miranda', 'Mike'),
       ('Violet', 'Augustus'),
       ('Miranda', 'Willy'),
       ('Charlie', 'Mike'),
       ('Veruca', 'Joe'),
       ('Miranda', 'Augustus'),
       ('Willy', 'Augustus'),
       ('Joe', 'Charlie'),
       ('Veruca', 'Augustus'),
       ('Miranda', 'Joe')]
```

The goal here is to create a program that can take a list of facts about who is friends with whom and generate an easy-to-interpret network diagram. This is usually done with a *mass-and-spring* algorithm. This type of algorithm is modeled on physics because the different nodes exert a push on each other and try to move apart, while the links try to pull connected nodes closer together. Thus, the network slowly assumes a layout where unconnected nodes are pushed apart and connected nodes are pulled close together—but not too close together.

Unfortunately, the mass-and-spring algorithm doesn't stop lines from crossing. In a network with a great number of links, this makes it difficult to see which nodes are connected because visually tracking the lines as they cross can be tricky. However, when you use optimization to create the layout, all you need to do is decide on a cost function and then try to minimize it. In this case, one interesting cost function to try is the number of lines that cross each other.

Counting Crossed Lines

In order to use the same optimizing functions that were defined earlier, it's necessary to represent a solution as a list of numbers. Fortunately, this particular problem is represented as a list of numbers very easily—every node has an x and y coordinate, so the coordinates for all the nodes can be put into a long list:

```
sol=[120,200,250,125 ...
```

In this solution, Charlie is placed at (120,200), Augustus at (250,125), and so on.

Right now, the new cost function will simply count the number of lines that cross each other. The derivation of the formula for two lines crossing is a bit beyond the scope of this chapter, but the basic idea is to calculate the fraction of the line where each line is crossed. If this fraction is between 0 (one end of the line) and 1 (the other end), for both lines, then they cross each other. If the fraction is not between 0 and 1, then the lines do not cross.

This function loops through every pair of links and uses the current coordinates of their endpoints to determine whether they cross. If they do, the function adds 1 to the total score. Add crosscount to *socialnetwork.py*:

```python
def crosscount(v):
    # Convert the number list into a dictionary of person:(x,y)
    loc=dict([(people[i],(v[i*2],v[i*2+1])) for i in range(0,len(people))])
    total=0

    # Loop through every pair of links
    for i in range(len(links)):
        for j in range(i+1,len(links)):

            # Get the locations
            (x1,y1),(x2,y2)=loc[links[i][0]],loc[links[i][1]]
            (x3,y3),(x4,y4)=loc[links[j][0]],loc[links[j][1]]

            den=(y4-y3)*(x2-x1)-(x4-x3)*(y2-y1)

            # den==0 if the lines are parallel
            if den==0: continue

            # Otherwise ua and ub are the fraction of the
            # line where they cross
            ua=((x4-x3)*(y1-y3)-(y4-y3)*(x1-x3))/den
            ub=((x2-x1)*(y1-y3)-(y2-y1)*(x1-x3))/den
```

```
      # If the fraction is between 0 and 1 for both lines
      # then they cross each other
      if ua>0 and ua<1 and ub>0 and ub<1:
         total+=1
   return total
```

The domain for this search is the range for each coordinate. For this example, you can assume that the network will be laid out in a 400×400 image, so the domain will be a little less than that to allow for a slight margin. Add this line to the end of *socialnetwork.py*:

```
domain=[(10,370)]*(len(people)*2)
```

Now you can try actually running some of the optimizations to find a solution where very few lines cross. Import *socialnetwork.py* to your Python session and try a couple of the optimization algorithms:

```
>>> import socialnetwork
>>> import optimization
>>> sol=optimization.randomoptimize(socialnetwork.domain,socialnetwork.crosscount)
>>> socialnetwork.crosscount(sol)
12
>>> sol=optimization.annealingoptimize(socialnetwork.domain,
      socialnetwork.crosscount,step=50,cool=0.99)
>>> socialnetwork.crosscount(sol)
1
>>> sol
[324, 190, 241, 329, 298, 237, 117, 181, 88, 106, 56, 10, 296, 370, 11, 312]
```

Simulated annealing is likely to find a solution where very few of the lines cross, but the list of coordinates is difficult to interpret. The next section will show you how to automatically draw the network.

Drawing the Network

You'll need the Python Imaging Library that was used in Chapter 3. If you haven't installed it yet, please consult Appendix A for instructions on getting the latest version and installing it with your Python instance.

The code for drawing the network is quite straightforward. All the code has to do is create an image, draw the links between the different people, and then draw the nodes for the people. The people's names are drawn afterward so that the lines don't cover them. Add this function to *socialnetwork.py*:

```
def drawnetwork(sol):
   # Create the image
   img=Image.new('RGB',(400,400),(255,255,255))
   draw=ImageDraw.Draw(img)

   # Create the position dict
   pos=dict([(people[i],(sol[i*2],sol[i*2+1])) for i in range(0,len(people))])
```

```
# Draw Links
for (a,b) in links:
    draw.line((pos[a],pos[b]),fill=(255,0,0))

# Draw people
for n,p in pos.items():
    draw.text(p,n,(0,0,0))

img.show()
```

To run this function in your Python session, just reload the module and call this function on your solution:

```
>>> reload(socialnetwork)
>>> drawnetwork(sol)
```

Figure 5-9 shows one possible outcome of the optimization.

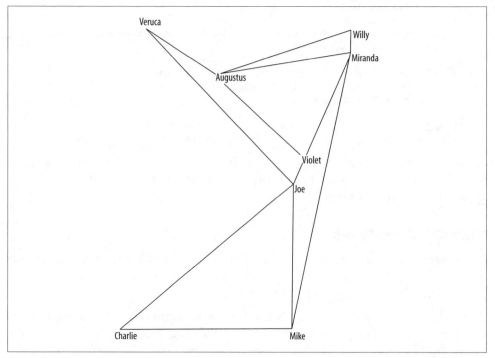

Figure 5-9. Layout resulting from a no-crossed-lines optimization

Of course, your solution will look different from this. Sometimes the solution will look pretty wacky—since the objective is just to minimize the number of crossed lines, the cost function never penalizes the layout for things like very tight angles between the lines or two nodes being very close together. In this respect, optimization is like a genie who grants your wishes very literally, so it's always important to be clear about what you want. There is often a solution that fits the original criteria of "best" but looks nothing like what you had in mind.

A simple way to penalize a solution that has put two nodes too close together is to calculate the distance between the nodes and divide by a desired minimum distance. You can add this code to the end of crosscount (before the return statement) to provide an additional penalty.

```
for i in range(len(people)):
  for j in range(i+1,len(people)):
    # Get the locations of the two nodes
    (x1,y1),(x2,y2)=loc[people[i]],loc[people[j]]

    # Find the distance between them
    dist=math.sqrt(math.pow(x1-x2,2)+math.pow(y1-y2,2))
    # Penalize any nodes closer than 50 pixels
    if dist<50:
      total+=(1.0-(dist/50.0))
```

This creates a higher cost for every pair of nodes that is less than 50 pixels apart, in proportion to how close together they are. If they are in exactly the same place, the penalty is 1. Run the optimization again to see if this results in a more spread-out layout.

Other Possibilities

This chapter has shown three completely different applications for optimization algorithms, but that's only a small fraction of what is possible. As stated throughout the chapter, the important steps are deciding on a representation and a cost function. If you can do these things, there's a good chance you can use optimization to find solutions to your problem.

An interesting activity might be to take a large group of people and divide them into teams in which the skills of the members are evenly divided. In a trivia contest, it might be desirable to create teams from a set of people so that each team has adequate knowledge of sports, history, literature, and television. Another possibility is to assign tasks in group projects by taking a combination of people's skills into account. Optimization can determine the best way to divide the tasks so that the task list is completed in the shortest possible time.

Given a long list of web sites tagged with keywords, it might be interesting to find an optimal group of web sites for a user-supplied set of keywords. The optimal group would contain a set of web sites that don't have many keywords in common with each other but represent as many of the user-supplied keywords as possible.

Exercises

1. *Group travel cost function.* Add total flight time as a cost equal to $0.50 per minute on the plane. Next try adding a penalty of $20 for making anyone get to the airport before 8 a.m.

2. *Annealing starting points.* The outcome of simulated annealing depends heavily on the starting point. Build a new optimization function that does simulated annealing from multiple starting solutions and returns the best one.

3. *Genetic optimization stopping criteria.* A function in this chapter runs the genetic optimizer for a fixed number of iterations. Change it so that it stops when there has been no improvement in any of the best solutions for 10 iterations.

4. *Round-trip pricing.* The function for getting flight data from Kayak right now only looks for one-way flights. Prices are probably cheaper when buying round-trip tickets. Modify the code to get round-trip prices, and modify the cost function to use a price lookup for a particular pair of flights instead of just summing their one-way prices.

5. *Pairing students.* Imagine if instead of listing dorm preferences, students had to express their preferences for a roommate. How would you represent solutions to pairing students? What would the cost function look like?

6. *Line angle penalization.* Add an additional cost to the network layout algorithm cost function when the angle between two lines attached to the same person is very small. (Hint: you can use the *vector cross-product*.)

## CHAPTER 6

Document Filtering

This chapter will demonstrate how to classify documents based on their contents, a very practical application of machine intelligence and one that is becoming more widespread. Perhaps the most useful and well-known application of document filtering is the elimination of spam. A big problem with the wide availability of email and the extremely low cost of sending email messages is that anyone whose address gets into the wrong hands is likely to receive unsolicited commercial email messages, making it difficult for them to read the messages that are actually of interest.

The problem of spam does not just apply to email, of course. Web sites have gotten more interactive over time, soliciting comments from users or asking them to create original content, which has compounded the spam problem. Public message boards like Yahoo! Groups and Usenet have long been victims of postings that are unrelated to the board's subject or that hawk dubious products. Blogs and Wikis are now experiencing the same problem. When building an application that allows the general public to contribute, you should always have a strategy for dealing with spam.

The algorithms described in this chapter are not specific to dealing with spam. Since they solve the more general problem of learning to recognize whether a document belongs in one category or another, they can be used for less unsavory purposes. One example might be automatically dividing your inbox into social and work-related email, based on the contents of the messages. Another possibility is identifying email messages that request information and automatically forwarding them to the most competent person to answer them. The example at the end of this chapter will demonstrate automatically filtering entries from an RSS feed into different categories.

Filtering Spam

Early attempts to filter spam were all rule-based classifiers, where a person would design a set of rules that was supposed to indicate whether or not a message was spam. Rules typically included things like overuse of capital letters, words related to pharmaceutical products, or particularly garish HTML colors. The problems with rule-based classifiers quickly became apparent—spammers learned all the rules and stopped exhibiting the obvious behaviors to get around the filters, while people whose parents never learned to turn off the Caps Lock key found their good email messages being classified as spam.

The other problem with rule-based filters is that what can be considered spam varies depending on where it's being posted and for whom it is being written. Keywords that would strongly indicate spam for one particular user, message board, or Wiki may be quite normal for others. To solve this problem, this chapter will look at programs that *learn*, based on you telling them what is spam email and what isn't, both initially and as you receive more messages. By doing this, you can create separate instances and datasets for individual users, groups, or sites that will each develop their own ideas about what is spam and what isn't.

Documents and Words

The classifier that you will be building needs *features* to use for classifying different items. A feature is anything that you can determine as being either present or absent in the item. When considering documents for classification, the items are the documents and the features are the words in the document. When using words as features, the assumption is that some words are more likely to appear in spam than in nonspam, which is the basic premise underlying most spam filters. Features don't have to be individual words, however; they can be word pairs or phrases or anything else that can be classified as absent or present in a particular document.

Create a new file called *docclass.py*, and add a function called getwords to extract the features from the text:

```
import re
import math

def getwords(doc):
  splitter=re.compile('\\W*')
  # Split the words by non-alpha characters
  words=[s.lower() for s in splitter.split(doc)
          if len(s)>2 and len(s)<20]

  # Return the unique set of words only
  return dict([(w,1) for w in words])
```

This function breaks up the text into words by dividing the text on any character that isn't a letter. This leaves only actual words, all converted to lowercase.

Determining which features to use is both very tricky and very important. The features must be common enough that they appear frequently, but not so common that they appear in every single document. In theory, the entire text of the document could be a feature, but that would almost certainly be useless unless you receive the exact same email message over and over. At the other extreme, the features could be individual characters, but since they would all likely appear in every email message, they would do a poor job of separating wanted from unwanted documents. Even the choice to use words as features poses questions of exactly how to divide words, which punctuation to include, and whether header information should be included.

The other thing to consider when deciding on features is how well they will divide the set of documents into the target categories. For example, the code for getwords above reduces the total number of features by converting them to lowercase. This means it will recognize that a capitalized word at the start of a sentence is the same as when that word is all lowercase in the middle of a sentence—a good thing, since words with different capitalization usually have the same meaning. However, this function will completely miss the SHOUTING style used in many spam messages, which may be vital for dividing the set into spam and nonspam. Another alternative might be to have a feature that is deemed present if more than half the words are uppercase.

As you can see, the choice of feature set involves many tradeoffs and is subject to endless tweaking. For now, you can use the simple getwords function given; later in the chapter, you'll see some ideas for improving the extraction of features.

Training the Classifier

The classifiers discussed in this chapter learn how to classify a document by being trained. Many of the other algorithms in this book, such as the neural network you saw in Chapter 4, learn by reading examples of correct answers. The more examples of documents and their correct classifications it sees, the better the classifier will get at making predictions. The classifier is also specifically designed to start off very uncertain and increase in certainty as it learns which features are important for making a distinction.

The first thing you'll need is a class to represent the classifier. This class will encapsulate what the classifier has learned so far. The advantage of structuring the module this way is that you can instantiate multiple classifiers for different users, groups, or queries, and train them differently to respond to a particular group's needs. Create a class called classifier in *docclass.py*:

```
class classifier:
  def __init__(self,getfeatures,filename=None):
    # Counts of feature/category combinations
    self.fc={}
    # Counts of documents in each category
    self.cc={}
    self.getfeatures=getfeatures
```

The three instance variables are fc, cc, and getfeatures. The fc variable will store the counts for different features in different classifications. For example:

```
{'python': {'bad': 0, 'good': 6}, 'the': {'bad': 3, 'good': 3}}
```

This indicates that the word "the" has appeared in documents classified as bad three times, and in documents that were classified as good three times. The word "Python" has only appeared in good documents.

The cc variable is a dictionary of how many times every classification has been used. This is needed for the probability calculations that we'll discuss shortly. The final instance variable, getfeatures, is the function that will be used to extract the features from the items being classified—in this example, it is the getwords function you just defined.

The methods in the class won't use the dictionaries directly because this restricts potential options for storing the training data in a file or database. Create these helper methods to increment and get the counts:

```
# Increase the count of a feature/category pair
def incf(self,f,cat):
  self.fc.setdefault(f,{})
  self.fc[f].setdefault(cat,0)
  self.fc[f][cat]+=1

# Increase the count of a category
def incc(self,cat):
  self.cc.setdefault(cat,0)
  self.cc[cat]+=1

# The number of times a feature has appeared in a category
def fcount(self,f,cat):
  if f in self.fc and cat in self.fc[f]:
    return float(self.fc[f][cat])
  return 0.0

# The number of items in a category
def catcount(self,cat):
  if cat in self.cc:
    return float(self.cc[cat])
  return 0

# The total number of items
def totalcount(self):
  return sum(self.cc.values())

# The list of all categories
def categories(self):
  return self.cc.keys()
```

The train method takes an item (a document in this case) and a classification. It uses the getfeatures function of the class to break the item into its separate features. It then calls incf to increase the counts for this classification for every feature. Finally, it increases the total count for this classification:

```
def train(self,item,cat):
    features=self.getfeatures(item)
    # Increment the count for every feature with this category
    for f in features:
        self.incf(f,cat)

    # Increment the count for this category
    self.incc(cat)
```

You can check to see if your class is working properly by starting a new Python session and importing this module:

```
$ python
>>> import docclass
>>> cl=docclass.classifier(docclass.getwords)
>>> cl.train('the quick brown fox jumps over the lazy dog','good')
>>> cl.train('make quick money in the online casino','bad')
>>> cl.fcount('quick','good')
1.0
>>> cl.fcount('quick','bad')
1.0
```

At this point, it's useful to have a method to dump some sample training data into the classifier so that you don't have to train it manually every time you create it. Add this function to the start of *docclass.py*:

```
def sampletrain(cl):
    cl.train('Nobody owns the water.','good')
    cl.train('the quick rabbit jumps fences','good')
    cl.train('buy pharmaceuticals now','bad')
    cl.train('make quick money at the online casino','bad')
    cl.train('the quick brown fox jumps','good')
```

Calculating Probabilities

You now have counts for how often an email message appears in each category, so the next step is to convert these numbers into probabilities. A probability is a number between 0 and 1, indicating how likely an event is. In this case, you can calculate the probability that a word is in a particular category by dividing the number of times the word appears in a document in that category by the total number of documents in that category.

Add a method called fprob to the classifier class:

```
def fprob(self,f,cat):
    if self.catcount(cat)==0: return 0
```

```
# The total number of times this feature appeared in this
# category divided by the total number of items in this category
return self.fcount(f,cat)/self.catcount(cat)
```

This is called *conditional probability*, and is usually written as *Pr(A | B)* and spoken "the probability of A given B." In this example, the numbers you have now are *Pr(word | classification)*; that is, for a given classification you calculate the probability that a particular word appears.

You can test this function in your Python session:

```
>>> reload(docclass)
<module 'docclass' from 'docclass.py'>
>>> cl=docclass.classifier(docclass.getwords)
>>> docclass.sampletrain(cl)
>>> cl.fprob('quick','good')
0.66666666666666663
```

You can see that the word "quick" appears in two of the three documents classified as good, which means there's a probability of *Pr(quick | good)* = 0.666 (a 2/3 chance) that a good document will contain that word.

Starting with a Reasonable Guess

The fprob method gives an accurate result for the features and classifications it has seen so far, but it has a slight problem—using only the information it has seen so far makes it incredibly sensitive during early training and to words that appear very rarely. In the sample training data, the word "money" only appears in one document and is classified as bad because it is a casino ad. Since the word "money" is in one bad document and no good ones, the probability that it will appear in the good category using fprob is now 0. This is a bit extreme, since "money" might be a perfectly neutral word that just happens to appear first in a bad document. It would be much more realistic for the value to gradually approach zero as a word is found in more and more documents with the same category.

To get around this, you'll need to decide on an *assumed probability*, which will be used when you have very little information about the feature in question. A good number to start with is 0.5. You'll also need to decide how much to *weight* the assumed probability—a weight of 1 means the assumed probability is weighted the same as one word. The weighted probability returns a weighted average of getprobability and the assumed probability.

In the "money" example, the weighted probability for the word "money" starts at 0.5 for all categories. After the classifier is trained with one bad document and finds that "money" fits into the bad category, its probability becomes 0.75 for bad. This is because:

```
(weight*assumedprob + count*fprob)/(count+weight)
= (1*1.0+1*0.5)/(1.0 + 1.0)
= 0.75
```

Add the method for `weightedprob` to your classifier class:

```
def weightedprob(self,f,cat,prf,weight=1.0,ap=0.5):
  # Calculate current probability
  basicprob=prf(f,cat)

  # Count the number of times this feature has appeared in
  # all categories
  totals=sum([self.fcount(f,c) for c in self.categories()])

  # Calculate the weighted average
  bp=((weight*ap)+(totals*basicprob))/(weight+totals)
  return bp
```

You can now test the function in your Python session. Reload the module and rerun the `sampletrain` method, since creating a new instance of the class will wipe out its existing training:

```
>>> reload(docclass)
<module 'docclass' from 'docclass.pyc'>
>>> cl=docclass.classifier(docclass.getwords)
>>> docclass.sampletrain(cl)
>>> cl.weightedprob('money','good',cl.fprob)
0.25
>>> docclass.sampletrain(cl)
>>> cl.weightedprob('money','good',cl.fprob)
0.16666666666666666
```

As you can see, rerunning the `sampletrain` method makes the classifier even more confident of the various word probabilities as they get pulled further from their assumed probability.

The assumed probability of 0.5 was chosen simply because it is halfway between 0 and 1. However, it's possible that you might have better background information than that, even on a completely untrained classifier. For example, one person who begins training a spam filter can use probabilities from other people's already-trained spam filters as the assumed probabilities. The user still gets a spam filter personalized for him, but the filter is better able to handle words that it has come across very infrequently.

A Naïve Classifier

Once you have the probabilities of a document in a category containing a particular word, you need a way to combine the individual word probabilities to get the probability that an entire document belongs in a given category. This chapter will consider two different classification methods. Both of them work in most situations, but they vary slightly in their level of performance for specific tasks. The classifier covered in this section is called a *naïve Bayesian classifier*.

This method is called *naïve* because it assumes that the probabilities being combined are *independent* of each other. That is, the probability of one word in the document being in a specific category is unrelated to the probability of the other words being in that category. This is actually a false assumption, since you'll probably find that documents containing the word "casino" are much more likely to contain the word "money" than documents about Python programming are.

This means that you can't actually use the probability created by the naïve Bayesian classifier as the actual probability that a document belongs in a category, because the assumption of independence makes it inaccurate. However, you can *compare* the results for different categories and see which one has the highest probability. In real life, despite the underlying flawed assumption, this has proven to be a surprisingly effective method for classifying documents.

Probability of a Whole Document

To use the naïve Bayesian classifier, you'll first have to determine the probability of an entire document being given a classification. As discussed earlier, you're going to assume the probabilities are independent, which means you can calculate the probability of all of them by multiplying them together.

For example, suppose you've noticed that the word "Python" appears in 20 percent of your bad documents—*Pr(Python | Bad)* = 0.2—and that the word "casino" appears in 80 percent of your bad documents *(Pr(Casino | Bad)* = 0.8). You would then expect the independent probability of both words appearing in a bad document—*Pr(Python & Casino | Bad)*—to be $0.8 \times 0.2 = 0.16$. From this you can see that calculating the entire document probability is just a matter of multiplying together all the probabilities of the individual words in that document.

In *docclass.py*, create a subclass of `classifier` called naivebayes, and create a `docprob` method that extracts the features (words) and multiplies all their probabilities together to get an overall probability:

```
class naivebayes(classifier):
  def docprob(self,item,cat):
    features=self.getfeatures(item)

    # Multiply the probabilities of all the features together
    p=1
    for f in features: p*=self.weightedprob(f,cat,self.fprob)
    return p
```

You now know how to calculate *Pr(Document | Category)*, but this isn't very useful by itself. In order to classify documents, you really need *Pr(Category | Document)*. In other words, given a *specific* document, what's the probability that it fits into this category? Fortunately, a British mathematician named Thomas Bayes figured out how to do this about 250 years ago.

A Quick Introduction to Bayes' Theorem

Bayes' Theorem is a way of flipping around conditional probabilities. It's usually written as:

Pr(A | B) = Pr(B | A) x Pr(A)/Pr(B)

In the example, this becomes:

Pr(Category | Document) = Pr(Document | Category) x Pr(Category) / Pr(Document)

The previous section showed how to calculate *Pr(Document | Category)*, but what about the other two values in the equation? Well, *Pr(Category)* is the probability that a randomly selected document will be in this category, so it's just the number of documents in the category divided by the total number of documents.

As for *Pr(Document)*, you could calculate it, but that would be unnecessary effort. Remember that the results of this calculation will not be used as a real probability. Instead, the probability for each category will be calculated separately, and then all the results will be compared. Since *Pr(Document)* is the same no matter what category the calculation is being done for, it will scale the results by the exact same amount, so you can safely ignore that term.

The prob method calculates the probability of the category, and returns the product of *Pr(Document | Category)* and *Pr(Category)*. Add this method to the naivebayes class:

```
def prob(self,item,cat):
  catprob=self.catcount(cat)/self.totalcount( )
  docprob=self.docprob(item,cat)
  return docprob*catprob
```

Try this function in Python to see how the numbers vary for different strings and categories:

```
>>> reload(docclass)
<module 'docclass' from 'docclass.pyc'>
>>> cl=docclass.naivebayes(docclass.getwords)
>>> docclass.sampletrain(cl)
>>> cl.prob('quick rabbit','good')
0.15624999999999997
>>> cl.prob('quick rabbit','bad')
0.050000000000000003
```

Based on the training data, the phrase "quick rabbit" is considered a much better candidate for the good category than the bad.

Choosing a Category

The final step in building the naïve Bayes classifier is actually deciding in which category a new item belongs. The simplest approach would be to calculate the probability of this item being in each of the different categories and to choose the category with the best probability. If you were just trying to decide the best place to put something, this would be a feasible strategy, but in many applications the categories can't be considered equal, and in some applications it's better for the classifier to admit that it doesn't know the answer than to decide that the answer is the category with a marginally higher probability.

In the case of spam filtering, it's much more important to avoid having good email messages classified as spam than it is to catch every single spam message. The occasional spam message in your inbox can be tolerated, but an important email that is automatically filtered to junk mail might get overlooked completely. If you have to search through your junk mail folder for important email messages, there's really no point in having a spam filter.

To deal with this problem, you can set up a minimum threshold for each category. For a new item to be classified into a particular category, its probability must be a specified amount larger than the probability for any other category. This specified amount is the *threshold*. For spam filtering, the threshold to be filtered to bad could be 3, so that the probability for bad would have to be 3 times higher than the probability for good. The threshold for good could be set to 1, so anything would be good if the probability were at all better than for the bad category. Any message where the probability for bad is higher, but not 3 times higher, would be classified as unknown.

To set up these thresholds, add a new instance variable to classifier by modifying the initialization method:

```
def __init__(self,getfeatures):
  classifier.__init__(self,getfeatures)
  self.thresholds={}
```

Add some simple methods to set and get the values, returning 1.0 as the default:

```
def setthreshold(self,cat,t):
  self.thresholds[cat]=t

def getthreshold(self,cat):
  if cat not in self.thresholds: return 1.0
  return self.thresholds[cat]
```

Now you can build the classify method. It will calculate the probability for each category, and will determine which one is the largest and whether it exceeds the next largest by more than its threshold. If none of the categories can accomplish this, the method just returns the default values. Add this method to classifier:

```
def classify(self,item,default=None):
  probs={}
  # Find the category with the highest probability
```

```
max=0.0
for cat in self.categories():
  probs[cat]=self.prob(item,cat)
  if probs[cat]>max:
    max=probs[cat]
    best=cat

# Make sure the probability exceeds threshold*next best
for cat in probs:
  if cat==best: continue
  if probs[cat]*self.getthreshold(best)>probs[best]: return default
return best
```

You're done! You've now built a complete system for classifying documents. This can also be extended to classify other things by creating different methods for getting the features. Try out the classifier in your Python session:

```
>>> reload(docclass)
<module 'docclass' from 'docclass.pyc'>
>>> cl=docclass.naivebayes(docclass.getwords)
>>> docclass.sampletrain(cl)
>>> cl.classify('quick rabbit',default='unknown')
'good'
>>> cl.classify('quick money',default='unknown')
'bad'
>>> cl.setthreshold('bad',3.0)
>>> cl.classify('quick money',default='unknown')
'unknown'
>>> for i in range(10): docclass.sampletrain(cl)
...
>>> cl.classify('quick money',default='unknown')
'bad'
```

Of course, you can alter the thresholds and see how the results are affected. Some spam-filtering plug-ins give users control over the thresholds so they can be adjusted if they're letting too much spam into the inbox or categorizing good messages as spam. The thresholds will also be different for other applications that involve document filtering; sometimes all categories will be equal, or filtering to "unknown" will be unacceptable.

The Fisher Method

The *Fisher method*, named for R. A. Fisher, is an alternative method that's been shown to give very accurate results, particularly for spam filtering. This is the method used by *SpamBayes*, an Outlook plug-in written in Python. Unlike the naïve Bayesian filter, which uses the feature probabilities to create a whole document probability, the Fisher method calculates the probability of a category for each feature in the document, then combines the probabilities and tests to see if the set of probabilities is more or less likely than a random set. This method also returns a probability for each category that can be compared to the others. Although this is a more complex method, it is worth learning because it allows much greater flexibility when choosing cutoffs for categorization.

Category Probabilities for Features

With the naïve Bayesian filter discussed earlier, you combined all of the *Pr(feature | category)* results to get an overall document probability, and then flipped it around at the end. In this section, you'll begin by calculating how likely it is that a document fits into a category given that a particular feature is in that document—that is, *Pr(category | feature)*. If the word "casino" appears in 500 documents, and 499 of those are in the bad category, "casino" will get a score very close to 1 for bad.

The normal way to calculate *Pr(category | feature)* would be:

> *(number of documents in this category with the feature) / (total number of documents with the feature)*

This calculation doesn't take into account the possibility that you may have received far more documents in one category than in another. If you have many good documents and only a few bad ones, a word that appears in all your bad documents will likely have a high probability for bad, even though the message is just as likely to be good. The methods perform better when they assume that in the future you will receive equal numbers of documents in each category, because this allows them to take advantage of the features that distinguish the categories.

To perform this normalization, the method calculates three things:

- *clf = Pr(feature | category) for this category*
- *freqsum = Sum of Pr(feature | category) for all the categories*
- *cprob = clf / (clf+nclf)*

Create a new subclass of `classifier` called `fisherclassifier` in *docclass.py* and add this method:

```
class fisherclassifier(classifier):
  def cprob(self,f,cat):
    # The frequency of this feature in this category
    clf=self.fprob(f,cat)
    if clf==0: return 0

    # The frequency of this feature in all the categories
    freqsum=sum([self.fprob(f,c) for c in self.categories()])

    # The probability is the frequency in this category divided by
    # the overall frequency
    p=clf/(freqsum)

    return p
```

This function will return the probability that an item with the specified feature belongs in the specified category, assuming there will be an equal number of items in each category. You can see what these numbers actually look like in your Python session:

```
>>> reload(docclass)
>>> cl=docclass.fisherclassifier(docclass.getwords)
>>> docclass.sampletrain(cl)
>>> cl.cprob('quick','good')
0.57142857142857151
>>> cl.cprob('money','bad')
1.0
```

This method shows us that documents containing the word "casino" have a 0.9 probability of being spam. This matches the training data, but again it suffers from the problem of only having been exposed to the words a small number of times, and it might be greatly overestimating the probabilities. So, like last time, it's better to use the weighted probability, which starts all probabilities at 0.5 and allows them to move toward other probabilities as the class is trained.

```
>>> cl.weightedprob('money','bad',cl.cprob)
0.75
```

Combining the Probabilities

You now have to combine the probabilities of the individual features to come up with an overall probability. In theory, you can just multiply them all together, which gives you a probability that you can use to compare this category with other categories. Of course, since the features aren't independent, this won't be a real probability, but it works much like the Bayesian classifier that you built in the previous section. The value returned by the Fisher method is a much better estimate of probability, which can be very useful when reporting results or deciding cutoffs.

The Fisher method involves multiplying all the probabilities together, then taking the natural log (*math.log* in Python), and then multiplying the result by −2. Add this method to fisherclassifier to do this calculation:

```
def fisherprob(self,item,cat):
  # Multiply all the probabilities together
  p=1
  features=self.getfeatures(item)
  for f in features:
    p*=(self.weightedprob(f,cat,self.cprob))

  # Take the natural log and multiply by -2
  fscore=-2*math.log(p)

  # Use the inverse chi2 function to get a probability
  return self.invchi2(fscore,len(features)*2)
```

Fisher showed that if the probabilities were independent and random, the result of this calculation would fit a *chi-squared distribution*. You would expect an item that doesn't belong in a particular category to contain words of varying feature probabilities for that category (which would appear somewhat random), and an item that does belong in that category to have many features with high probabilities. By feeding the result of the Fisher calculation to the *inverse chi-square function*, you get the probability that a random set of probabilities would return such a high number.

Add the inverse chi-square function to the `fisherclassifier` class:

```
def invchi2(self,chi,df):
  m = chi / 2.0
  sum = term = math.exp(-m)
  for i in range(1, df//2):
      term *= m / i
      sum += term
  return min(sum, 1.0)
```

Again, you can try this function in your Python session and see how the Fisher method scores some example strings:

```
>>> reload(docclass)
>>> cl=docclass.fisherclassifier(docclass.getwords)
>>> docclass.sampletrain(cl)
>>> cl.cprob('quick','good')
0.57142857142857151
>>> cl.fisherprob('quick rabbit','good')
0.78013986588957995
>>> cl.fisherprob('quick rabbit','bad')
0.35633596283335256
```

As you can see, these results are always between 0 and 1. They are, on their own, a good measure of how well a document fits into a category. Because of this, the classifier itself can be more sophisticated.

Classifying Items

You can use the values returned by `fisherprob` to determine the classification. Rather than having multiplication thresholds like the Bayesian filter, you can specify the lower bounds for each classification. The classifier will then return the highest value that's within its bounds. In the spam filter, you might set the minimum for the bad classification quite high, perhaps 0.6. You might set the minimum for the good classification a lot lower, perhaps 0.2. This would minimize the chance of good email messages being classified as bad, and allow a few spam email messages into the inbox. Anything that scores lower than 0.2 for good and lower than 0.6 for bad would be classified as unknown.

Create an init method in `fisherclassifier` with another variable to store the cutoffs:

```
def __init__(self,getfeatures):
  classifier.__init__(self,getfeatures)
  self.minimums={}
```

Add a couple of methods for getting and setting these values, with a default value of 0:

```
def setminimum(self,cat,min):
  self.minimums[cat]=min

def getminimum(self,cat):
  if cat not in self.minimums: return 0
  return self.minimums[cat]
```

Finally, add a method to calculate the probabilities for each category and determine the best result that exceeds the specified minimum:

```
def classify(self,item,default=None):
  # Loop through looking for the best result
  best=default
  max=0.0
  for c in self.categories():
    p=self.fisherprob(item,c)
    # Make sure it exceeds its minimum
    if p>self.getminimum(c) and p>max:
      best=c
      max=p
  return best
```

Now you can try the classifier on the test data using the Fisher scoring method. Enter the following in your Python session:

```
>>> reload(docclass)
<module 'docclass' from 'docclass.py'>
>>> docclass.sampletrain(cl)
>>> cl.classify('quick rabbit')
'good'
>>> cl.classify('quick money')
'bad'
>>> cl.setminimum('bad',0.8)
>>> cl.classify('quick money')
'good'
>>> cl.setminimum('good',0.4)
>>> cl.classify('quick money')
>>>
```

The results are similar to those of the naïve Bayesian classifier. The Fisher classifier is believed to perform better for spam filtering in practice; however, this is unlikely to be apparent with such a small training set. The classifier you should use depends on your application, and there's no easy way to predict in advance which will perform better or what cutoffs you should use. Fortunately, the code given here should make it very easy to experiment with the two algorithms and with different settings.

Persisting the Trained Classifiers

In any real-world application, it's unlikely that all the training and classification will be done entirely in one session. If the classifier is used as part of a web-based application, it will probably have to save any training that the user does while using the application, and then restore the training data the next time the user logs on.

Using SQLite

This section will show you how to persist the training information for your classifier using a database, in this case, SQLite. If your application involves many users concurrently training and querying the classifier, it's probably wise to store the counts in a database. SQLite is the same database we used in Chapter 4. You'll need to download and install pysqlite if you haven't already; details on how to do this are in Appendix A. Accessing SQLite from Python is similar to accessing other databases, so this should adapt quite easily.

To import pysqlite, add this statement to the top of *docclass.py*:

```
from pysqlite2 import dbapi2 as sqlite
```

The code in this section will replace the dictionary structures currently in the classifier class with a persistent data store. Add a classifier method that opens a database for this classifier and creates tables if necessary. The tables match the structure of the dictionaries that they replace:

```
def setdb(self,dbfile):
  self.con=sqlite.connect(dbfile)
  self.con.execute('create table if not exists fc(feature,category,count)')
  self.con.execute('create table if not exists cc(category,count)')
```

If you're planning to adapt this for another database, you may need to modify the create table statements to work with the system you're using.

You'll have to replace all the helper methods for getting and incrementing the counts:

```
def incf(self,f,cat):
  count=self.fcount(f,cat)
  if count==0:
    self.con.execute("insert into fc values ('%s','%s',1)"
                     % (f,cat))
  else:
    self.con.execute(
      "update fc set count=%d where feature='%s' and category='%s'"
      % (count+1,f,cat))

def fcount(self,f,cat):
  res=self.con.execute(
    'select count from fc where feature="%s" and category="%s"'
    %(f,cat)).fetchone()
```

```
    if res==None: return 0
    else: return float(res[0])

  def incc(self,cat):
    count=self.catcount(cat)
    if count==0:
      self.con.execute("insert into cc values ('%s',1)" % (cat))
    else:
      self.con.execute("update cc set count=%d where category='%s'"
                       % (count+1,cat))

  def catcount(self,cat):
    res=self.con.execute('select count from cc where category="%s"'
                         %(cat)).fetchone()
    if res==None: return 0
    else: return float(res[0])
```

The methods that get the list of all the categories and the total number of documents should also be replaced:

```
  def categories(self):
    cur=self.con.execute('select category from cc');
    return [d[0] for d in cur]

  def totalcount(self):
    res=self.con.execute('select sum(count) from cc').fetchone();
    if res==None: return 0
    return res[0]
```

Finally, you'll need to add a commit after training so that the data is stored after all the counts have been updated. Add this line to the end of the train method in classifier:

```
    self.con.commit()
```

That's it! After you initialize a classifier, you need to call the setdb method with the name of a database file. All training will be automatically stored and can be used by anyone else. You can even use the training from one type of classifier to do classifications in another type:

```
>>> reload(docclass)
<module 'docclass' from 'docclass.py'>
>>> cl=docclass.fisherclassifier(docclass.getwords)
>>> cl.setdb('test1.db')
>>> docclass.sampletrain(cl)
>>> cl2=docclass.naivebayes(docclass.getwords)
>>> cl2.setdb('test1.db')
>>> cl2.classify('quick money')
u'bad'
```

Filtering Blog Feeds

To try out the classifier on real data and show the different ways it can be used, you can apply it to entries from a blog or other RSS feed. To do this, you'll need to get the Universal Feed Parser, which we used in Chapter 3. If you haven't already downloaded it, you can get it from *http://feedparser.org*. More information on installing the Feed Parser is given in Appendix A.

Although a blog will not necessarily contain spam in its entries, many blogs contain some articles that interest you and some that don't. This can be because you only want to read articles in a certain category or by a certain writer, but it's often more complicated than that. Again, you can set up specific rules for things that do and do not interest you—maybe you read a gadget blog and are not interested in entries that contain the word "cell phone"—but it's much less work to use the classifier you've built to figure out these rules for you.

A benefit of classifying entries in an RSS feed is that if you use a blog-searching tool like Google Blog Search, you can set up the results of your searches in a feed reader. Many people do this to track products, things that interest them, even their own names. You'll find, though, that spam-based or useless blogs trying to make money from blog traffic can also appear in these searches.

For this example, you can use any feed you like, although many feeds have too few entries to do any effective training. This particular example uses the results of a Google Blog Search for the word "Python" in RSS format. You can download these results from *http://kiwitobes.com/feeds/python_search.xml*.

Create a new file called *feedfilter.py* and add the following code:

```python
import feedparser
import re

# Takes a filename of URL of a blog feed and classifies the entries
def read(feed,classifier):
  # Get feed entries and loop over them
  f=feedparser.parse(feed)
  for entry in f['entries']:
    print
    print '-----'
    # Print the contents of the entry
    print 'Title:     '+entry['title'].encode('utf-8')
    print 'Publisher: '+entry['publisher'].encode('utf-8')
    print
    print entry['summary'].encode('utf-8')


    # Combine all the text to create one item for the classifier
    fulltext='%s\n%s\n%s' % (entry['title'],entry['publisher'],entry['summary'])
```

```
# Print the best guess at the current category
print 'Guess: '+str(classifier.classify(fulltext))

# Ask the user to specify the correct category and train on that
cl=raw_input('Enter category: ')
classifier.train(fulltext,cl)
```

This function loops over all the entries and uses the classifier to get a best guess at the classification. It shows this best guess to the user and then asks what the correct category should have been. When you run this with a new classifier, the guesses will at first be random, but they should improve over time.

The classifier you have built is completely generic. Although spam filtering was used as an example to help explain what each piece of code does, the categories can be anything. If you're using *python_search.xml*, you might have four categories—one for the programming language, one for Monty Python, one for python snakes, and one for everything else. Try running the interactive filter in your Python session by setting up a classifier and passing it to feedfilter:

```
>>> import feedfilter
>>> cl=docclass.fisherclassifier(docclass.getwords)
>>> cl.setdb('python_feed.db')  # Only if you implemented SQLite
>>> feedfilter.read('python_search.xml',cl)

-----
Title:     My new baby boy!
Publisher: Shetan Noir, the zombie belly dancer! - MySpace Blog

This is my new baby, Anthem. He is a 3 and half month old ball <b>python</b>,
orange shaded normal pattern. I have held him about 5 times since I brought him
home tonight at 8:00pm...
Guess: None
Enter category: snake

-----
Title:     If you need a laugh...
Publisher: Kate&#39;s space

Even does 'funny walks' from Monty <b>Python</b>. He talks about all the ol'
Guess: snake
Enter category: monty

-----
Title:     And another one checked off the list..New pix comment ppl
Publisher: And Python Guru - MySpace Blog

Now the one of a kind NERD bred Carplot male is in our possesion. His name is Broken
(not because he is sterile) lol But check out the pic and leave one
Guess: snake
Enter category: snake
```

You'll see the guesses improving over time. There aren't many samples for snakes, so the classifier often gets them wrong, especially since they are further divided into pet snakes and fashion-related posts. After you've run through the training, you can get probabilities for a specific feature—both the probability of a word given a category and the probability of a category given a word:

```
>>> cl.cprob('python','prog')
0.33333333333333331
>>> cl.cprob('python','snake')
0.33333333333333331
>>> cl.cprob('python','monty')
0.33333333333333331
>>> cl.cprob('eric','monty')
1.0
>>> cl.fprob('eric','monty')
0.25
```

The probabilities for the word "python" are evenly divided, since every entry contains that word. The word "Eric" occurs in 25 percent of entries related to Monty Python and does not occur at all in other entries. Thus, the probability of the word given the category is 0.25, and the probability for the category given the word is 1.0.

Improving Feature Detection

In all the examples so far, the function for creating the list of features uses just a simple nonalphanumeric split to break up the words. The function also converts all words to lowercase, so there's no way to detect the overuse of uppercase words. There are several different ways this can be improved:

- Without actually making uppercase and lowercase tokens completely distinct, use the fact that there are many uppercase words as a feature.
- Use sets of words in addition to individual words.
- Capture more metainformation, such as who sent an email message or what category a blog entry was posted under, and annotate it as metainformation.
- Keep URLs and numbers intact.

Remember that it's not simply a matter of making the features more specific. Features have to occur in multiple documents for them to be of any use to the classifier.

The classifier class will take any function as getfeatures and run it on the items passed in, expecting a list or dictionary of all the features for that item to be returned. Because it is so generic, you can easily create a function that works on types more complicated than just strings. For example, when classifying entries in a blog feed, you can use a function that takes the whole entry instead of the extracted text and annotates where the different words come from. You can also pull out word pairs from the body of the text and only the individual words from the subject. It's also probably pointless to tokenize the creator field, since the postings of someone named "John Smith" will not likely tell you anything about the postings of someone else with the first name John.

Add this new feature-extraction function to *feedfilter.py*. Notice that it expects a feed entry and not a string as its parameter:

```
def entryfeatures(entry):
  splitter=re.compile('\\W*')
  f={}

  # Extract the title words and annotate
  titlewords=[s.lower() for s in splitter.split(entry['title'])
          if len(s)>2 and len(s)<20]
  for w in titlewords: f['Title:'+w]=1

  # Extract the summary words
  summarywords=[s.lower() for s in splitter.split(entry['summary'])
          if len(s)>2 and len(s)<20]

  # Count uppercase words
  uc=0
  for i in range(len(summarywords)):
    w=summarywords[i]
    f[w]=1
    if w.isupper(): uc+=1

    # Get word pairs in summary as features
    if i<len(summarywords)-1:
      twowords=' '.join(summarywords[i:i+1])
      f[twowords]=1

  # Keep creator and publisher whole
  f['Publisher:'+entry['publisher']]=1

  # UPPERCASE is a virtual word flagging too much shouting
  if float(uc)/len(summarywords)>0.3: f['UPPERCASE']=1

  return f
```

This function extracts the words from the title and the summary, just like getwords did earlier. It marks all the words in the title as such and adds them as features. The words in the summary are added as features, and then pairs of consecutive words are added as well. The function adds the creator and publisher as features without dividing them up, and finally, it counts the number of words in the summary that are uppercase. If more than 30 percent of the words are uppercase, the function adds an additional feature called UPPERCASE to the set. Unlike a rule that says uppercase words mean a particular thing, this is just an additional feature that the classifier can use for training—in some cases, it may decide it's completely useless to distinguish document categories.

If you want to use this new version with `filterfeed`, you'll have to change the function to pass the entries to the classifier rather than to `fulltext`. Just change the end to:

```
# Print the best guess at the current category
print 'Guess: '+str(classifier.classify(entry))

# Ask the user to specify the correct category and train on that
cl=raw_input('Enter category: ')
classifier.train(entry,cl)
```

You can then initialize the classifier to use `entryfeatures` as its feature-extraction function:

```
>>> reload(feedfilter)
<module 'feedfilter' from 'feedfilter.py'>
>>> cl=docclass.fisherclassifier(feedfilter.entryfeatures)
>>> cl.setdb('python_feed.db')  # Only if using the DB version
>>> feedfilter.read('python_search.xml',cl)
```

There's a lot more you can do with features. The basic framework you've built allows you to define a function for extracting features and set up the classifier to use the function. It will classify any object you pass to it as long as the feature-extraction function you specify can return a set of features from the object.

Using Akismet

Akismet is a slight detour from the study of text-classification algorithms, but for a specific class of applications, it may solve your spam-filtering needs with minimal effort and eliminate the need for you to build your own classifier.

Akismet started out as a WordPress plug-in that allowed people to report spam comments posted on their blogs, and to filter new comments based on their similarity to spam reported by other people. Now the API is open and you can query Akismet with any string to find out if Akismet thinks the string is spam.

The first thing you'll need is an Akismet API key, which you can get at *http://akismet. com*. These keys are free for personal use and there are several options available for commercial use. The Akismet API is called with regular HTTP requests, and libraries have been written for various languages. The one used in this section is available at *http://kemayo.wordpress.com/2005/12/02/akismet-py*. Download *akismet.py* and put it in your code directory or in your Python Libraries directory.

Using the API is very simple. Create a new file called *akismettest.py* and add this function:

```
import akismet

defaultkey = "YOURKEYHERE"
pageurl="http://yoururlhere.com"
```

```
defaultagent="Mozilla/5.0 (Windows; U; Windows NT 5.1; en-US; rv:1.8.0.7) "
defaultagent+="Gecko/20060909 Firefox/1.5.0.7"

def isspam(comment,author,ipaddress,
           agent=defaultagent,
           apikey=defaultkey):
  try:
    valid = akismet.verify_key(apikey,pageurl)
    if valid:
      return akismet.comment_check(apikey,pageurl,
        ipaddress,agent,comment_content=comment,
        comment_author_email=author,comment_type="comment")
    else:
      print 'Invalid key'
      return False
  except akismet.AkismetError, e:
      print e.response, e.statuscode
      return False
```

You now have a method you can call with any string to see if it is similar to those in blog comments. Try it in your Python session:

```
>>> import akismettest
>>> msg='Make money fast! Online Casino!'
>>> akismettest.isspam(msg,'spammer@spam.com','127.0.0.1')
True
```

Experiment with different usernames, agents, and IP addresses to see how the results vary.

Because Akismet is primarily used for spam comments posted on blogs, it may not perform well on other types of documents, such as email messages. Also, unlike the classifier, it doesn't allow any tweaking of parameters, nor does it let you see the calculations it uses to come up with the answer. It is, however, very accurate for spam-comment filtering, and it's worth trying on your applications if you are receiving a similar kind of spam because Akismet has a far larger collection of documents for comparison than you are likely to have gathered.

Alternative Methods

Both of the classifiers built in this chapter are examples of *supervised learning methods*, methods that are trained with correct results and gradually get better at making predictions. The *artificial neural network* described in Chapter 4 for weighting search results for ranking purposes was another example of supervised learning. That neural network can be adapted to work on the same problems in this chapter by using the features as inputs and having outputs representing each of the possible classifications. Likewise, *support vector machines*, which are described in Chapter 9, can be applied to the problems in this chapter.

The reason Bayesian classifiers are often used for document classification is that they require far less computing power than other methods do. An email message might have hundreds or even thousands of words in it, and simply updating the counts takes vastly less memory and processor cycles than training a neural network of that size does; as shown, it can be done entirely within a database. Depending on the speed required for training and querying, and on the environment in which it is run, a neural network may be a viable alternative. The complexity of a neural network also brings with it a lack of interpretability; in this chapter you were able to look at the word probabilities and see exactly how much they contribute to the final score, while the connection strengths between the neurons in a network has no equally simple interpretation.

On the other hand, neural networks and support-vector machines have one big advantage over the classifiers presented in this chapter: they can capture more complex relationships between the input features. In a Bayesian classifier, every feature has a probability for each category, and you combine the probabilities to get an overall likelihood. In a neural network, the probability of a feature can change depending on the presence or absence of other features. It may be that you're trying to block online-casino spam but you're also interested in horse betting, in which case the word "casino" is bad unless the word "horse" is somewhere else in the email message. Naïve Bayesian classifiers cannot capture this interdependence, and neural networks can.

Exercises

1. *Varying assumed probabilities.* Change the `classifier` class so it supports different assumed probabilities for different features. Change the `init` method so that it will take another classifier and start with a better guess than 0.5 for the assumed probabilities.

2. *Calculate Pr(Document).* In the naïve Bayesian classifier, the calculation of *Pr(Document)* was skipped since it wasn't required to compare the probabilities. In cases where the features are independent, it can actually be used to calculate the overall probability. How would you calculate *Pr(Document)*?

3. *A POP-3 email filter.* Python comes with a library called *poplib* for downloading email messages. Write a script that downloads email messages from a server and attempts to classify them. What are the different properties of an email message, and how might you build a feature-extraction function to take advantage of these?

4. *Arbitrary phrase length.* This chapter showed you how to extract word pairs as well as individual words. Make the feature extraction configurable to extract up to a specified number of words as a single feature.

5. *Preserving IP addresses*. IP addresses, phone numbers, and other numerical information can be helpful in identifying spam. Modify the feature-extraction function to return these items as features. (IP addresses have periods embedded in them, but you still need to get rid of the periods between sentences.)

6. *Other virtual features*. There are many virtual features like UPPERCASE that can be useful in classifying documents. Documents of excessive length or with a preponderance of long words may also be clues. Implement these as features. Can you think of any others?

7. *Neural network classifier*. Modify the neural network from Chapter 4 to be used for document classification. How do its results compare? Write a program that classifies and trains on documents thousands of times. Time how long it takes with each of the algorithms. How do they compare?

## CHAPTER 7

Modeling with Decision Trees

You've now seen a few different automatic classifiers, and this chapter will expand on them by introducing a very useful method called *decision tree learning*. Unlike most other classifiers, the models produced by decision trees are easy to interpret— the list of numbers in a Bayesian classifier will tell you how important each word is, but you really have to do the calculation to know what the outcome will be. A neural network is even more difficult to interpret, since the weight of the connection between two neurons has very little meaning on its own. You can understand the reasoning process of a decision tree just by looking at it, and you can even convert it to a simple series of if-then statements.

This chapter will cover three different examples that employ decision trees. The first shows how to predict which of a site's users are likely to pay for premium access. Many online applications that are priced by subscription or on a per-use basis offer users a way to try the applications before spending money. In the case of subscriptions, the sites usually offer a time-limited free trial or a feature-limited free version. Sites that employ per-use pricing may offer a free session or similar incentive.

The other examples, covered later in the chapter, will use decision trees to model housing prices and "hotness."

Predicting Signups

Sometimes when a high-traffic site links to a new application that offers free accounts and subscription accounts, the application will get thousands of new users. Many of these users are driven by curiosity and are not really looking for that particular type of application, so there is a very low likelihood that they will become paying customers. This makes it difficult to distinguish and follow up with likely customers, so many sites resort to mass-emailing everyone who has signed up, rather than using a more targeted approach.

To help with this problem, it would be useful to be able to predict the likelihood that a user will become a paying customer. You know by now that you can use a Bayesian classifier or neural network to do this. However, clarity is very important in this case—if you know the factors that indicate a user will become a customer, you can use that information to guide an advertising strategy, to make certain aspects of the site more accessible, or to use other strategies that will help increase the number of paying customers.

For this example, imagine an online application that offers a free trial. Users sign up for the trial and use the site for a certain number of days, after which they can choose to upgrade to a basic or premium service. As users sign up for the free trial, information about them is collected, and at the end of the trial, the site owners note which users chose to become paying customers.

To minimize annoyance for users and sign them up as quickly as possible, the site doesn't ask them a lot of questions about themselves—instead, it collects information from the server logs, such as the site that referred them, their geographical location, how many pages they viewed before signing up, and so on. If you collect the data and put it in a table, it might look like Table 7-1.

Table 7-1. User behavior and final purchase decision for a web site

Referrer	Location	Read FAQ	Pages viewed	Service chosen
Slashdot	USA	Yes	18	None
Google	France	Yes	23	Premium
Digg	USA	Yes	24	Basic
Kiwitobes	France	Yes	23	Basic
Google	UK	No	21	Premium
(direct)	New Zealand	No	12	None
(direct)	UK	No	21	Basic
Google	USA	No	24	Premium
Slashdot	France	Yes	19	None
Digg	USA	No	18	None
Google	UK	No	18	None
Kiwitobes	UK	No	19	None
Digg	New Zealand	Yes	12	Basic
Google	UK	Yes	18	Basic
Kiwitobes	France	Yes	19	Basic

Arrange the data in a list of rows, with each row being a list of columns. The final column in each row indicates whether or not the user signed up; this Service column is the value you want to be able to predict. Create a new file called *treepredict.py* to work with throughout this chapter. If you'd like to enter the data manually, add this to the top of the file:

```
my_data=[['slashdot','USA','yes',18,'None'],
        ['google','France','yes',23,'Premium'],
        ['digg','USA','yes',24,'Basic'],
        ['kiwitobes','France','yes',23,'Basic'],
        ['google','UK','no',21,'Premium'],
        ['(direct)','New Zealand','no',12,'None'],
        ['(direct)','UK','no',21,'Basic'],
        ['google','USA','no',24,'Premium'],
        ['slashdot','France','yes',19,'None'],
        ['digg','USA','no',18,'None'],
        ['google','UK','no',18,'None'],
        ['kiwitobes','UK','no',19,'None'],
        ['digg','New Zealand','yes',12,'Basic'],
        ['slashdot','UK','no',21,'None'],
        ['google','UK','yes',18,'Basic'],
        ['kiwitobes','France','yes',19,'Basic']]
```

If you'd prefer to download the dataset, it's available at *http://kiwitobes.com/tree/ decision_tree_example.txt*.

To load in the file, add this line to the top of *treepredict.py*:

```
my_data=[line.split('\t') for line in file('decision_tree_example.txt')]
```

You now have information about users' locations, where they connected from, and how much time they spent on your site before signing up; you just need a way to fill in the Service column with a good guess.

Introducing Decision Trees

Decision trees are one of the simpler machine-learning methods. They are a completely transparent method of classifying observations, which, after training, look like a series of if-then statements arranged into a tree. Figure 7-1 shows an example of a decision tree for classifying fruit.

Once you have a decision tree, it's quite easy to see how it makes all of its decisions. Just follow the path down the tree that answers each question correctly and you'll eventually arrive at an answer. Tracing back from the node where you ended up gives a rationale for the final classification.

This chapter will look at a way to represent a decision tree, at code for constructing the tree from real data, and at code for classifying new observations. The first step is to create a representation of a tree. Create a new class called decisionnode, which represents each node in the tree:

```
class decisionnode:
  def __init__(self,col=-1,value=None,results=None,tb=None,fb=None):
    self.col=col
    self.value=value
    self.results=results
    self.tb=tb
    self.fb=fb
```

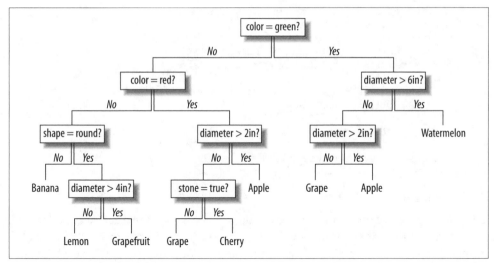

Figure 7-1. Example decision tree

Each node has five instance variables, all of which may be set in the initializer:

- `col` is the column index of the criteria to be tested.
- `value` is the value that the column must match to get a true result.
- `tb` and `fb` are `decisionnodes`, which are the next nodes in the tree if the result is true or false, respectively.
- `results` stores a dictionary of results for this branch. This is `None` for everything except endpoints.

The functions that create a tree return the root node, which can be traversed by following its True or False branches until a branch with results is reached.

Training the Tree

This chapter uses an algorithm called *CART* (Classification and Regression Trees). To build the decision tree, the algorithm first creates a root node. By considering all the observations in the table, it chooses the best variable to divide up the data. To do this, it looks at all the different variables and decides which condition (for example, "Did the user read the FAQ?") would separate the outcomes (which service the user signed up for) in a way that makes it easier to guess what the user will do.

`divideset` is a function that divides the rows into two sets based on the data in a specific column. This function takes a list of rows, a column number, and a value to divide into the column. In the case of Read FAQ, the possible values are Yes or No, and for Referrer, there are several possibilities. It then returns two lists of rows: the first containing the rows where the data in the specified column matches the value, and the second containing the rows where it does not.

```
# Divides a set on a specific column. Can handle numeric
# or nominal values
def divideset(rows,column,value):
    # Make a function that tells us if a row is in
    # the first group (true) or the second group (false)
    split_function=None
    if isinstance(value,int) or isinstance(value,float):
        split_function=lambda row:row[column]>=value
    else:
        split_function=lambda row:row[column]==value

    # Divide the rows into two sets and return them
    set1=[row for row in rows if split_function(row)]
    set2=[row for row in rows if not split_function(row)]
    return (set1,set2)
```

The code creates a function to divide the data called split_function, which depends on knowing if the data is numerical or not. If it is, the true criterion is that the value in this column is greater than value. If the data is not numeric, split_function simply determines whether the column's value is the same as value. It uses this function to divide the data into two sets, one where split_function returns true and one where it returns false.

Start a Python session and try dividing the results by the Read FAQ column:

```
$ python
>>> import treepredict
>>> treepredict.divideset(treepredict.my_data,2,'yes')
([['slashdot', 'USA', 'yes', 18, 'None'], ['google', 'France', 'yes', 23,
'Premium'],...]]
[['google', 'UK', 'no', 21, 'Premium'], ['(direct)', 'New Zealand', 'no', 12,
'None'],...])
```

Table 7-2 shows the division.

Table 7-2. Outcomes based on Read FAQ column values

True	False
None	Premium
Premium	None
Basic	Basic
Basic	Premium
None	None
Basic	None
Basic	None

This doesn't look like a good variable for separating the outcomes at this stage, since both sides seem pretty well mixed. We need a way to choose the best variable.

Choosing the Best Split

Our casual observation that the chosen variable isn't very good may be accurate, but to choose which variable to use in a software solution, you need a way to measure how mixed a set is. What you want to do is find the variable that creates the two sets with the least possible mixing. The first function you'll need is one to get the counts of each result in a set. Add this to *treepredict.py*:

```
# Create counts of possible results (the last column of
# each row is the result)
def uniquecounts(rows):
    results={}
    for row in rows:
        # The result is the last column
        r=row[len(row)-1]
        if r not in results: results[r]=0
        results[r]+=1
    return results
```

uniquecounts finds all the different possible outcomes and returns them as a dictionary of how many times they each appear. This is used by the other functions to calculate how mixed a set is. There are a few different metrics for measuring this, and two will be considered here: Gini impurity and entropy.

Gini Impurity

Gini impurity is the expected error rate if one of the results from a set is randomly applied to one of the items in the set. If every item in the set is in the same category, the guess will always be correct, so the error rate is 0. If there are four possible results evenly divided in the group, there's a 75 percent chance that the guess would be incorrect, so the error rate is 0.75.

The function for Gini impurity looks like this:

```
# Probability that a randomly placed item will
# be in the wrong category
def giniimpurity(rows):
    total=len(rows)
    counts=uniquecounts(rows)
    imp=0
    for k1 in counts:
        p1=float(counts[k1])/total
        for k2 in counts:
            if k1==k2: continue
            p2=float(counts[k2])/total
            imp+=p1*p2
    return imp
```

This function calculates the probability of each possible outcome by dividing the number of times that outcome occurs by the total number of rows in the set. It then adds up the products of all these probabilities. This gives the overall chance that a row would be randomly assigned to the wrong outcome. The higher this probability, the worse the split. A probability of zero is great because it tells you that everything is already in the right set.

Entropy

Entropy, in information theory, is the amount of disorder in a set—basically, how mixed a set is. Add this function to *treepredict.py*:

```
# Entropy is the sum of p(x)log(p(x)) across all
# the different possible results
def entropy(rows):
    from math import log
    log2=lambda x:log(x)/log(2)
    results=uniquecounts(rows)
    # Now calculate the entropy
    ent=0.0
    for r in results.keys():
        p=float(results[r])/len(rows)
        ent=ent-p*log2(p)
    return ent
```

The entropy function calculates the frequency of each item (the number of times it appears divided by the total number of rows), and applies these formulas:

p(i) = frequency(outcome) = count(outcome) / count(total rows)
Entropy = sum of p(i) x log(p(i)) for all outcomes

This is a measurement of how different the outcomes are from each other. If they're all the same (e.g., if you were really lucky and everyone became a premium subscriber), then the entropy is 0. The more mixed up the groups are, the higher their entropy. Our goal in dividing the data into two new groups is to reduce the entropy.

Try testing the Gini impurity and entropy metrics in your Python session:

```
>>> reload(treepredict)
<module 'treepredict' from 'treepredict.py'>
>>> treepredict.giniimpurity(treepredict.my_data)
0.6328125
>>> treepredict.entropy(treepredict.my_data)
1.5052408149441479
>>> set1,set2=treepredict.divideset(treepredict.my_data,2,'yes')
>>> treepredict.entropy(set1)
1.2987949406953985
>>> treepredict.giniimpurity(set1)
0.53125
```

The main difference between entropy and Gini impurity is that entropy peaks more slowly. Consequently, it tends to penalize mixed sets a little more heavily. The rest of this chapter will use entropy as the metric because it is used more commonly, but it's easy to swap it out for the Gini impurity.

Recursive Tree Building

To see how good an attribute is, the algorithm first calculates the entropy of the whole group. Then it tries dividing up the group by the possible values of each attribute and calculates the entropy of the two new groups. To determine which attribute is the best to divide on, the *information gain* is calculated. Information gain is the difference between the current entropy and the weighted-average entropy of the two new groups. The algorithm calculates the information gain for every attribute and chooses the one with the highest information gain.

After the condition for the root node has been decided, the algorithm creates two branches corresponding to true or false for that condition, as shown in Figure 7-2.

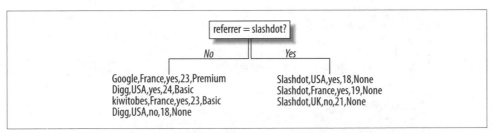

Figure 7-2. Decision tree after a single split

The observations are divided into those that meet the condition and those that don't. For each branch, the algorithm then determines if the branch can be divided further or if it has reached a solid conclusion. If one of the new branches can be divided, the same method as above is used to determine which variable to use. The second division is shown in Figure 7-3.

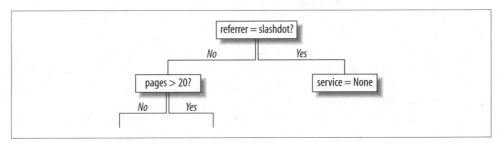

Figure 7-3. Decision tree after two splits

The branches keep dividing, creating a tree by calculating the best attribute for each new node. A branch stops dividing when the information gain from splitting a node is not more than zero.

Create a new function called buildtree in *treepredict.py*. This is a recursive function that builds the tree by choosing the best dividing criteria for the current set:

```
def buildtree(rows,scoref=entropy):
  if len(rows)==0: return decisionnode( )
  current_score=scoref(rows)

  # Set up some variables to track the best criteria
  best_gain=0.0
  best_criteria=None
  best_sets=None

  column_count=len(rows[0])-1
  for col in range(0,column_count):
    # Generate the list of different values in
    # this column
    column_values={}
    for row in rows:
       column_values[row[col]]=1
    # Now try dividing the rows up for each value
    # in this column
    for value in column_values.keys( ):
      (set1,set2)=divideset(rows,col,value)

      # Information gain
      p=float(len(set1))/len(rows)
      gain=current_score-p*scoref(set1)-(1-p)*scoref(set2)
      if gain>best_gain and len(set1)>0 and len(set2)>0:
        best_gain=gain
        best_criteria=(col,value)
        best_sets=(set1,set2)
  # Create the subbranches
  if best_gain>0:
    trueBranch=buildtree(best_sets[0])
    falseBranch=buildtree(best_sets[1])
    return decisionnode(col=best_criteria[0],value=best_criteria[1],
                        tb=trueBranch,fb=falseBranch)
  else:
    return decisionnode(results=uniquecounts(rows))
```

This function is first called with the list of rows. It loops through every column (except the last one, which has the result in it), finds every possible value for that column, and divides the dataset into two new subsets. It calculates the weighted-average entropy for every pair of new subsets by multiplying each set's entropy by the fraction of the items that ended up in each set, and remembers which pair has the lowest entropy.

If the best pair of subsets doesn't have a lower weighted-average entropy than the current set, that branch ends and the counts of the possible outcomes are stored. Otherwise, buildtree is called on each set and they are added to the tree. The results of the calls on each subset are attached to the True and False branches of the nodes, eventually constructing an entire tree.

Now you can finally apply the algorithm to the original dataset. The code above is flexible enough to handle both text and numeric data. It also assumes that the last row is the target value, so you can simply pass the rows of data to build the tree:

```
>>> reload(treepredict)
<module 'treepredict' from 'treepredict.py'>
>>> tree=treepredict.buildtree(treepredict.my_data)
```

tree now holds a trained decision tree. In a moment you'll learn how to look at the tree, and later, how to use it to make predictions.

Displaying the Tree

So now that you have a tree, what should you do with it? Well, one thing you'll definitely want to do is look at it. printtree is a simple function for displaying the tree in plain text. The output isn't pretty, but it's a simple way to view small trees:

```
def printtree(tree,indent=''):
    # Is this a leaf node?
    if tree.results!=None:
        print str(tree.results)
    else:
        # Print the criteria
        print str(tree.col)+':'+str(tree.value)+'? '

        # Print the branches
        print indent+'T->',
        printtree(tree.tb,indent+'  ')
        print indent+'F->',
        printtree(tree.fb,indent+'  ')
```

This is another recursive function. It takes a tree returned by buildtree and traverses down it, and it knows it has reached the end of a branch when it reaches the node with results. Until it reaches that point, it prints the criteria for the True and False branches and calls printtree on each of them, each time increasing the indent string.

Call this function with the tree you just built, and you'll get something like this:

```
>>> reload(treepredict)
>>> treepredict.printtree(tree)
0:google?
T-> 3:21?
  T-> {'Premium': 3}
  F-> 2:yes?
    T-> {'Basic': 1}
    F-> {'None': 1}
F-> 0:slashdot?
  T-> {'None': 3}
  F-> 2:yes?
    T-> {'Basic': 4}
    F-> 3:21?
      T-> {'Basic': 1}
      F-> {'None': 3}
```

This is a visual representation of the process that the decision tree will go through when trying to make a new classification. The condition on the root node is "is Google in column 0?" If this condition is met, it proceeds to the T-> branch and finds that anyone referred from Google will become a paid subscriber if they have viewed 21 pages or more. If the condition is not met, it jumps to the F-> branch and evaluates the condition "is Slashdot in column 0?" This continues until it reaches a branch that has a result. As mentioned earlier, the ability to view the logic behind the reasoning process is one of the big advantages of decision trees.

Graphical Display

The textual display of the tree is fine for small trees, but as they get larger, visually tracking your way through the tree can be quite difficult. Here you'll see how to make a graphical representation of the tree that will be useful for viewing trees you'll build in later sections.

The code for drawing the tree is similar to the code for drawing dendrograms in Chapter 3. Both involve drawing a binary tree with nodes of arbitrary depth, so you'll first need functions to decide how much space a given node will take up—both the total width of all its children and how deep the node goes, which tells you much vertical space it will need for all its branches. The total width of a branch is the combined width of its child branches, or 1 if it doesn't have any child branches:

```
def getwidth(tree):
  if tree.tb==None and tree.fb==None: return 1
  return getwidth(tree.tb)+getwidth(tree.fb)
```

The depth of a branch is 1 plus the total depth of its longest child branch:

```
def getdepth(tree):
  if tree.tb==None and tree.fb==None: return 0
  return max(getdepth(tree.tb),getdepth(tree.fb))+1
```

To actually draw the tree, you'll need to have the Python Imaging Library installed. You can get this library from *http://pythonware.com*, and Appendix A has more information on installing it. Add this import statement at the beginning of *treepredict.py*:

```
from PIL import Image,ImageDraw
```

The drawtree function determines the appropriate total size and sets up a canvas. It then passes this canvas and the top node of the tree to drawnode. Add this function to *treepredict.py*:

```
def drawtree(tree,jpeg='tree.jpg'):
  w=getwidth(tree)*100
  h=getdepth(tree)*100+120

  img=Image.new('RGB',(w,h),(255,255,255))
  draw=ImageDraw.Draw(img)

  drawnode(draw,tree,w/2,20)
  img.save(jpeg,'JPEG')
```

The drawnode function actually draws the decision nodes of the tree. It works recursively, first drawing the current node and calculating the positions of the child nodes, then calling drawnode on each of the child nodes. Add this function to *treepredict.py*:

```python
def drawnode(draw,tree,x,y):
  if tree.results==None:
    # Get the width of each branch
    w1=getwidth(tree.fb)*100
    w2=getwidth(tree.tb)*100

    # Determine the total space required by this node
    left=x-(w1+w2)/2
    right=x+(w1+w2)/2

    # Draw the condition string
    draw.text((x-20,y-10),str(tree.col)+':'+str(tree.value),(0,0,0))

    # Draw links to the branches
    draw.line((x,y,left+w1/2,y+100),fill=(255,0,0))
    draw.line((x,y,right-w2/2,y+100),fill=(255,0,0))

    # Draw the branch nodes
    drawnode(draw,tree.fb,left+w1/2,y+100)
    drawnode(draw,tree.tb,right-w2/2,y+100)
  else:
    txt=' \n'.join(['%s:%d'%v for v in tree.results.items()])
    draw.text((x-20,y),txt,(0,0,0))
```

You can now try drawing the current tree in your Python session:

```
>>> reload(treepredict)
<module 'treepredict' from 'treepredict.pyc'>
>>> treepredict.drawtree(tree,jpeg='treeview.jpg')
```

This should produce a new file called *treeview.jpg*, which is shown in Figure 7-4.

The code does not print the True and False branch labels, and they would likely just contribute to the clutter of larger diagrams. In the generated tree diagrams, the True branch is always the righthand branch, so you can follow the reasoning process through.

Classifying New Observations

Now you'll need a function that takes a new observation and classifies it according to the decision tree. Add this function to *treepredict.py*:

```python
def classify(observation,tree):
  if tree.results!=None:
    return tree.results
  else:
    v=observation[tree.col]
    branch=None
    if isinstance(v,int) or isinstance(v,float):
```

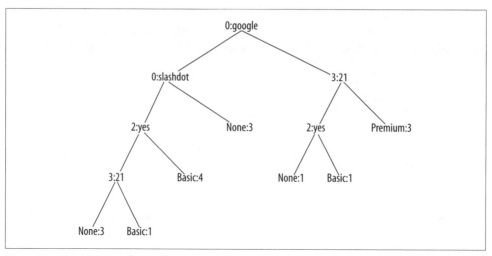

Figure 7-4. Decision tree for predicting subscribers

```
    if v>=tree.value: branch=tree.tb
    else: branch=tree.fb
  else:
    if v==tree.value: branch=tree.tb
    else: branch=tree.fb
  return classify(observation,branch)
```

This function traverses the tree in much the same manner as `printtree`. After each call, it checks to see if it has reached the end of this branch by looking for `results`. If not, it evaluates the observation to see if the column matches the value. If it does, it calls `classify` again on the True branch; if not, it calls `classify` on the False branch.

Now you can call `classify` to get the prediction for a new observation:

```
>>> reload(treepredict)
<module 'treepredict' from 'treepredict.pyc'>
>>> treepredict.classify(['(direct)','USA','yes',5],tree)
{'Basic': 4}
```

You now have functions for creating a decision tree from any dataset, for displaying and interpreting the tree, and for classifying new results. These functions can be applied to any dataset that consists of multiple rows, each containing a set of observations and an outcome.

Pruning the Tree

One problem with training the tree using the methods described so far is that it can become *overfitted*—that is, it can become too specific to the training data. An overfitted tree may give an answer as being more certain than it really is by creating branches that decrease entropy slightly for the training set, but whose conditions are actually completely arbitrary.

Decision Trees in the Real World

Because decision trees are so easy to interpret, they are among the most widely used data-mining methods in business analysis, medical decision-making, and policy-making. Often, a decision tree is created automatically, and an expert uses it to understand the key factors and then refines it to better match her beliefs. This process allows machines to assist experts and to clearly show the reasoning process so that individuals can judge the quality of the prediction.

Decision trees have been used in this manner for such wide-ranging applications as customer profiling, financial risk analysis, assisted diagnosis, and traffic prediction.

Since the algorithm above continually splits the branches until it can't reduce the entropy any further, one possibility is to stop splitting when the entropy is not reduced by a minimum amount. This strategy is employed frequently, but it suffers from a minor drawback—it is possible to have a dataset where the entropy is not reduced much by one split but is reduced greatly by subsequent splits. An alternative strategy is to build the entire tree as described earlier, and then try to eliminate superfluous nodes. This process is known as *pruning*.

Pruning involves checking pairs of nodes that have a common parent to see if merging them would increase the entropy by less than a specified threshold. If so, the leaves are merged into a single node with all the possible outcomes. This helps avoid overfitting and stops the tree from making predictions that are more confident than what can really be gleaned from the data.

Add a new function to *treepredict.py* for pruning the tree:

```
def prune(tree,mingain):
  # If the branches aren't leaves, then prune them
  if tree.tb.results==None:
    prune(tree.tb,mingain)
  if tree.fb.results==None:
    prune(tree.fb,mingain)

  # If both the subbranches are now leaves, see if they
  # should merged
  if tree.tb.results!=None and tree.fb.results!=None:
    # Build a combined dataset
    tb,fb=[],[]
    for v,c in tree.tb.results.items():
      tb+=[[v]]*c
    for v,c in tree.fb.results.items():
      fb+=[[v]]*c

    # Test the reduction in entropy
    delta=entropy(tb+fb)-(entropy(tb)+entropy(fb)/2)
```

```
    if delta<mingain:
        # Merge the branches
        tree.tb,tree.fb=None,None
        tree.results=uniquecounts(tb+fb)
```

When this function is called on the root node, it will traverse all the way down the tree to the nodes that only have leaf nodes as children. It will create a combined list of results from both of the leaves and will test the entropy. If the change in entropy is less than the mingain parameter, the leaves will be deleted and all their results moved to their parent node. The combined node then becomes a possible candidate for deletion and merging with another node.

Try it on your current dataset to see if it merges any of the nodes:

```
>>> reload(treepredict)
<module 'treepredict' from 'treepredict.pyc'>
>>> treepredict.prune(tree,0.1)
>>> treepredict.printtree(tree)
0:google?
T-> 3:21?
  T-> {'Premium': 3}
  F-> 2:yes?
    T-> {'Basic': 1}
    F-> {'None': 1}
F-> 0:slashdot?
  T-> {'None': 3}
  F-> 2:yes?
    T-> {'Basic': 4}
    F-> 3:21?
      T-> {'Basic': 1}
      F-> {'None': 3}
>>> treepredict.prune(tree,1.0)
>>> treepredict.printtree(tree)
0:google?
T-> 3:21?
  T-> {'Premium': 3}
  F-> 2:yes?
    T-> {'Basic': 1}
    F-> {'None': 1}
F-> {'None': 6, 'Basic': 5}
```

In the example, the data divides quite easily, so pruning with a reasonable minimum gain doesn't really do anything. Only when the minimum gain is turned up very high does one of the leaves get merged. As you'll see later, real datasets tend not to break as cleanly as this one does, so pruning is much more effective in those cases.

Dealing with Missing Data

Another advantage of decision trees is their ability to deal with missing data. Your dataset may be missing some piece of information—in the current example, for instance, the geographical location of a user may not be discernable from her IP address, so the field may be blank. To adapt the decision tree to handle this, you'll need to implement a different prediction function.

If you are missing a piece of data that is required to decide which branch of the tree to follow, you can actually follow *both* branches. However, instead of counting the results equally, the results from either side are weighted. In the basic decision tree, everything has an implied weight of 1, meaning that the observations count fully for the probability that an item fits into a certain category. If you are following multiple branches instead, you can give each branch a weight equal to the fraction of all the other rows that are on that side.

The function for doing this, `mdclassify`, is a simple modification of `classify`. Add it to *treepredict.py*:

```
def mdclassify(observation,tree):
  if tree.results!=None:
    return tree.results
  else:
    v=observation[tree.col]
    if v==None:
      tr,fr=mdclassify(observation,tree.tb),mdclassify(observation,tree.fb)
      tcount=sum(tr.values())
      fcount=sum(fr.values())
      tw=float(tcount)/(tcount+fcount)
      fw=float(fcount)/(tcount+fcount)
      result={}
      for k,v in tr.items(): result[k]=v*tw
      for k,v in fr.items(): result[k]=v*fw
      return result
    else:
      if isinstance(v,int) or isinstance(v,float):
        if v>=tree.value: branch=tree.tb
        else: branch=tree.fb
      else:
        if v==tree.value: branch=tree.tb
        else: branch=tree.fb
      return mdclassify(observation,branch)
```

The only difference is at the end where, if the important piece of data is missing, the results for each branch are calculated and then combined with their respective weightings.

Try out `mdclassify` on a row with a crucial piece of information missing and see how your results look:

```
>>> reload(treepredict)
<module 'treepredict' from 'treepredict.py'>
>>> treepredict.mdclassify(['google',None,'yes',None],tree)
{'Premium': 1.5, 'Basic': 1.5}
>>> treepredict2.mdclassify(['google','France',None,None],tree)
{'None': 0.125, 'Premium': 2.25, 'Basic': 0.125}
```

As expected, leaving out the Pages variable returns a strong chance of Premium and a slight chance of Basic. Leaving out the Read FAQ variable yields a different distribution, with each possibility in the end weighted by how many items were placed on each side.

Dealing with Numerical Outcomes

The user behavior example and the fruit tree were both classification problems, since the outcomes were categories rather than numbers. The remaining examples in this chapter, home prices and hotness, are both problems with numerical outcomes.

While it's possible to run buildtree on a dataset with numbers as outcomes, the result probably won't be very good. If all the numbers are treated as different categories, the algorithm won't take into account the fact that some numbers are close together and others are far apart; they will all be treated as completely separate. To deal with this, when you have a tree with numerical outcomes, you can use variance as a scoring function instead of entropy or Gini impurity. Add the variance function to *treepredict.py*:

```
def variance(rows):
  if len(rows)==0: return 0
  data=[float(row[len(row)-1]) for row in rows]
  mean=sum(data)/len(data)
  variance=sum([(d-mean)**2 for d in data])/len(data)
  return variance
```

This function is a possible parameter for buildtree, and it calculates the statistical variance for a set of rows. A low variance means that the numbers are all very close together, and a high variance means that they are widely dispersed. When building a tree using variance as the scoring function, node criteria will be picked that split the numbers so that higher values are on one side and lower values are on the other. Splitting the data this way reduces the overall variance on the branches.

Modeling Home Prices

There are many potential uses for decision trees, but they are most useful when there are several possible variables and you're interested in the reasoning process. In some cases, you already know the outcomes, and the interesting part is modeling the outcomes to understand why they are as they are. One area in which this is potentially very interesting is understanding prices of goods, particularly those that have a lot of variability in measurable ways. This section will look at building decision trees for modeling real estate prices, because houses vary greatly in price and have many numerical and nominal variables that are easily measured.

The Zillow API

Zillow is a free web service that tracks real estate prices and uses this information to create price estimates for other houses. It works by looking at comps (similar houses) and using their values to predict a new value, which is similar to what real estate appraisers do. A section of a Zillow web page showing information about a house and its estimate value is shown in Figure 7-5.

Figure 7-5. Screenshot from zillow.com

Fortunately, Zillow also has an API that lets you get details and the estimated value of houses. The page for the Zillow API is *http://www.zillow.com/howto/api/APIOverview.htm.*

You'll need to get a developer key to access the API, which is free and available from the web site. The API itself is quite simple—it involves requesting a URL with all your search parameters in the query, and then parsing the returned XML to get details like number of bedrooms and estimated price. Create a new file called *zillow.py* and add the following code:

```
import xml.dom.minidom
import urllib2

zwskey="X1-ZWz1chwxis15aj_9skq6"
```

As you did in Chapter 5, you're going to use the *minidom* API to parse XML results of your queries. The function getaddressdata takes an address and a city, and constructs the URL to query Zillow for property information. It parses the results and extracts the important information, which it returns as a tuple of results. Add this function to *zillow.py*:

```
def getaddressdata(address,city):
  escad=address.replace(' ','+')

  # Construct the URL
  url='http://www.zillow.com/webservice/GetDeepSearchResults.htm?'
  url+='zws-id=%s&address=%s&citystatezip=%s' % (zwskey,escad,city)

  # Parse resulting XML
  doc=xml.dom.minidom.parseString(urllib2.urlopen(url).read())
  code=doc.getElementsByTagName('code')[0].firstChild.data

  # Code 0 means success; otherwise, there was an error
  if code!='0': return None

  # Extract the info about this property
  try:
    zipcode=doc.getElementsByTagName('zipcode')[0].firstChild.data
    use=doc.getElementsByTagName('useCode')[0].firstChild.data
    year=doc.getElementsByTagName('yearBuilt')[0].firstChild.data
    bath=doc.getElementsByTagName('bathrooms')[0].firstChild.data
    bed=doc.getElementsByTagName('bedrooms')[0].firstChild.data
    rooms=doc.getElementsByTagName('totalRooms')[0].firstChild.data
    price=doc.getElementsByTagName('amount')[0].firstChild.data
  except:
    return None

  return (zipcode,use,int(year),float(bath),int(bed),int(rooms),price)
```

The tuple returned by this function is suitable to put in a list as an observation, since the "result," the price bucket, is at the end. To use this function to generate an entire dataset, you'll need a list of addresses. You can generate this yourself or download a list of randomly generated addresses in Cambridge, MA at *http://kiwitobes.com/ addresslist.txt*.

Create a new function called getpricelist to read this file and generate a list of data:

```
def getpricelist():
  l1=[]
  for line in file('addresslist.txt'):
    data=getaddressdata(line.strip(),'Cambridge,MA')
    l1.append(data)
  return l1
```

You can now use these functions to generate a dataset and build a decision tree. Try this in your Python session:

```
>>> import zillow
>>> housedata=zillow.getpricelist()
>>> reload(treepredict)
>>> housetree=treepredict.buildtree(housedata,scoref=treepredict.variance)
>>> treepredict.drawtree(housetree,'housetree.jpg')
```

One possible generated file, *housetree.jpg*, is shown in Figure 7-6.

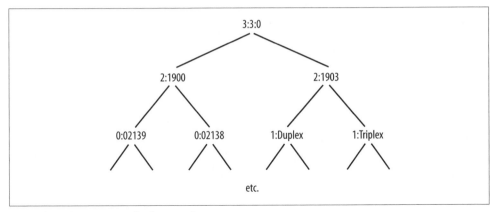

Figure 7-6. *Decision tree for house prices*

Of course, if you were only interested in guessing the price of particular property, you could just use the Zillow API to get an estimate. What's interesting here is that you actually built a model of the factors to be considered in determining housing prices. Notice that the top of the tree is Bathrooms, which means that you reduce the variance the most by dividing the dataset on the total number of bathrooms. The main deciding factor in the price of a house in Cambridge is whether or not it has three or more bathrooms (usually this indicates that the property is a large multifamily house).

The obvious downside of using a decision tree here is that it's necessary to create buckets of price data, since they're all different and have to be grouped in some way to create useful endpoints. It's possible that a different prediction technique would have worked better on the actual price data. Chapter 8 discusses a different method for making price predictions.

Modeling "Hotness"

Hot or Not is a site that allows users to upload photos of themselves. Its original concept was to let users rank other users on their physical appearance, and to aggregate the results to create a score between 1 and 10 for each person. It has since evolved into a dating site, and now has an open API that allows you to get demographic information about members along with their "hotness" rating. This makes it an interesting test case for a decision tree model because there is a set of input variables, an output variable, and a possibly interesting reasoning process. The site itself is also a good example of what might be considered collective intelligence.

Again, you'll need to get an application key to access the API. You can sign up and get one at *http://dev.hotornot.com/signup*.

The Hot or Not API works in much the same way as the other APIs that have been covered. You simply pass the parameters of a query to a URL and parse the XML that is returned. To get started, create a new file called *hotornot.py* and add the import statements and your key definition:

```
import urllib2
import xml.dom.minidom

api_key="479NUNJHETN"
```

Next, get a list of random people to make up the dataset. Fortunately, Hot or Not provides an API call that returns a list of people with specified criteria. In this example, the only criteria will be that the people have "meet me" profiles, since only from these profiles can you get other information like location and interests. Add this function to *hotornot.py*:

```
def getrandomratings(c):
  # Construct URL for getRandomProfile
  url="http://services.hotornot.com/rest/?app_key=%s" % api_key
  url+="&method=Rate.getRandomProfile&retrieve_num=%d" % c
  url+="&get_rate_info=true&meet_users_only=true"

  f1=urllib2.urlopen(url).read()

  doc=xml.dom.minidom.parseString(f1)

  emids=doc.getElementsByTagName('emid')
  ratings=doc.getElementsByTagName('rating')

  # Combine the emids and ratings together into a list
  result=[]
  for e,r in zip(emids,ratings):
    if r.firstChild!=None:
      result.append((e.firstChild.data,r.firstChild.data))
  return result
```

Once you've generated a list of user IDs and ratings, you'll need another function to download information about people—in this case, gender, age, location, and keywords. Having all 50 states as possible location variables will lead to too many branching possibilities. In order to reduce the number of possibilities for location, you can divide the states into regions. Add the following code to specify regions:

```
stateregions={'New England':['ct','mn','ma','nh','ri','vt'],
              'Mid Atlantic':['de','md','nj','ny','pa'],
              'South':['al','ak','fl','ga','ky','la','ms','mo',
                       'nc','sc','tn','va','wv'],
              'Midwest':['il','in','ia','ks','mi','ne','nd','oh','sd','wi'],
              'West':['ak','ca','co','hi','id','mt','nv','or','ut','wa','wy']}
```

The API provides a method to download demographic data for individuals, so the function getpeopledata just loops through all the results of the first search and queries the API for their details. Add this function to *hotornot.py*:

```
def getpeopledata(ratings):
  result=[]
  for emid,rating in ratings:
    # URL for the MeetMe.getProfile method
    url="http://services.hotornot.com/rest/?app_key=%s" % api_key
    url+="&method=MeetMe.getProfile&emid=%s&get_keywords=true" % emid

    # Get all the info about this person
    try:
      rating=int(float(rating)+0.5)
      doc2=xml.dom.minidom.parseString(urllib2.urlopen(url).read())
      gender=doc2.getElementsByTagName('gender')[0].firstChild.data
      age=doc2.getElementsByTagName('age')[0].firstChild.data
      loc=doc2.getElementsByTagName('location')[0].firstChild.data[0:2]

      # Convert state to region
      for r,s in stateregions.items():
        if loc in s: region=r

      if region!=None:
        result.append((gender,int(age),region,rating))
    except:
      pass
  return result
```

You can now import this module into your Python session and generate a dataset:

```
>>> import hotornot
>>> l1=hotornot.getrandomratings(500)
>>> len(l1)
442
>>> pdata=hotornot.getpeopledata(l1)
>>> pdata[0]
(u'female', 28, 'West', 9)
```

The list contains information about each user with their rating as the last field. This data structure can be passed directly to the buildtree method to build a tree:

```
>>> hottree=treepredict.buildtree(pdata,scoref=treepredict.variance)
>>> treepredict.prune(hottree,0.5)
>>> treepredict.drawtree(hottree,'hottree.jpg')
```

A possible output for the final tree is shown in Figure 7-7.

The central node at the top that divides the dataset the best is gender. The remainder of the tree is actually quite complicated and difficult to read. However, you can certainly use it to make predictions about previously unseen people. Also, because the algorithms support missing data, you can aggregate people across large variables. For example, maybe you want to compare the hotness of everyone in the South against everyone in the Mid-Atlantic:

```
>>> south=treepredict2.mdclassify((None,None,'South'),hottree)
>>> midat=treepredict2.mdclassify((None,None,'Mid Atlantic'),hottree)
```

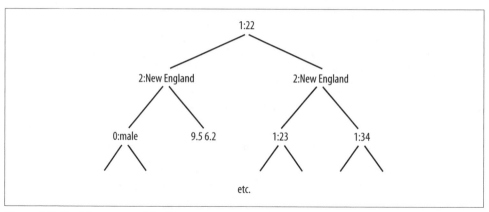

Figure 7-7. Decision tree model of hotness

```
>>> south[10]/sum(south.values())
0.055820815183261735
>>> midat[10]/sum(midat.values())
0.048972797320600864
```

For this dataset, there are slightly more super-hot people in the South. You can try other things like considering age groups, or testing whether men get better scores than women.

When to Use Decision Trees

Probably the biggest advantage of decision trees is how easy it is to interpret a trained model. After running the algorithm on our example problem, we not only end up with a tree that can make predictions about new users, we also get the list of questions used to make those determinations. From this you can see that, for instance, users who find the site through Slashdot never become paid subscribers, but users who find the site through Google and view at least 20 pages are likely to become premium subscribers. This, in turn, might allow you to alter your advertising strategy to target sites that give you the highest quality traffic. We also learn that certain variables, such as the user's country of origin, are not important in determining the outcome. If data is difficult or expensive to collect and we learn that it is not important, we know that we can stop collecting it.

Unlike some other machine-learning algorithms, decision trees can work with both categorical and numerical data as inputs. In the first example problem, we used a combination of pages viewed with several categorical inputs. Furthermore, while many algorithms require you to prepare or normalize data before you can run them, the code in this chapter will take any list of data containing category or numerical data and build the appropriate decision tree.

Decision trees also allow for probabilistic assignment of data. With some problems, there is not enough information to always make a correct distinction—a decision tree may have a node that has several possibilities and can't be divided any more. The code in this chapter returns a dictionary of the counts of different outcomes, and this information can help us decide how confident we are in the results. Not all algorithms can estimate the probability of an uncertain result.

However, there are definitely drawbacks to the decision tree algorithm used here. While it can be very effective for problems with only a few possible results, it can't be used effectively on datasets with many possibilities. In the first example, the only outcomes are none, basic, and premium. If there were hundreds of outcomes instead, the decision tree would grow very complicated and would probably make poor predictions.

The other big disadvantage of the decision trees described here is that while they can handle simple numerical data, they can only create greater-than/less-than decision points. This makes it difficult for decision trees to classify data where the class is determined by a more complex combination of the variables. For instance, if the results were determined by the differences of two variables, the tree would get very large and would quickly become inaccurate.

In sum, decision trees are probably not a good choice for problems with many numerical inputs and outputs, or with many complex relationships between numerical inputs, such as in interpreting financial data or image analysis. Decision trees are great for datasets with a lot of categorical data and numerical data that has breakpoints. These trees are the best choice if understanding the decision-making process is important; as you've observed, seeing the reasoning can be as important as knowing the final prediction.

Exercises

1. *Result probabilities.* Currently, the classify and mdclassify functions give their results as total counts. Modify them to give the probabilities of the results being one of the categories.

2. *Missing data ranges.* mdclassify allows the use of "None" to specify a missing value. For numerical values the result may not be completely unknown, but may be known to be in a range. Modify mdclassify to allow a tuple such as (20,25) in place of a value and traverse down both branches when necessary.

3. *Early stopping.* Rather than pruning the tree, buildtree can just stop dividing when it reaches a point where the entropy is not reduced enough. This may not be ideal in some cases, but it does save an extra step. Modify buildtree to take a minimum gain parameter and stop dividing the branch if this condition is not met.

4. *Building with missing data.* You built a function that can classify a row with missing data, but what if there is missing data in the training set? Modify `buildtree` so that it will check for missing data and, in cases where it's not possible to send a result down a particular branch, will send it down both branches.

5. *Multiway splits.* (Hard) All the trees built in this chapter are binary decision trees. However, some datasets might create simpler trees if they allowed a node to split into more than two branches. How would you represent this? How would you train the tree?

## CHAPTER 8

Building Price Models

So far we have examined several classifiers, most of which are well suited for predicting to which category a new piece of data belongs. However, Bayesian classifiers, decision trees, and support-vector machines (which you'll see in the next chapter) are not the best algorithms for making predictions about numerical data based on many different attributes, such as prices. This chapter will look at algorithms that can be trained to make numerical predictions based on examples they have seen before, and even display probability distributions for the predictions to help the user interpret how the prediction is being made.

We'll be looking at how to use these algorithms for building models that predict prices. Economists consider prices, particularly auction prices, to be a good method of using collective intelligence to determine the real value of something; in a large market with many buyers and sellers, the price will usually reach the optimal value for both sides of the transaction. Price prediction is also a good test for algorithms of this kind, since there are usually many different factors to consider when determining a price. When considering bidding on a laptop, for example, you have to take into account processor speed, installed RAM, hard drive size, screen resolution, and other factors.

An important part of making numerical predictions is determining which variables are important and in what combinations. In the laptop example, there are likely to be several variables that will barely, if at all, affect the price, such as free accessories or some bundled software. Further, the screen size may have a greater effect on the final price than the hard drive size. You'll be using the optimization techniques developed in Chapter 5 to automatically determine the best weights for the variables.

Building a Sample Dataset

A challenging dataset for testing a numerical prediction algorithm should have a few properties that make the dataset more difficult to make predictions from. If you are looking at TVs, it's easy to infer that bigger is better, and such problems can more easily be solved with traditional statistical techniques. For this reason, it's more interesting to look at a dataset where price doesn't simply increase in proportion to size or the number of characteristics.

In this section, you'll create a dataset of wine prices based on a simple artificial model. The prices are based on a combination of the rating and the age of the wine. The model assumes that wine has a peak age, which is older for good wines and almost immediate for bad wines. A high-rated wine will start at a high price and increase in value until its peak age, and a low-rated wine will start cheap and get cheaper.

To model this, create a new file called *numpredict.py* and add the wineprice function:

```
from random import random,randint
import math

def wineprice(rating,age):
  peak_age=rating-50

  # Calculate price based on rating
  price=rating/2
  if age>peak_age:
    # Past its peak, goes bad in 5 years
    price=price*(5-(age-peak_age))
  else:
    # Increases to 5x original value as it
    # approaches its peak
    price=price*(5*((age+1)/peak_age))
  if price<0: price=0
  return price
```

You'll also need a function to build a dataset of wine prices. The following function generates 200 bottles of wine and calculates their prices from the model. It then randomly adds or subtracts 20 percent to capture things like taxes and local variations in prices, and also to make the numerical prediction a bit more difficult. Add wineset1 to *numpredict.py*:

```
def wineset1():
  rows=[]
  for i in range(300):
    # Create a random age and rating
    rating=random()*50+50
    age=random()*50

    # Get reference price
    price=wineprice(rating,age)

    # Add some noise
    price*=(random()*0.4+0.8)

    # Add to the dataset
    rows.append({'input':(rating,age),
                 'result':price})
  return rows
```

Start up a Python session, and test some wine prices and build a new dataset:

```
$ python
>>> import numpredict
>>> numpredict.wineprice(95.0,3.0)
21.111111111111114
>>> numpredict.wineprice(95.0,8.0)
47.5
>>> numpredict.wineprice(99.0,1.0)
10.102040816326529
>>> data=numpredict.wineset1( )
>>> data[0]
{'input': (63.602840187200407, 21.574120872184949), 'result': 34.565257353086487}
>>> data[1]
{'input': (74.994980945756794, 48.052051269308649), 'result': 0.0}
```

In the dataset shown, the second bottle is too old and has expired, while the first has aged well. The interplay of variables makes this a good dataset on which to test algorithms.

k-Nearest Neighbors

The easiest approach to our wine pricing problem is the same one you would use if you were trying to price something manually—that is, to find a few of the most similar items and assume the prices will be roughly the same. By finding a set of items similar to the item that interests you, the algorithm can average their prices and make a guess at what the price should be for this item. This approach is called *k-nearest neighbors* (kNN).

Number of Neighbors

The k in kNN refers to the number of items that will be averaged to get the final result. If the data were perfect, you could use k=1, meaning you would just pick the nearest neighbor and use its price as the answer. But in real-world situations, there are always aberrations. In the example, you deliberately add "noise" to simulate this (the random addition or subtraction of 20 percent). Someone might get a great deal, or an uninformed customer might drastically overpay for the nearest neighbor. For this reason, it's better to take a few neighbors and average them to reduce any noise.

To visualize the problem of choosing too few neighbors, consider a problem where there's only one descriptive variable, say, age. Figure 8-1 shows a graph of price (on the y-axis) versus age (on the x-axis). Also on the graph is the line that you get if you only use a single nearest neighbor.

Notice how the predicted price is far too dependent on random variations. If you were using the squiggly line to make a prediction, you would decide that there's a big price jump between wine that is 15 years old and wine that is 16 years old, when that's really just the result of variation in the prices of two particular bottles.

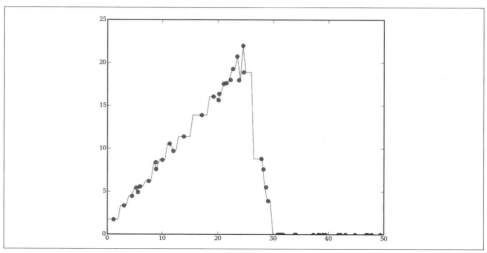

Figure 8-1. kNN using too few neighbors

On the other hand, choosing too many neighbors will reduce accuracy because the algorithm will be averaging in data from items that are not at all similar to the query. Figure 8-2 shows the same dataset; the line averages 20 of the nearest neighbors.

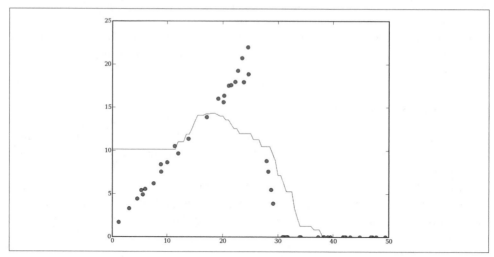

Figure 8-2. kNN using too many neighbors

It's clear that averaging too many prices greatly underestimates the prices of wine around the 25-year mark. Choosing the correct number of neighbors can be done manually for different datasets, or it can be done with optimization.

Defining Similarity

The first thing you'll need for the kNN algorithm is a way to measure how similar two items are. You've seen a few different metrics for measuring this throughout the book. For now, you'll be using Euclidean distance, a function that we covered in several earlier chapters. Add the euclidian function to *numpredict.py*:

```
def euclidean(v1,v2):
  d=0.0
  for i in range(len(v1)):
    d+=(v1[i]-v2[i])**2
  return math.sqrt(d)
```

In your Python session, try the function on some of the points in your dataset, along with a new data point:

```
>>> reload(numpredict)
<module 'numpredict' from 'numpredict.py'>
>>> data[0]['input']
(82.720398223643514, 49.21295829683897)
>>> data[1]['input']
(98.942698715228076, 25.702723509372749)
>>> numpredict.euclidean(data[0]['input'],data[1]['input'])
28.56386131112269
```

You'll notice that this function treats both age and rating the same when calculating distance, even though in almost any real problem, some of variables have a greater impact on the final price than others. This is a well-known weakness of kNN, and ways to correct for this problem will be shown later in this chapter.

Code for k-Nearest Neighbors

kNN is a relatively simple algorithm to implement. It is computationally intensive, but it does have the advantage of not requiring retraining every time new data is added. Add the getdistances function to *numpredict.py* to get the distances between a given item and every item in the original dataset:

```
def getdistances(data,vec1):
  distancelist=[]
  for i in range(len(data)):
    vec2=data[i]['input']
    distancelist.append((euclidean(vec1,vec2),i))
  distancelist.sort()
  return distancelist
```

This function calls the distance function on the vector given against every other vector in the dataset and puts them in a big list. The list is sorted so that the closest item is at the top.

The kNN function uses the list of distances and averages the top k results. Add knnestimate to *numpredict.py*:

```
def knnestimate(data,vec1,k=3):
  # Get sorted distances
  dlist=getdistances(data,vec1)
  avg=0.0

  # Take the average of the top k results
  for i in range(k):
    idx=dlist[i][1]
    avg+=data[idx]['result']
  avg=avg/k
  return avg
```

You can now get a price estimate for a new item:

```
>>> reload(numpredict)
>>> numpredict.knnestimate(data,(95.0,3.0))
29.176138546872018
>>> numpredict.knnestimate(data,(99.0,3.0))
22.356856188108672
>>> numpredict.knnestimate(data,(99.0,5.0))
37.610888778473793
>>> numpredict.wineprice(99.0,5.0)  # Get the actual price
30.306122448979593
>>> numpredict.knnestimate(data,(99.0,5.0),k=1) # Try with fewer neighbors
38.078819347238685
```

Try different parameters and different values for k to see how the results are affected.

Weighted Neighbors

One way to compensate for the fact that the algorithm may be using neighbors that are too far away is to weight them according to their distance. This is similar to the method used in Chapter 2, where people's preferences were weighted according to how similar they were to the preferences of a person seeking a recommendation.

The more similar the items are, the smaller the distance between them, so you'll need a way of converting distances to weights. There are a few different ways of doing this, each with advantages and drawbacks. This section will look at three functions that you can use.

Inverse Function

The function you used in Chapter 4 to convert distances to weights was an inverse function. Figure 8-3 shows what this looks like if you plot weight on one axis and price on the other.

The simplest form of this function returns 1 divided by the distance. However, in some cases, items are exactly the same or very close, leading to a very high or infinite weight. For this reason, it's necessary to add a small number to the distance before inverting it.

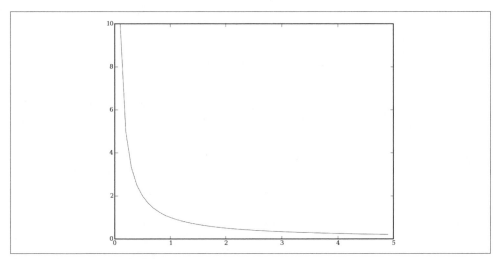

Figure 8-3. Inverse weight function

Add the inverseweight function to *numpredict.py*:

```
def inverseweight(dist,num=1.0,const=0.1):
  return num/(dist+const)
```

This function is fast and easy to implement, and you can experiment with different values of num to see what produces good results. Its main potential drawback is that it applies very heavy weights to items that are close and falls off quickly after that. This may be desirable, but in some cases it will make the algorithm much more sensitive to noise.

Subtraction Function

A second option is a *subtraction function*, the graph for which is shown in Figure 8-4.

This is a simple function that subtracts the distance from a constant. The weight is the result of this subtraction if the result is greater than zero; otherwise, the result is zero. Add the subtractweight function to *numpredict.py*:

```
def subtractweight(dist,const=1.0):
  if dist>const:
    return 0
  else:
    return const-dist
```

This function overcomes the potential issue of overweighting close items, but it has its own limitation. Because the weight eventually falls to 0, it's possible that there will be nothing close enough to be considered a close neighbor, which means that for some items the algorithm won't make a prediction at all.

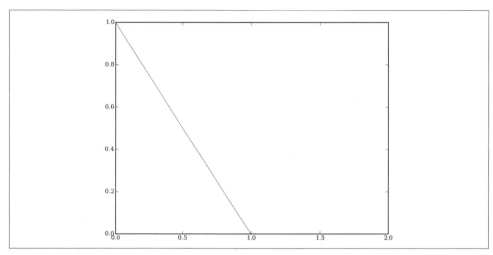

Figure 8-4. Subtraction weight function

Gaussian Function

The final function to consider is a *Gaussian function*, also known as a *bell curve*. It is a little more complex that the other functions considered here, but as you'll see, it overcomes some of their limitations. The Gaussian function is shown in Figure 8-5.

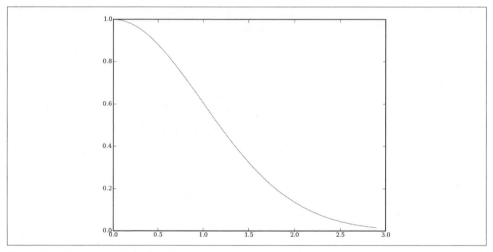

Figure 8-5. Gaussian weight function

The weight in this function is 1 when the distance is 0, and the weight declines as the distance increases. However, unlike the subtraction function, the weight never falls all the way to 0, so it will always be possible to make a prediction. The code for this function is more complex and will not evaluate as quickly as the other two functions.

Add gaussian to *numpredict.py*:

```
def gaussian(dist,sigma=10.0):
  return math.e**(-dist**2/(2*sigma**2))
```

You can now try the different functions on some of the items with varying parameters and see how they differ:

```
>>> reload(numpredict)
<module 'numpredict' from 'numpredict.py'>
>>> numpredict.subtractweight(0.1)
0.9
>>> numpredict.inverseweight(0.1)
5.0
>>> numpredict.gaussian(0.1)
0.99501247919268232
>>> numpredict.gaussian(1.0)
0.60653065971263342
>>> numpredict.subtractweight(1)
0.0
>>> numpredict.inverseweight(1)
0.90909090909090906
>>> numpredict.gaussian(3.0)
0.01110899653824231
```

You can see that all the functions have their highest values at 0.0 and decrease in different ways from there.

Weighted kNN

The code for doing weighted kNN works the same way as the regular kNN function, by first getting the sorted distances and taking the k closest elements. The important difference is that instead of just averaging them, the weighted kNN calculates a *weighted average*. The weighted average is calculated by multiplying each item's weight by its value before adding them together. After the sum is calculated, it is divided by the sum of all the weights.

Add weightedknn to *numpredict.py*:

```
def weightedknn(data,vec1,k=5,weightf=gaussian):
  # Get distances
  dlist=getdistances(data,vec1)
  avg=0.0
  totalweight=0.0

  # Get weighted average
  for i in range(k):
    dist=dlist[i][0]
    idx=dlist[i][1]
    weight=weightf(dist)
    avg+=weight*data[idx]['result']
    totalweight+=weight
  avg=avg/totalweight
  return avg
```

The function loops over the k nearest neighbors and passes each of their distances to one of the weight functions you defined earlier. The `avg` variable is calculated by multiplying these weights by the neighbor's value. The `totalweight` variable is the sum of the weights. At the end, `avg` is divided by `totalweight`.

You can try this function in your Python session and compare its performance to that of the regular kNN function:

```
>>> reload(numpredict)
<module 'numpredict' from 'numpredict.py'>
>>> numpredict.weightedknn(data,(99.0,5.0))
32.640981119354301
```

In this example, the results show that `weightedknn` gets closer to the correct answer than `knnestimate`. However, this is just for a couple of samples. A rigorous test would involve a lot of different items from the dataset, which you could actually use to decide the best algorithm and best parameters. Next you'll see ways to perform a test like this.

Cross-Validation

Cross-validation is the name given to a set of techniques that divide up data into *training sets* and *test sets*. The training set is given to the algorithm, along with the correct answers (in this case, prices), and becomes the set used to make predictions. The algorithm is then asked to make predictions for each item in the test set. The answers it gives are compared to the correct answers, and an overall score for how well the algorithm did is calculated.

Usually this procedure is performed several times, dividing the data up differently each time. Typically, the test set will be a small portion, perhaps 5 percent of the all the data, with the remaining 95 percent making up the training set. To start, create a function called `dividedata` in *numpredict.py*, which divides up the dataset into two smaller sets given a ratio that you specify:

```
def dividedata(data,test=0.05):
  trainset=[]
  testset=[]
  for row in data:
    if random()<test:
      testset.append(row)
    else:
      trainset.append(row)
  return trainset,testset
```

The next step is to test the algorithm by giving it a training set and calling it with each item in the test set. The function calculates the differences and combines them to create an aggregate score for how far off it was in general. This is usually done by adding up the squares of all the differences.

Add a new function, testalgorithm, to *numpredict.py*:

```
def testalgorithm(algf,trainset,testset):
  error=0.0
  for row in testset:
    guess=algf(trainset,row['input'])
    error+=(row['result']-guess)**2
  return error/len(testset)
```

testalgorithm takes an algorithm, algf, which accepts a dataset and query. It loops over every row in the test set and then calculates the best guess by applying algf. It then subtracts the guess from the real result.

Squaring the numbers is common practice because it makes large differences count for even more. This means an algorithm that is very close most of the time but far off occasionally will fare worse than an algorithm that is always somewhat close. This is often desired behavior, but there are situations in which making a big mistake is occasionally acceptable if accuracy is very high the rest of the time. When this is the case, you can modify the function to just add up the absolute values of the differences.

The final step is to create a function that makes several different divisions of data and runs testalgorithm on each, adding up all the results to get a final score. Add crossvalidate to *numpredict.py*:

```
def crossvalidate(algf,data,trials=100,test=0.05):
  error=0.0
  for i in range(trials):
    trainset,testset=dividedata(data,test)
    error+=testalgorithm(algf,trainset,testset)
  return error/trials
```

The code that you've built so far has many possible variations to compare. You can try, for example, testing knnestimate with different values of k.

```
>>> reload(numpredict)
<module 'numpredict' from 'numpredict.py'>
>>> numpredict.crossvalidate(numpredict.knnestimate,data)
254.06864176819553
>>> def knn3(d,v): return numpredict.knnestimate(d,v,k=3)
...
>>> numpredict.crossvalidate(knn3,data)
166.97339783733005
>>> def knn1(d,v): return numpredict.knnestimate(d,v,k=1)
...
>>> numpredict.crossvalidate(knn1,data)
209.54500183486215
```

As expected, using too few neighbors or too many neighbors leads to poor results. In this example, a value of 3 performs better than a value of 1 or 5. You can also try the different weighting functions that you defined for weighted kNN to see which one gives the best results:

```
>>> numpredict.crossvalidate(numpredict.weightedknn,data)
200.34187674254176
>>> def knninverse(d,v):
...    return numpredict.weightedknn(d,v,\\
       weightf=numpredict.inverseweight)
>>> numpredict.crossvalidate(knninverse,data)
148.85947702660616
```

When the parameters are set properly, weighted kNN seems to give better results for this dataset. Choosing the correct parameters may be time consuming, but you only have to do it once for a particular training set, possibly updating them occasionally as the training set grows. In the "Optimizing the Scale" section later in the chapter, you'll be looking at ways to determine some of the parameters automatically.

Heterogeneous Variables

The dataset you built at the start of this chapter was designed to be artificially simple—specifically, all the variables used to predict the price are roughly comparable and are all important to the final result.

Since all the variables fall within the same range, it's meaningful to calculate distances using all of them at once. Imagine, however, if you introduced a new variable that influenced the price, such as the size of the bottle in milliliters. Unlike the variables you've used so far, which were between 0 and 100, its range would be up to 1,500. Look at Figure 8-6 to see how this would affect the nearest neighbor or distance-weighting calculations.

Clearly, this new variable has a far greater impact on the calculated distances than the original ones do—it will overwhelm any distance calculation, which essentially means that the other variables are not taken into account.

A different problem is the introduction of entirely irrelevant variables. If the dataset also included the number of the aisle in which you found the wine, this variable would be included in the distance calculations. Two items identical in every respect but with very different aisles would be considered very far apart, which would badly hinder the ability of the algorithms to make accurate predictions.

Adding to the Dataset

In order to simulate these effects, you're going to add some new variables to your dataset. You can copy the code in wineset1 to create a new function called wineset2 and modify it by adding the parts shown in bold:

```
def wineset2():
  rows=[]
  for i in range(300):
    rating=random()*50+50
    age=random()*50
```

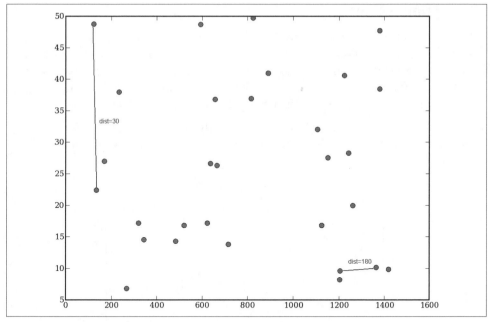

Figure 8-6. Heterogeneous variables cause distance problems

```
aisle=float(randint(1,20))
bottlesize=[375.0,750.0,1500.0,3000.0][randint(0,3)]
price=wineprice(rating,age)
price*=(bottlesize/750)
price*=(random( )*0.9+0.2)
rows.append({'input':(rating,age,aisle,bottlesize),
             'result':price})
return rows
```

Now you can create new datasets with aisles and bottle sizes:

```
>>> reload(numpredict)
<module 'numpredict' from 'numpredict.py'>
>>> data=numpredict.wineset2( )
```

To see how this affects the kNN predictors, try them out on the new datasets with the best parameters you managed to find earlier:

```
>>> numpredict.crossvalidate(knn3,data)
1427.3377833596137
>>> numpredict.crossvalidate(numpredict.weightedknn,data)
1195.0421231227463
```

You'll notice that even though the dataset now contains even more information and less noise than it did before (which should theoretically lead to better predictions), the values returned by crossvalidate have actually gotten a lot worse. This is because the algorithms do not yet know how to treat the variables differently.

Scaling Dimensions

What we need here is not a way to base distance on the actual values, but a way to normalize the values so that it makes sense to consider them all in the same space. It would also be helpful to find a way to eliminate the superfluous variables or to at least reduce their impact on the calculations. One way to accomplish both things is to rescale the dimensions before performing any of the calculations.

The simplest form of rescaling is multiplying the values in each dimension by a constant for that dimension. An example of rescaling is shown in Figure 8-7.

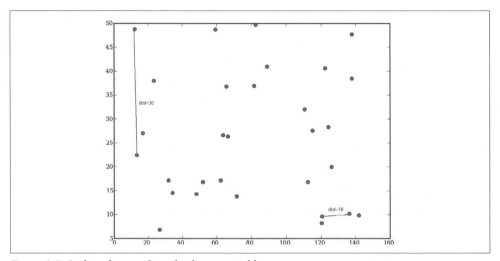

Figure 8-7. Scaling the axes fixes the distance problem

You can see that the bottle-size axis has been scaled down by a factor of 10, and consequently the nearest neighbors for several of the items have changed. This solves the problem of some variables being naturally much larger than others, but what about unimportant variables? Consider what happens if every item's value in a dimension is multiplied by 0, as shown in Figure 8-8.

Notice how everything is now in the same place in the aisle dimension, so the distances between the items are entirely dependent on their placement in the age dimension. That is, aisle has become totally meaningless in the calculation of the nearest neighbors, and has been entirely eliminated from consideration. If all the unimportant variables are collapsed to 0, the algorithms will be far more accurate.

The rescale function takes a list of items and a parameter called scale, which is a list of real numbers. It returns a new dataset with all the values multiplied by the values in scale. Add rescale to *numpredict.py*:

```
def rescale(data,scale):
  scaleddata=[]
  for row in data:
```

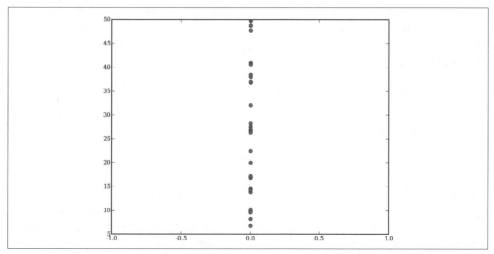

Figure 8-8. Unimportant axes are scaled to 0

```
        scaled=[scale[i]*row['input'][i] for i in range(len(scale))]
        scaleddata.append({'input':scaled,'result':row['result']})
    return scaleddata
```

You can try this out by rescaling a dataset by some cleverly chosen parameters and see if this makes for good predictions:

```
>>> reload(numpredict)
<module 'numpredict' from 'numpredict.py'>
>>> sdata=numpredict.rescale(data,[10,10,0,0.5])
>>> numpredict.crossvalidate(knn3,sdata)
660.9964024835578
>>> numpredict.crossvalidate(numpredict.weightedknn,sdata)
852.32254222973802
```

The results are pretty good for those few examples; certainly better than before. Try changing the scale parameter and see if you can improve the results even more.

Optimizing the Scale

In this case, it's not difficult to choose good parameters for scaling because you know in advance which variables are important. However, most of the time you'll be working with datasets that you didn't build yourself, and you won't necessarily know which variables are unimportant and which ones have a significant impact.

In theory, you could try out a lot of numbers in different combinations until you found one that worked well enough, but there might be hundreds of variables to consider and it would be very tedious. Fortunately, if you worked through Chapter 5, you already know how to automatically find a good solution when there are many input variables to consider—by using *optimization*.

You'll recall that optimization simply requires you to specify a domain that gives the number of variables, a range, and a cost function. The crossvalidate function returns a higher value for a worse solution, so it's already essentially a cost function. The only thing you need to do is wrap it so that it takes a list of values as its parameter, rescales the data, and calculates the cross-validation error. Add createcostfunction to *numpredict.py*:

```
def createcostfunction(algf,data):
  def costf(scale):
    sdata=rescale(data,scale)
    return crossvalidate(algf,sdata,trials=10)
  return costf
```

The domain is the range of weights for each dimension. In this case, the lowest possible value is 0 because negative numbers will just create a mirror image of the data, which for distance calculations doesn't change anything. In theory, the weights can be as high as you want, but for practical purposes, let's restrict them to 20 for now. Add this line to *numpredict.py*:

```
weightdomain=[(0,20)]*4
```

You now have everything you need to automatically optimize the weights. Make sure *optimization.py*, the file you created in Chapter 5, is in your current directory and try an annealing optimization in your Python session:

```
>>> import optimization
>>> reload(numpredict)
<module 'numpredict' from 'numpredict.pyc'>
>>> costf=numpredict.createcostfunction(numpredict.knnestimate,data)
>>> optimization.annealingoptimize(numpredict.weightdomain,costf,step=2)
[11,18,0,6]
```

Perfect! The algorithm not only determines that aisle is a useless variable and reduces its scale almost to 0, but it also figures out that bottle size is disproportionately large compared to its impact, and increases the scales of the other two variables accordingly.

You can also try the slower but often more accurate geneticoptimize function and see if it returns similar results:

```
>>> optimization.geneticoptimize(numpredict.weightdomain,costf,popsize=5,\\
    lrate=1,maxv=4,iters=20)
[20,18,0,12]
```

An advantage of optimizing the variable scales in this way is that you immediately see which variables are important and how important they are. In some cases, some of the data may be difficult or expensive to collect, and if you determine that it's not very valuable, you can avoid the extra cost. In other cases, just knowing which variables are important—particularly in determining price—may affect what you choose to emphasize as part of a marketing effort, or may reveal how products can be designed differently to fetch the highest prices.

Uneven Distributions

So far we've been assuming that if you take an average or weighted average of the data, you'll get a pretty good estimate of the final price. In many cases this will be accurate, but in some situations there may be an unmeasured variable that can have a big effect on the outcome. Imagine that in the wine example there were buyers from two separate groups: people who bought from the liquor store, and people who bought from a discount store and received a 50 percent discount. Unfortunately, this information isn't tracked in the dataset.

The createhiddendataset function creates a dataset that simulates these properties. It drops some of the complicating variables and just focuses on the original ones. Add this function to *numericalpredictor.py*:

```
def wineset3():
  rows=wineset1()
  for row in rows:
    if random()<0.5:
      # Wine was bought at a discount store
      row['result']*=0.6
  return rows
```

Consider what will happen if you ask for an estimate of the price of a different item using the kNN or weighted kNN algorithms. Since the dataset doesn't actually contain any information about whether the buyer bought from the liquor store or a discount store, the algorithm won't be able to take this into account, so it will bring in the nearest neighbors regardless of where the purchase was made. The result is that it will give the average of items from both groups, perhaps representing a 25 percent discount. You can verify this by trying it in your Python session:

```
>>> reload(numpredict)
<module 'numpredict' from 'numpredict.py'>
>>> data=numpredict.wineset3()
>>> numpredict.wineprice(99.0,20.0)
106.07142857142857
>>> numpredict.weightedknn(data,[99.0,20.0])
83.475441632209339
>>> numpredict.crossvalidate(numpredict.weightedknn,data)
599.51654107008562
```

While this is not a bad way to make an estimate if you just want a single number, it does not accurately reflect what someone will actually end up paying for an item. In order to get beyond averages, you need a way to look closer at the data at that point.

Estimating the Probability Density

Rather than taking the weighted average of the neighbors and getting a single price estimate, it might be interesting in this case to know the probability that an item falls within a certain price range. In the example, given inputs of 99 percent and 20 years, you'd like a function that tells you there's a 50 percent chance that the price is between $40 and $80, and a 50 percent chance that it's between $80 and $100.

To do this, you need a function that returns a value between 0 and 1 representing the probability. The function first calculates the weights of the neighbors within that range, and then calculates the weights of all the neighbors. The probability is the sum of the neighbor weights within the range divided by the sum of all the weights. Create a new function called probguess in *numpredict.py* to perform this calculation:

```python
def probguess(data,vec1,low,high,k=5,weightf=gaussian):
  dlist=getdistances(data,vec1)
  nweight=0.0
  tweight=0.0

  for i in range(k):
    dist=dlist[i][0]
    idx=dlist[i][1]
    weight=weightf(dist)
    v=data[idx]['result']

    # Is this point in the range?
    if v>=low and v<=high:
      nweight+=weight
    tweight+=weight
  if tweight==0: return 0

  # The probability is the weights in the range
  # divided by all the weights
  return nweight/tweight
```

Like kNN, this function sorts the data by the distance from vec1 and determines the weights of the nearest neighbors. It adds the weights of all the neighbors together to get tweight. It also considers whether each neighbor's price is within the range (between low and high); if so, it adds the weight to nweight. The probability that the price for vec1 is between low and high is nweight divided by tweight.

Now try this function on your dataset:

```python
>>> reload(numpredict)
<module 'numpredict' from 'numpredict.py'>
>>> numpredict.probguess(data,[99,20],40,80)
0.62305988451497296
>>> numpredict.probguess(data,[99,20],80,120)
0.37694011548502687
>>> numpredict.probguess(data,[99,20],120,1000)
0.0
>>> numpredict.probguess(data,[99,20],30,120)
1.0
```

The function gives good results. The ranges that are well outside the actual prices have probabilities of 0, and the ones that capture the full range of possibilities are close to 1. By breaking it down into smaller buckets, you can determine the actual ranges in which things tend to cluster. However, this requires that you guess at the ranges and enter them until you have a clear picture of the structure of the data. In the next section, you'll see ways to get an overall picture of the probability distribution.

Graphing the Probabilities

To avoid having to guess which ranges to try, you can create a graphical representation of the probability density. An excellent free library for making mathematical graphs in Python is *matplotlib*, which you can download from *http://matplotlib. sourceforge.net*.

Installation instructions are on the web site, and there is more information on matplotlib in Appendix A. This library is very powerful and has a huge number of features, only a few of which you'll be using in this chapter. After you install it, you can try creating a simple graph in your Python session:

```
>>> from pylab import *
>>> a=array([1,2,3,4])
>>> b=array([4,2,3,1])
>>> plot(a,b)
>>> show( )
>>> t1=arange(0.0,10.0,0.1)
>>> plot(t1,sin(t1))
[<matplotlib.lines.Line2D instance at 0x00ED9300>]
>>> show( )
```

This should give you a simple graph like the one shown in Figure 8-9. The arange function creates a list of numbers as an array in much the same way as the range function. In this case, you are plotting a sine curve from 0 to 10.

This section will show two different ways at looking at a probability distribution. The first is called the *cumulative probability*. A graph of cumulative probability shows the probability that the result is less than a given value. With prices, the graph starts with 0 probability that the price is less than 0, and increases as it hits groups of items at a certain price. At the maximum price, the graph reaches 1 because there's a 100 percent chance that the actual price is less than or equal to the maximum possible price.

Creating the data for the cumulative probability graph is simply a matter of looping over a range of prices that call the probabilityguess function with 0 as the lower bound and a specified price as the upper bound. The results of these calls can be passed to the plot function to create a graph. Add cumulativegraph to *numpredict.py*:

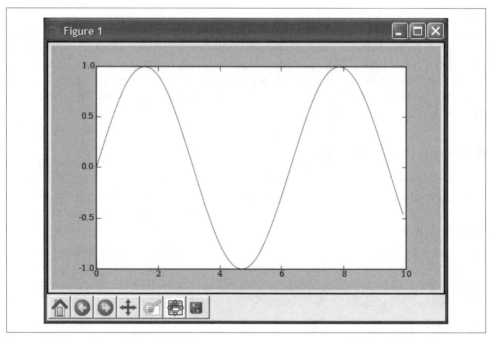

Figure 8-9. Sample use of matplotlib

```
def cumulativegraph(data,vec1,high,k=5,weightf=gaussian):
  t1=arange(0.0,high,0.1)
  cprob=array([probguess(data,vec1,0,v,k,weightf) for v in t1])
  plot(t1,cprob)
  show( )
```

You can now call this from your Python session to create the graph:

```
>>> reload(numpredict)
<module 'numpredict' from 'numpredict.py'>
>>> numpredict.cumulativegraph(data,(1,1),6)
```

The graph will look something like Figure 8-10. As expected, the cumulative probability starts at 0 and increases all the way to 1. What's interesting about the graph is the way it increases. The probability value stays at 0 until around $50 and then climbs fairly quickly, settling at 0.6 until the price hits $110, where it jumps again.

It's clear from reading the graph that the probabilities are grouped around $60 and $110, since that's where the cumulative probability jumps. Knowing this in advance allows you to do the probability calculation without having to guess.

The other option is to try to graph the actual probabilities for different price points. This is trickier because the probability that any item will be an exact price is very low. Graphing this would show 0 almost everywhere with spikes at the predicted prices. Instead, you'll need a way to combine probabilities over certain windows.

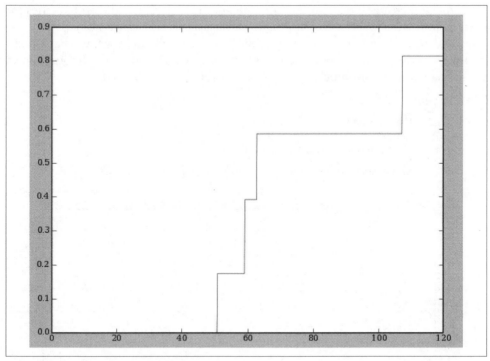

Figure 8-10. A cumulative probability graph

One way to do this is to assume the probability at each point is a weighted average of the surrounding probabilities, much the same as the weighted kNN algorithm.

To see this in action, add probabilitygraph to *numpredict.py*:

```
def probabilitygraph(data,vec1,high,k=5,weightf=gaussian,ss=5.0):
  # Make a range for the prices
  t1=arange(0.0,high,0.1)

  # Get the probabilities for the entire range
  probs=[probguess(data,vec1,v,v+0.1,k,weightf) for v in t1]

  # Smooth them by adding the gaussian of the nearby probabilites
  smoothed=[]
  for i in range(len(probs)):
    sv=0.0
    for j in range(0,len(probs)):
      dist=abs(i-j)*0.1
      weight=gaussian(dist,sigma=ss)
      sv+=weight*probs[j]
    smoothed.append(sv)
  smoothed=array(smoothed)

  plot(t1,smoothed)
  show( )
```

This function creates a range from 0 to high and then calculates the probabilities for every point. Because this would normally be very jagged, the function loops over the array and creates a smoothed array by adding close probabilities together. Each point on the smoothed probability is the Gaussian-weighted sum of its neighbors. The `ss` parameter specifies how much the probabilities should be smoothed.

Try it in your Python session:

```
>>> reload(numpredict)
<module 'numpredict' from 'numpredict.py'>
>>> numpredict.probabilitygraph(data,(1,1),6)
```

You should get a graph similar to the one shown in Figure 8-11.

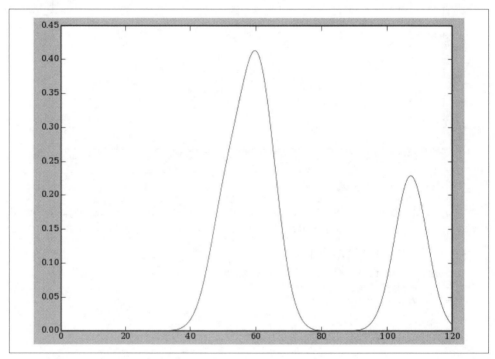

Figure 8-11. A probability density graph

This graph makes it even easier to see where the results are grouped together. Try varying the window `ss` and see how the results change. This probability distribution makes it clear that in guessing prices for a bottle of wine, you are missing a key piece of data about how some people get better deals than others. In some cases, you'll be able to figure out what this data is, but in others, you'll simply see that you need to shop around for items in the lower price range.

Using Real Data—the eBay API

eBay is an online auction site and one of the most popular sites on the Internet. It has millions of listings and millions of users bidding and jointly setting prices, making it a great example of collective intelligence. As it happens, eBay also has a free XML-based API that you can use to perform searches, get detailed item information, and even post items for sale. In this section, you'll see how to use the eBay API to get price data and convert the data so that the algorithms in this chapter can be used for prediction.

Getting a Developer Key

The process of accessing eBay's API takes several steps, but it's relatively simple and automatic. A good overview of the process is in the Quick Start Guide, which is online at *http://developer.ebay.com/quickstartguide*.

This guide will take you through the process of creating a developer account, getting your production keys, and creating a token. When you're finished, you should have four strings that will be needed for the example in this chapter:

- A developer key
- An application key
- A certificate key
- An authentication token, which is very long

Create a new file called *ebaypredict.py* and add the following code, which imports some modules and includes the abovementioned strings:

```
import httplib
from xml.dom.minidom import parse, parseString, Node

devKey = 'developerkey'
appKey = 'applicationkey'
certKey = 'certificatekey'
userToken = 'token'
serverUrl = 'api.ebay.com'
```

There is no official Python API for eBay, but there is an XML API that you can access using *httplib* and *minidom*. This section will only cover two calls to this API, GetSearchResults and GetItem, but much of the code given here can be reused for other calls, too. For more information on all the calls supported by the API, you can look at the full documentation at *http://developer.ebay.com/DevZone/XML/docs/WebHelp/index.htm*.

Setting Up a Connection

Once you have your keys, it's time to set up a connection to the eBay API. The API requires that you pass a lot of headers, which include the keys and the call you're going to make. To do this, create a function called getHeaders to take the call name and return a dictionary of headers that can be passed to httplib. Add this function to *ebaypredict.py*:

```
def getHeaders(apicall,siteID="0",compatabilityLevel = "433"):
  headers = {"X-EBAY-API-COMPATIBILITY-LEVEL": compatabilityLevel,
             "X-EBAY-API-DEV-NAME": devKey,
             "X-EBAY-API-APP-NAME": appKey,
             "X-EBAY-API-CERT-NAME": certKey,
             "X-EBAY-API-CALL-NAME": apicall,
             "X-EBAY-API-SITEID": siteID,
             "Content-Type": "text/xml"}
  return headers
```

In addition to the headers, the eBay API requires you to send XML with parameters for your request. It returns an XML document that can be parsed with the *parseString* from the minidom library.

The function to send the request opens a connection to the server, posts the parameters' XML, and parses the result. Add sendrequest to *ebaypredict.py*:

```
def sendRequest(apicall,xmlparameters):
  connection = httplib.HTTPSConnection(serverUrl)
  connection.request("POST", '/ws/api.dll', xmlparameters, getHeaders(apicall))
  response = connection.getresponse( )
  if response.status != 200:
    print "Error sending request:" + response.reason
  else:
    data = response.read( )
    connection.close( )
  return data
```

These functions can be used to make any call to the eBay API. For the different API calls, you'll need to generate the request XML and a way to interpret the parsed results.

Because DOM parsing can be tedious, you should also create a simple convenience method, getSingleValue, which finds a node and returns its contents:

```
def getSingleValue(node,tag):
  nl=node.getElementsByTagName(tag)
  if len(nl)>0:
    tagNode=nl[0]
    if tagNode.hasChildNodes( ):
      return tagNode.firstChild.nodeValue
  return '-1'
```

Performing a Search

Performing a search is just a matter of creating the XML parameters for the GetSearchResults API call and passing them to the sendrequest function that you defined previously. The XML parameters are in the form:

```
<GetSearchResultsRequest xmlns="urn:ebay:apis:eBLBaseComponents">
<RequesterCredentials><eBayAuthToken>token</eBayAuthToken></RequesterCredentials>
<parameter1>value</parameter1>
<parameter2>value</parameter2>
</GetSearchResultsRequest>
```

Dozens of parameters can be passed to this API call, but for this example we'll just consider two of them:

Query

A string containing the search terms. Using this parameter is exactly like typing in a search from the eBay home page.

CategoryID

A numerical value specifying the category you wish to search. eBay has a large hierarchy of categories, which you can request with the GetCategories API call. This can be used alone or in combination with Query.

The doSearch function takes these two parameters and performs a search. It then returns a list of the item IDs (which you'll use later with the GetItem call), along with their descriptions and current prices. Add doSearch to *ebaypredict.py*:

```python
def doSearch(query,categoryID=None,page=1):
  xml = "<?xml version='1.0' encoding='utf-8'?>"+\
        "<GetSearchResultsRequest xmlns=\"urn:ebay:apis:eBLBaseComponents\">"+\
        "<RequesterCredentials><eBayAuthToken>" +\
        userToken +\
        "</eBayAuthToken></RequesterCredentials>" + \
        "<Pagination>"+\
          "<EntriesPerPage>200</EntriesPerPage>"+\
          "<PageNumber>"+str(page)+"</PageNumber>"+\
        "</Pagination>"+\
        "<Query>" + query + "</Query>"
  if categoryID!=None:
    xml+="<CategoryID>"+str(categoryID)+"</CategoryID>"
  xml+="</GetSearchResultsRequest>"

  data=sendRequest('GetSearchResults',xml)
  response = parseString(data)
  itemNodes = response.getElementsByTagName('Item');
  results = []
  for item in itemNodes:
    itemId=getSingleValue(item,'ItemID')
    itemTitle=getSingleValue(item,'Title')
    itemPrice=getSingleValue(item,'CurrentPrice')
    itemEnds=getSingleValue(item,'EndTime')
    results.append((itemId,itemTitle,itemPrice,itemEnds))
  return results
```

In order to use the category parameter, you'll also need a function to retrieve the category hierarchy. This is another straightforward API call, but the XML file for all the category data is very large, takes a long time to download, and is very difficult to parse. For this reason, you'll want to limit the category data to the general area in which you're interested.

The getCategory function takes a string and a parent ID and returns all the categories containing that string within that top-level category. If the parent ID is missing, the function simply displays a list of all the top-level categories. Add this function to *ebaypredict.py*:

```
def getCategory(query='',parentID=None,siteID='0'):
  lquery=query.lower()
  xml = "<?xml version='1.0' encoding='utf-8'?>"+\
        "<GetCategoriesRequest xmlns=\"urn:ebay:apis:eBLBaseComponents\">"+\
        "<RequesterCredentials><eBayAuthToken>" +\
        userToken +\
        "</eBayAuthToken></RequesterCredentials>"+\
        "<DetailLevel>ReturnAll</DetailLevel>"+\
        "<ViewAllNodes>true</ViewAllNodes>"+\
        "<CategorySiteID>"+siteID+"</CategorySiteID>"
  if parentID==None:
    xml+="<LevelLimit>1</LevelLimit>"
  else:
    xml+="<CategoryParent>"+str(parentID)+"</CategoryParent>"
  xml += "</GetCategoriesRequest>"
  data=sendRequest('GetCategories',xml)
  categoryList=parseString(data)
  catNodes=categoryList.getElementsByTagName('Category')
  for node in catNodes:
    catid=getSingleValue(node,'CategoryID')
    name=getSingleValue(node,'CategoryName')
    if name.lower().find(lquery)!=-1:
      print catid,name
```

You can now try this function in your Python session:

```
>>> import ebaypredict
>>> laptops=ebaypredict.doSearch('laptop')
>>> laptops[0:10]
[(u'110075464522', u'Apple iBook G3 12" 500MHZ Laptop , 30 GB HD ', u'299.99',
u'2007-01-11T03:16:14.000Z'),
 (u'150078866214', u'512MB PC2700 DDR Memory 333MHz 200-Pin Laptop SODIMM', u'49.99',
u'2007-01-11T03:16:27.000Z'),
 (u'120067807006', u'LAPTOP USB / PS2 OPTICAL MOUSE 800 DPI SHIP FROM USA', u
'4.99', u'2007-01-11T03:17:00.000Z'),
 ...
```

Oops, it looks like the search for "laptop" returns all sorts of vaguely laptop-related accessories. Fortunately, you can search for the "Laptops, Notebooks" category and limit your search to results that are really laptops. You'll need to get the top-level list first, and then search within "Computers and Networking" to find the category ID for laptops, then you can search for "laptop" within the correct category:

```
>>> ebaypredict.getCategory('computers')
58058 Computers & Networking
>>> ebaypredict.getCategory('laptops',parentID=58058)
25447 Apple Laptops, Notebooks
...
31533 Drives for Laptops
51148 Laptops, Notebooks...
>>> laptops=ebaypredict.doSearch('laptop',categoryID=51148)
>>> laptops[0:10]
[(u'150078867562', u'PANASONIC TOUGHBOOK Back-Lit KeyBoard 4 CF-27 CF-28',
  u'49.95', u'2007-01-11T03:19:49.000Z'),
 (u'270075898309', u'mini small PANASONIC CFM33 CF M33 THOUGHBOOK ! libretto',
  u'171.0', u'2007-01-11T03:19:59.000Z'),
 (u'170067141814', u'Sony VAIO "PCG-GT1" Picturebook Tablet Laptop MINT   ',
  u'760.0', u'2007-01-11T03:20:06.000Z'),...
```

As of this writing, the ID for the "Laptops, Notebooks" category is 51148. You can see that limiting the search to the "iPod" category eliminates many of the unrelated results that are returned by using just the query "iPod." Having more consistency makes this a much better dataset to use for a price model.

Getting Details for an Item

The listings in the search results give the title and price, and it may be possible to extract details such as capacity or color from the text of the title. eBay also provides attributes specific to different item types. A laptop is listed with attributes like processor type and installed RAM, while an iPod has attributes like capacity. In addition to these details, it's also possible to get details such as the seller's rating, the number of bids, and the starting price.

To get these details, you need to make an eBay API call to GetItem, passing the item's ID as returned by the search function. To do this, create a function called getItem in *ebaypredict.py*:

```python
def getItem(itemID):
  xml = "<?xml version='1.0' encoding='utf-8'?>"+\
        "<GetItemRequest xmlns=\"urn:ebay:apis:eBLBaseComponents\">"+\
        "<RequesterCredentials><eBayAuthToken>" +\
        userToken +\
        "</eBayAuthToken></RequesterCredentials>" + \
        "<ItemID>" + str(itemID) + "</ItemID>"+\
        "<DetailLevel>ItemReturnAttributes</DetailLevel>"+\
        "</GetItemRequest>"
  data=sendRequest('GetItem',xml)
  result={}
  response=parseString(data)
  result['title']=getSingleValue(response,'Title')
  sellingStatusNode = response.getElementsByTagName('SellingStatus')[0];
  result['price']=getSingleValue(sellingStatusNode,'CurrentPrice')
  result['bids']=getSingleValue(sellingStatusNode,'BidCount')
  seller = response.getElementsByTagName('Seller')
  result['feedback'] = getSingleValue(seller[0],'FeedbackScore')
```

```
attributeSet=response.getElementsByTagName('Attribute');
attributes={}
for att in attributeSet:
  attID=att.attributes.getNamedItem('attributeID').nodeValue
  attValue=getSingleValue(att,'ValueLiteral')
  attributes[attID]=attValue
result['attributes']=attributes
return result
```

This function retrieves the item's XML using sendrequest and then parses out the interesting data. Since attributes are different for each item, they are all returned in a dictionary. Try this function on one of the results you get from your search:

```
>>> reload(ebaypredict)
>>> ebaypredict.getItem(laptops[7][0])
{'attributes': {u'13': u'Windows XP', u'12': u'512', u'14': u'Compaq',
                u'3805': u'Exchange', u'3804': u'14 Days',
                u'41': u'-', u'26445': u'DVD+/-RW', u'25710': u'80.0',
                u'26443': u'AMD Turion 64', u'26444': u'1800', u'26446': u'15',
                u'10244': u'-'},
 'price': u'515.0', 'bids': u'28', 'feedback': u'2797',
 'title': u'COMPAQ V5210US 15.4" AMD Turion 64 80GB Laptop Notebook'}
```

From these results, it looks like attribute 26444 represents processor speed, 26446 represents screen size, 12 represents installed RAM, and 25710 represents hard-drive size. Along with the seller rating, the number of bids, and the starting price, this makes a potentially interesting dataset for doing price predictions.

Building a Price Predictor

To use the predictor you built in this chapter, you'll need to take a set of items from eBay and turn them into lists of numbers that can be used as a dataset to be passed to the cross-validate function. To do this, the makeLaptopDataset function first calls doSearch to get a list of laptops, and then requests each one individually. Using the attributes determined in the previous section, the function creates a list of numbers that can be used for prediction, and puts data in the structure appropriate for the kNN functions.

Add makeLaptopDataset to *ebaypredict.py*:

```
def makeLaptopDataset():
  searchResults=doSearch('laptop',categoryID=51148)
  result=[]
  for r in searchResults:
    item=getItem(r[0])
    att=item['attributes']
    try:
      data=(float(att['12']),float(att['26444']),
            float(att['26446']),float(att['25710']),
            float(item['feedback'])
            )
      entry={'input':data,'result':float(item['price'])}
```

```
        result.append(entry)
    except:
      print item['title']+' failed'
  return result
```

The function ignores any items that do not have the necessary attributes. Downloading and processing all the results will take a little while, but you'll have an interesting dataset of real prices and attributes to play with. To get the data, call the function from your Python session:

```
>>> reload(ebaypredict)
<module 'ebaypredict' from 'ebaypredict.py'>
>>> set1=ebaypredict.makeLaptopDataset()
...
```

You can now try some kNN estimates for various configurations:

```
>>> numpredict.knnestimate(set1,(512,1000,14,40,1000))
667.89999999999998
>>> numpredict.knnestimate(set1,(1024,1000,14,40,1000))
858.42599999999982
>>> numpredict.knnestimate(set1,(1024,1000,14,60,0))
482.02600000000001
>>> numpredict.knnestimate(set1,(1024,2000,14,60,1000))
1066.8
```

These show some of the impact from differing amounts of RAM, processor speed, and feedback score. Now you can try experimenting with different variables, scaling the data, and plotting the probability distributions.

When to Use k-Nearest Neighbors

The k-nearest neighbors method has a few disadvantages. Making predictions is very computationally intensive because the distance to every point has to be calculated. Furthermore, in a dataset with many variables, it can be difficult to determine the appropriate weights or whether some variables should be eliminated. Optimization can help with this, but it can take a very long time to find a good solution with big datasets.

Still, as you've seen in this chapter, kNN offers a number of advantages over other methods. The flip side to the computational intensity of making a prediction is that new observations can be added to the data without any computational effort. It's also easy to interpret exactly what's happening because you know it's using the weighted value of other observation to make its predictions.

Although determining weights can be tricky, once the best weights have been determined, you can use them to better understand the characteristics of the dataset. Finally, you can create probability functions for times when you suspect there are other unmeasured variables in the dataset.

Exercises

1. *Optimizing the number of neighbors*. Create a cost function for optimization that determines the ideal number of neighbors for a simple dataset.

2. *Leave-one-out cross-validation*. Leave-one-out cross-validation is an alternative method of calculating prediction error that treats every row in the dataset individually as a test set, and treats the rest of the data as a training set. Implement a function to do this. How does it compare to the method described in this chapter?

3. *Eliminating variables*. Rather than trying to optimize variable scales for a large set of variables that are probably useless, you could try to eliminate variables that make the prediction much worse before doing anything else. Can you think of a way to do this?

4. *Varying* ss *for graphing probability*. The ss parameter in probabilityguess dictates how smoothly the probability is graphed. What happens if this number is too high? Too low? Can you think of any way to determine what a good value will be without looking at the graph?

5. *The laptop dataset*. Try running the optimization on the laptop dataset from eBay. Which variables are important? Now try running the functions for graphing probability density. Are there any noticeable peaks?

6. *Other item types*. Which other items on eBay have suitable numerical attributes? iPods, cell phones, and cars all have a lot of interesting information. Try building another dataset for numerical prediction.

7. *Search attributes*. The eBay API has a lot of functionality that was not covered in this chapter. The GetSearchResults call has many options, including the ability to restrict searches to certain attributes. Modify the function to support this and try finding only Core Duo laptops.

## CHAPTER 9

Advanced Classification: Kernel Methods and SVMs

Previous chapters have considered several classifiers, including decision trees, Bayesian classifiers, and neural networks. This chapter will introduce the concept of linear classifiers and kernel methods as a prelude to covering one of the most advanced classifiers, and one that remains an active area of research, called *support-vector machines* (SVMs).

The dataset used throughout much of the chapter pertains to matching people on a dating site. Given information about two people, can we predict whether they will be a good match? This is an interesting problem because there are many variables, both numerical and nominal, and many nonlinear relationships. This dataset will be used to demonstrate some of the weaknesses of the previously described classifiers, and to show how the dataset can be tweaked to work better with these algorithms. An important thing to take away from this chapter is that it's rarely possible to throw a complex dataset at an algorithm and expect it to learn how to classify things accurately. Choosing the right algorithm and preprocessing the data appropriately is often required to get good results. I hope that going through the process of tweaking this dataset will give you ideas for how to modify others in the future.

At the end of the chapter, you'll learn how to build a dataset of real people from *Facebook*, a popular social networking site, and you'll use the algorithms to predict whether people with certain characteristics are likely to be friends.

Matchmaker Dataset

The dataset you'll use in this chapter is based on an imaginary online dating site. Most dating sites collect a lot of interesting information about their members, including demographic information, interests, and behavior. Imagine that this site collects the following information:

- Age
- Smoker?

- Want children?
- List of interests
- Location

Furthermore, this site collects information about whether two people have made a good match, whether they initially made contact, and if they decided to meet in person. This data is used to create the matchmaker dataset. There are two files to download:

> *http://kiwitobes.com/matchmaker/agesonly.csv*
> *http://kiwitobes.com/matchmaker/matchmaker.csv*

The *matchmaker.csv* file looks like this:

```
39,yes,no,skiing:knitting:dancing,220 W 42nd St New York
NY,43,no,yes,soccer:reading:scrabble,824 3rd Ave New York NY,0
23,no,no,football:fashion,102 1st Ave New York
NY,30,no,no,snowboarding:knitting:computers:shopping:tv:travel,
151 W 34th St New York NY,1
50,no,no,fashion:opera:tv:travel,686 Avenue of the Americas
New York NY,49,yes,yes,soccer:fashion:photography:computers:
camping:movies:tv,824 3rd Ave New York NY,0
```

Each row has information about a man and a woman and, in the final column, a 1 or a 0 to indicate whether or not they are considered a good match. (Your author is aware of the simplifying assumption made here; computer models are never quite as complicated as real life.) For a site with a large number of profiles, this information might be used to build a predictive algorithm that assists users in finding other people who are likely to be good matches. It might also indicate particular types of people that the site is lacking, which would be useful in strategies for promoting the site to new members. The *agesonly.csv* file has match information based only on age, which we will use to illustrate how the classifiers work, since two variables are much easier to visualize.

The first step is to build a function for loading this dataset. This is just a matter of reading all the fields into a list, but for experimental purposes, the function will have one optional parameter to load only in certain fields. Create a new file called *advancedclassify.py* and add the matchrow class and the loadmatch function:

```
class matchrow:
  def __init__(self,row,allnum=False):
    if allnum:
      self.data=[float(row[i]) for i in range(len(row)-1)]
    else:
      self.data=row[0:len(row)-1]
    self.match=int(row[len(row)-1])

def loadmatch(f,allnum=False):
  rows=[]
  for line in file(f):
    rows.append(matchrow(line.split(','),allnum))
  return rows
```

loadmatch creates a list of matchrow classes, each containing the raw data and whether or not there was a match. Use this function to load both the ages-only dataset and the full matchmaker set:

```
>>> import advancedclassify
>>> agesonly=advancedclassify.loadmatch('agesonly.csv',allnum=True)
>>> matchmaker=advancedclassify.loadmatch('matchmaker.csv')
```

Difficulties with the Data

Two interesting aspects of this dataset are the nonlinearity and the interplay of the variables. If you installed *matplotlib* (*http://matplotlib.sourceforge.net*) in Chapter 8 you can visualize some of the variables using advancedclassify and generating a couple of lists from it. (This step is not necessary to work through the rest of the chapter.) Try this in your Python session:

```
from pylab import *
def plotagematches(rows):
  xdm,ydm=[r.data[0] for r in rows if r.match==1],\
          [r.data[1] for r in rows if r.match==1]
  xdn,ydn=[r.data[0] for r in rows if r.match==0],\
          [r.data[1] for r in rows if r.match==0]

  plot(xdm,ydm,'go')
  plot(xdn,ydn,'ro')

  show()
```

Call this method from your Python session:

```
>>> reload(advancedclassify)
<module 'advancedclassify' from 'advancedclassify.py'>
>>> advancedclassify.plotagematches(agesonly)
```

This will generate a *scatter plot* of the man's age versus the woman's age. The points will be O if the people are a match and X if they are not. You'll get a window like the one shown in Figure 9-1.

Although there are obviously many other factors that determine whether two people are a match, this figure is based on the simplified age-only dataset, and it shows an obvious boundary that indicates people do not go far outside their own age range. The boundary also appears to curve and become less defined as people get older, showing that people will tolerate greater age differences as they get older.

Decision Tree Classifier

Chapter 7 covered decision tree classifiers, which try to automatically classify data using a tree. The decision tree algorithm described there will split the data based on numerical boundaries. This presents a problem when the dividing line can be expressed more accurately as a function of two variables. In this case, the difference

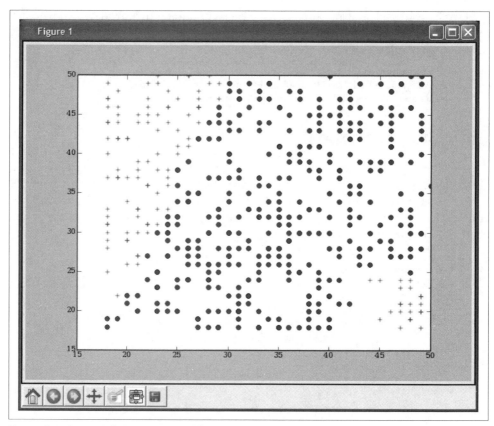

Figure 9-1. Generated age-age scatter plot

between the ages is a much better variable for prediction. You can imagine that training a decision directly on the data would give you a result like the one shown in Figure 9-2.

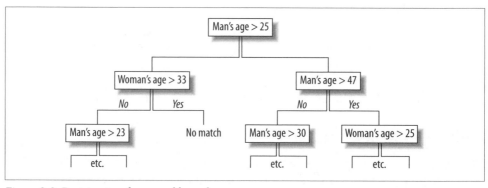

Figure 9-2. Decision tree for curved boundary

This is obviously quite useless for interpretation. It may work for automatic classification, but it is very messy and rigid. Had the other variables besides age been considered, the result would have been even more confusing. To understand what the decision tree is doing, consider the scatter plot and the *decision boundary* that has been created by the decision tree, as shown in Figure 9-3.

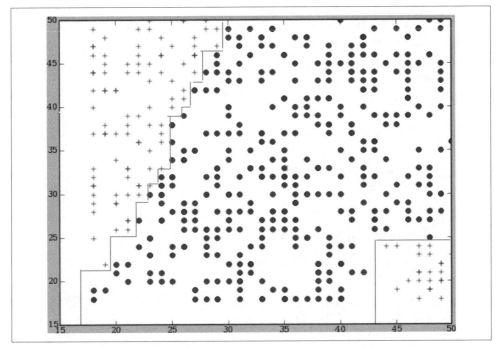

Figure 9-3. Boundary created by a decision tree

The decision boundary is the line at which every point on one side will be assigned to one category and every point on the other side will be assigned to the other category. It's clear from the figure that the constraints on the decision tree have forced the boundaries to be vertical or horizontal.

There are two main points here. The first is that it's not a good idea to naïvely use the data you're given without considering what it means and how it can be transformed to be easier to interpret. Creating a scatter plot can help you find out how data is really divided. The second point is that despite their strengths, the decision trees described in Chapter 7 are often a poor way to determine the class in problems with multiple numerical inputs that don't exhibit simple relationships.

Basic Linear Classification

This is one of the simplest classifiers to construct, but it's a good basis for further work. It works by finding the average of all the data in each class and constructing a point that represents the center of the class. It can then classify new points by determining to which center point they are closest.

To do this, you'll first need a function that calculates the *average point* in the classes. In this case, the classes are just 0 and 1. Add lineartrain to *advancedclassify.py*:

```
def lineartrain(rows):
  averages={}
  counts={}

  for row in rows:
    # Get the class of this point
    cl=row.match

    averages.setdefault(cl,[0.0]*(len(row.data)))
    counts.setdefault(cl,0)

    # Add this point to the averages
    for i in range(len(row.data)):
      averages[cl][i]+=float(row.data[i])

    # Keep track of how many points in each class
    counts[cl]+=1

  # Divide sums by counts to get the averages
  for cl,avg in averages.items():
    for i in range(len(avg)):
      avg[i]/=counts[cl]

  return averages
```

You can run this function in your Python session to get the averages:

```
>>> reload(advancedclassify)
<module 'advancedclassify' from 'advancedclassify.pyc'>
>>> avgs=advancedclassify.lineartrain(agesonly)
```

To see why this is useful, consider again the plot of the age data, shown in Figure 9-4.

The Xs in the figure represent the average points as calculated by lineartrain. The line dividing the data is halfway between the two Xs. This means that all the points on the left side of the line are closer to the "no match" average point, and all the points on the right side are closer to the "match" average. Whenever you have a new pair of ages and want to guess if two people will be a match, you can just imagine the point on this chart and see to which average it's closer.

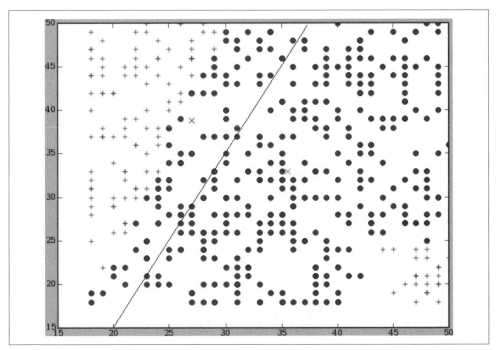

Figure 9-4. Linear classifier using averages

There are a couple of ways to determine the closeness of a new point. You learned about Euclidean distance in previous chapters; one approach would be to calculate the distance from the point to the averages for each of the classes, and choose the one with the smaller distance. While this approach will work for this classifier, in order to extend it later, you'll need to take a different approach using *vectors* and *dot-products*.

A vector has a magnitude and a direction, and it's often drawn as an arrow in a plane or written as a set of numbers. Figure 9-5 shows an example of a vector. The figure also shows how subtracting one point from another gives the vector that joins them.

A dot-product gives a single number from two vectors by multiplying each value in the first vector by the corresponding value in the second vector and adding them all together. Create a new function called dotproduct in *advancedclassify.py*:

```
def dotproduct(v1,v2):
    return sum([v1[i]*v2[i] for i in range(len(v1))])
```

The dot-product is also equal to the lengths of the two vectors multiplied together times the cosine of the angle between them. Most importantly, the cosine of an angle is negative if the angle is greater than 90 degrees, which means the dot-product will also be negative in this case. To see how you can take advantage of this, take a look at Figure 9-6.

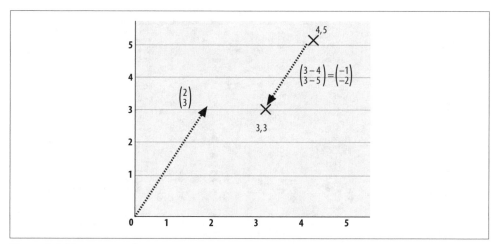

Figure 9-5. Vector examples

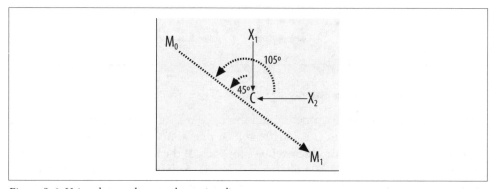

Figure 9-6. Using dot-products to determine distance

In the diagram you see the two average points for "match" (M_0) and "no match" (M_1), and C, which is the halfway point between them. There are two other points, X_0 and X_1, which are examples that have to be classified. The vector joining M_0 to M_1 is shown, as are the vectors joining X_1 and X_2 to C.

In this figure, X_1 is closer to M_0, so it should be classified as being a match. You'll notice that the angle between the vectors $X_1 \rightarrow C$ and $M_0 \rightarrow M_1$ is 45 degrees, which is less than 90 degrees, so the dot-product of $X_1 \rightarrow C$ and $M_0 \rightarrow M_1$ is positive.

On the other hand, the angle between $X_2 \rightarrow C$ and $M_0 \rightarrow M_1$ is more than 90 degrees because the vectors point in opposing directions. This means that the dot-product of $X_2 \rightarrow C$ and $M_0 \rightarrow M_1$ is negative.

The dot-product is negative for the big angle and positive for the small angle, so you only need to look at the sign of the dot-product to see in which class the new point belongs.

The point C is the average of M_0 and M_1, or $(M_0+M_1)/2$, so the formula for finding the class is:

```
class=sign((X - (M₀+M₁)/2) . (M₀-M₁))
```

Multiplying this out gives:

```
class=sign(X.M₀ - X.M₁ + (M₀.M₀ - M₁.M₁)/2)
```

This is the formula we will use to determine the class. Add a new function called dpclassify to *advancedclassify.py*:

```
def dpclassify(point,avgs):
  b=(dotproduct(avgs[1],avgs[1])-dotproduct(avgs[0],avgs[0]))/2
  y=dotproduct(point,avgs[0])-dotproduct(point,avgs[1])+b
  if y>0: return 0
  else: return 1
```

Now you can use the classifier to try to get some results for the data in your Python session:

```
>>> reload(advancedclassify)
<module 'advancedclassify' from 'advancedclassify.py'>
>>> advancedclassify.dpclassify([30,30],avgs)
1
>>> advancedclassify.dpclassify([30,25],avgs)
1
>>> advancedclassify.dpclassify([25,40],avgs)
0
>>> advancedclassify.dpclassify([48,20],avgs)
1
```

Remember that this is a linear classifier, so it just finds a dividing line. This means that if there isn't a straight line dividing the data or if there are multiple sections, as there are with the age-age comparison, the classifier will get some of the answers incorrect. In this example, the age comparison of 48 versus 20 really should have been a mismatch, but since only one line was found and this point falls to the right of it, the function decides that this is a match. In the "Understanding Kernel Methods" section later in this chapter, you'll see how to improve this classifier to do nonlinear classification.

Categorical Features

The matchmaker dataset contains numerical data and categorical data. Some classifiers, like the decision tree, can handle both types without any preprocessing, but the classifiers in the remainder of this chapter work only with numerical data. To handle this, you'll need a way to turn data into numbers so that it will be useful to the classifier.

Yes/No Questions

The simplest thing to convert to a number is a yes/no question because you can turn a "yes" into 1 and a "no" into −1. This also leaves the option of converting missing or ambiguous data (such as "I don't know") to 0. Add the yesno function to *advancedclassify.py* to do this conversion for you:

```
def yesno(v):
  if v=='yes': return 1
  elif v=='no': return -1
  else: return 0
```

Lists of Interests

There are a couple of different ways you can record people's interests in the dataset. The simplest is to treat every possible interest as a separate numerical variable, and assign a 0 if the person has that interest and a 1 if he doesn't. If you are dealing with individual people, that is the best approach. In this case, however, you have pairs of people, so a more intuitive approach is to use the number of common interests as a variable.

Add a new function called matchcount to *advancedclassify.py*, which returns the number of matching items in a list as a float:

```
def matchcount(interest1,interest2):
  l1=interest1.split(':')
  l2=interest2.split(':')
  x=0
  for v in l1:
    if v in l2: x+=1
  return x
```

The number of common interests is an interesting variable, but it definitely eliminates some potentially useful information. It's possible that certain combinations of different interests work well together, such as skiing and snowboarding or drinking and dancing. A classifier that wasn't trained on the original data would never be able to learn these combinations.

An alternative to creating a new variable for every interest, leading to a lot of variables and thus to much more complex classifiers, is to arrange interests in a hierarchy. You could say, for example, that skiing and snowboarding are both examples of snow sports, which is a subcategory of sports; a pair who are both interested in snow sports but not in the same one might get 0.8 added to their matchcount instead of a full point. The farther up the hierarchy you have to go to find a match, the smaller fraction of a point it would be worth. Although the matchmaker dataset doesn't have this hierarchy, it's something you can consider when similar problems arise.

Determining Distances Using Yahoo! Maps

The most difficult thing to deal with in this dataset is the location. It's certainly arguable that people living closer together are more likely to be a match, but the locations in the data file are given as a mix of addresses and zip codes. A very simple approach would be to use "live in the same zip code" as a variable, but this would be extremely limiting—it's quite possible for people to live on adjacent blocks that are in different zip codes. Ideally, you could create a new variable based on distance.

Of course, it's not possible to figure out the distances between two addresses without additional information. Fortunately, Yahoo! Maps provides an API service called *Geocoding*, which takes an address in the United States and returns its longitude and latitude. By doing this for pairs of addresses, you can calculate an approximate distance between them.

If for any reason you can't use the Yahoo! API, just add a dummy function for milesdistance to *advancedclassify.py*:

```
def milesdistance(a1,a2):
    return 0
```

Getting a Yahoo! Application Key

To use the Yahoo! API, you'll first need to get an application key that is used in your queries to identify your application. You can get a key by going to *http://api.search. yahoo.com/webservices/register_application* and answering a few questions. If you don't already have a Yahoo! account, you'll have to create one. You'll get the key right away, so you won't have to wait for an email response.

Using the Geocoding API

The Geocoding API requires that you request a URL of the form. You can do this at *http://api.local.yahoo.com/MapsService/V1/geocode?appid=appid&location=location*.

The location is free text and can be an address, a zip code, or even just a city and state. The returned result is an XML file that looks like this:

```
<ResultSet>
<Result precision="address">
<Latitude>37.417312</Latitude>
<Longitude>-122.026419</Longitude>
<Address>755 FIRST AVE</Address>
<City>SUNNYVALE</City>
<State>CA</State>
<Zip>94089-1019</Zip>
<Country>US</Country>
</Result>
</ResultSet>
```

The fields you're interested in are longitude and latitude. To parse this, you'll use the minidom API you used in previous chapters. Add getlocation to *advancedclassify.py*:

```
yahookey="Your Key Here"
from xml.dom.minidom import parseString
from urllib import urlopen,quote_plus

loc_cache={}
def getlocation(address):
  if address in loc_cache: return loc_cache[address]
  data=urlopen('http://api.local.yahoo.com/MapsService/V1/'+\
               'geocode?appid=%s&location=%s' %
               (yahookey,quote_plus(address))).read()
  doc=parseString(data)
  lat=doc.getElementsByTagName('Latitude')[0].firstChild.nodeValue
  long=doc.getElementsByTagName('Longitude')[0].firstChild.nodeValue
  loc_cache[address]=(float(lat),float(long))
  return loc_cache[address]
```

This function creates the URL with your application key and the location, and it returns and extracts the longitude and latitude. Although this is the only information you'll need for calculating distance, you can use the Yahoo! Geocoding API for other things as well, such as determining the zip code of a given address or finding out where a certain zip code is.

Calculating the Distance

Converting the longitudes and latitudes of two points into a distance in miles is actually quite tricky if you require complete accuracy. However, the distances in this case are very small and you're only calculating them for the sake of comparison, so you can use an approximation instead. The approximation is similar to the Euclidean distance you've seen in previous chapters, except that the difference between the latitudes is first multiplied by 69.1, and the difference between the longitudes is multiplied by 53.

Add the milesdistance function to *advancedclassify.py*:

```
def milesdistance(a1,a2):
  lat1,long1=getlocation(a1)
  lat2,long2=getlocation(a2)
  latdif=69.1*(lat2-lat1)
  longdif=53.0*(long2-long1)
  return (latdif**2+longdif**2)**.5
```

This function calls the previously defined getlocation on both addresses and then calculates the distance between them. If you like, you can try it in your Python session:

```
>>> reload(advancedclassify)
<module 'advancedclassify' from 'advancedclassify.py'>
>>> advancedclassify.getlocation('1 alewife center, cambridge, ma')
(42.398662999999999, -71.140512999999999)
>>> advancedclassify.milesdistance('cambridge, ma','new york,ny')
191.77952424273104
```

The distances calculated by the approximation will generally be less than 10 percent off, which is fine for this application.

Creating the New Dataset

You now have all the parts required to create a dataset for training the classifier. What you need now is a function that puts them all together. This function will load the dataset from the data file using the loadmatch function, and will apply the appropriate transformations to the columns. Add loadnumerical to *advancedclassify.py*:

```
def loadnumerical():
  oldrows=loadmatch('matchmaker.csv')
  newrows=[]
  for row in oldrows:
    d=row.data
    data=[float(d[0]),yesno(d[1]),yesno(d[2]),
          float(d[5]),yesno(d[6]),yesno(d[7]),
          matchcount(d[3],d[8]),
          milesdistance(d[4],d[9]),
          row.match]
    newrows.append(matchrow(data))
  return newrows
```

This function generates a new data row for every row in the original set. It calls the functions you defined previously to convert all the data to numbers, including the distance calculation and the interest overlap count.

Call this function from your Python session to create the new dataset:

```
>>> reload(advancedclassify)
>>> numericalset=advancedclassify.loadnumerical()
>>> numericalset[0].data
[39.0, 1, -1, 43.0, -1, 1, 0, 0.90110601059793416]
```

Again, it's easy to create subsets by specifying the columns that interest you. This is useful for visualizing the data and understanding how the classifiers work on different variables.

Scaling the Data

When you were only making comparisons based on people's ages, it was fine to keep the data as it was and to use averages and distances, since it makes sense to compare variables that mean the same thing. However, now you've introduced some new variables that aren't really comparable to age, since their values are much smaller. Having differing opinions about children—a gap of 2, between 1 and –1—may be much more significant in reality than having an age gap of six years, but if you used the data as is, the age difference would count for three times as much.

To resolve this issue, it's a good idea to put all the data on a common scale so that differences are comparable in every variable. You can do this by determining the lowest and highest values for every variable, and scaling the data so that the lowest value is now 0 and the highest value is now 1, with all the other values somewhere between 0 and 1.

Add scaledata to *advancedclassifier.py*:

```python
def scaledata(rows):
  low=[999999999.0]*len(rows[0].data)
  high=[-999999999.0]*len(rows[0].data)
  # Find the lowest and highest values
  for row in rows:
    d=row.data
    for i in range(len(d)):
      if d[i]<low[i]: low[i]=d[i]
      if d[i]>high[i]: high[i]=d[i]

  # Create a function that scales data
  def scaleinput(d):
    return [(d.data[i]-low[i])/(high[i]-low[i])
            for i in range(len(low))]

  # Scale all the data
  newrows=[matchrow(scaleinput(row.data)+[row.match])
          for row in rows]

  # Return the new data and the function
  return newrows,scaleinput
```

This function defines an internal function, scaleinput, which finds the lowest value and subtracts that amount from all the values to bring the range to a 0 starting point. It then divides the values by the difference between the lowest and highest values to convert them all to values between 0 and 1. The function applies scaleinput to every row in the dataset and returns the new dataset along with the function so you can also scale your queries.

Now you can try the linear classifier on a bigger set of variables:

```
>>> reload(advancedclassify)
<module 'advancedclassify' from 'advancedclassify.py'>
>>> scaledset,scalef=advancedclassify.scaledata(numericalset)
>>> avgs=advancedclassify.lineartrain(scaledset)
>>> numericalset[0].data
[39.0, 1, -1, 43.0, -1, 1, 0, 0.90110601059793416]
>>> numericalset[0].match
0
>>> advancedclassify.dpclassify(scalef(numericalset[0].data),avgs)
1
>>> numericalset[11].match
1
>>> advancedclassify.dpclassify(scalef(numericalset[11].data),avgs)
1
```

Notice that you need to scale the numerical examples first to fit them into the new space. Although the classifier works for some examples, the limitations of simply trying to find a dividing line now become clearer. To improve the results, you'll need to get beyond linear classification.

Understanding Kernel Methods

Consider what would happen if you tried to use the linear classifier on a dataset similar to the one in Figure 9-7.

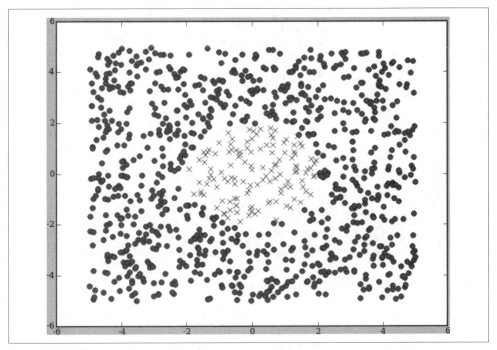

Figure 9-7. A class encircling another class

Where would the average points be for each class? They would both be in exactly the same place! Even though it's clear to you and me that anything inside the circle is an X and everything outside the circle is an O, the linear classifier is unable to distinguish these two classes.

But consider what happens if you square every x and y value first. A point that was at (–1,2) would now be at (1,4), a point that was at (0.5,1) would now be at (0.25,1), and so on. The new plot would look like Figure 9-8.

All the Xs have moved into the corner and all the Os are outside that corner. It's now very easy to divide the Xs and Os with a straight line, and any time a new piece of data has to be classified, you can just square its x and y values and see on which side of the line it falls.

This example shows that by transforming the points first, it's possible to create a new dataset that can be divided with a straight line. However, this example was chosen precisely because it can be transformed very easily; in real problems, the transformation will likely be a lot more complicated and will involve transforming

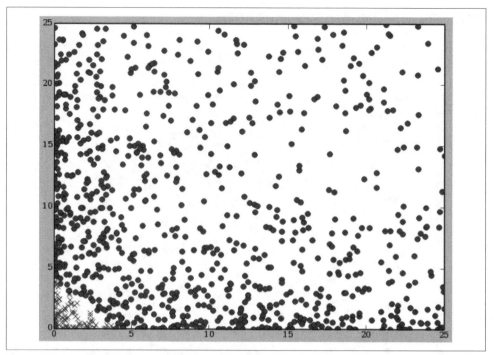

Figure 9-8. Moving the points into a different space

the data into more dimensions. For example, you might take a dataset of x and y coordinates and create a new dataset with a, b, and c coordinates where a=x^2, b=x*y, and c=y^2. Once the data has been put into more dimensions, it's easier to find the dividing line between two classes.

The Kernel Trick

While you could write code to transform the data into a new space like this, it isn't usually done in practice because finding a dividing line when working with real datasets can require casting the data into hundreds or thousands of dimensions, and this is quite impractical to implement. However, with any algorithm that uses dot-products—including the linear classifier—you can use a technique called the *kernel trick*.

The kernel trick involves replacing the dot-product function with a new function that returns what the dot-product would have been if the data had first been transformed to a higher dimensional space using some mapping function. There is no limit to the number of possible transformations, but only a few are actually used in practice. The one that is usually recommended (and the one that you'll use here) is called the *radial-basis function*.

The radial-basis function is like the dot-product in that it takes two vectors and returns a value. Unlike the dot-product, it is not linear and can thus map more complex spaces. Add rbf to *advancedclassify.py*:

```
def rbf(v1,v2,gamma=20):
  dv=[v1[i]-v2[i] for i in range(len(v1))]
  l=veclength(dv)
  return math.e**(-gamma*l)
```

This function takes a single parameter, gamma, which can be adjusted to get the best linear separation for a given dataset.

You now need a new function that calculates the distances from the average points in the transformed space. Unfortunately, the averages were calculated in the original space, so they can't be used here—in fact, the averages can't be calculated at all because you won't actually be calculating the locations of the points in the new space. Thankfully, averaging a set of vectors and taking the dot-product of the average with vector A gives the same result as averaging the dot-products of vector A with every vector in the set.

So, instead of calculating the dot-product between the point you're trying to classify and the average point for a class, you calculate the dot-product or the radial-basis function between the point and every other point in the class, and then average them. Add nonlinearclassify to *advancedclassify.py*:

```
def nlclassify(point,rows,offset,gamma=10):
  sum0=0.0
  sum1=0.0
  count0=0
  count1=0

  for row in rows:
    if row.match==0:
      sum0+=rbf(point,row.data,gamma)
      count0+=1
    else:
      sum1+=rbf(point,row.data,gamma)
      count1+=1
  y=(1.0/count0)*sum0-(1.0/count1)*sum1+offset

  if y<0: return 0
  else: return 1

def getoffset(rows,gamma=10):
  l0=[]
  l1=[]
  for row in rows:
    if row.match==0: l0.append(row.data)
    else: l1.append(row.data)
  sum0=sum(sum([rbf(v1,v2,gamma) for v1 in l0]) for v2 in l0)
  sum1=sum(sum([rbf(v1,v2,gamma) for v1 in l1]) for v2 in l1)

  return (1.0/(len(l1)**2))*sum1-(1.0/(len(l0)**2))*sum0
```

The offset value is also different in the transformed space and can be a little slow to calculate. For this reason, you should calculate it once for a dataset and pass it to nlclassify each time.

Try using this new classifier with just the ages and see if it fixes the problem that you identified earlier:

```
>>> advancedclassify.nlclassify([30,30],agesonly,offset)
1
>>> advancedclassify.nlclassify([30,25],agesonly,offset)
1
>>> advancedclassify.nlclassify([25,40],agesonly,offset)
0
>>> advancedclassify.nlclassify([48,20],agesonly,offset)
0
```

Excellent! The transformation allows the classifier to recognize that there is a band of matches where the ages are close together, and that on either side of the band a match is very unlikely. Now it recognizes that 48 versus 20 is not a good match. Try it again with the other data included:

```
>>> ssoffset=advancedclassify.getoffset(scaledset)
>>> numericalset[0].match
0
>>> advancedclassify.nlclassify(scalef(numericalset[0].data),scaledset,ssoffset)
0
>>> numericalset[1].match
1
>>> advancedclassify.nlclassify(scalef(numericalset[1].data),scaledset,ssoffset)
1
>>> numericalset[2].match
0
>>> advancedclassify.nlclassify(scalef(numericalset[2].data),scaledset,ssoffset)
0
>>> newrow=[28.0,-1,-1,26.0,-1,1,2,0.8] # Man doesn't want children, woman does
>>> advancedclassify.nlclassify(scalef(newrow),scaledset,ssoffset)
0
>>> newrow=[28.0,-1,1,26.0,-1,1,2,0.8] # Both want children
>>> advancedclassify.nlclassify(scalef(newrow),scaledset,ssoffset)
1
```

The performance of the classifier has improved a lot. In the session above, you can see that if the man doesn't want children and the woman does, it's a deal breaker, even though they are close in age and have two common interests. Try changing the other variables to see what affects the outcome.

Support-Vector Machines

Consider again the challenge of finding a straight line that divides two classes. Figure 9-9 illustrates an example. The averages for each class are shown in the figure, along with the dividing line that they imply.

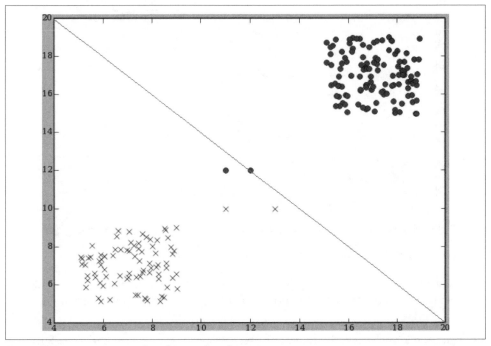

Figure 9-9. Linear average classifier misclassifies points

Notice that the dividing line calculated by using the averages misclassifies two of the points because they are much closer to the line than the majority of the data. The problem is that since most of the data is far away from the line, it's not relevant for including in the dividing line.

Support-vector machines are a well known set of methods for creating classifiers that solve this problem. They do this by trying to find the line that is as far away as possible from each of the classes. This line is called the *maximum-margin hyperplane*, and is shown in Figure 9-10.

The dividing line has been chosen so that the parallel lines that touch the items from each class are as far from it as possible. Again, you can determine into which class a new data point fits simply by seeing which side of the line it is on. Notice that only the points at the margin are needed to determine the placement of the dividing line; you could get rid of all the other data and the line would be in the same place. The

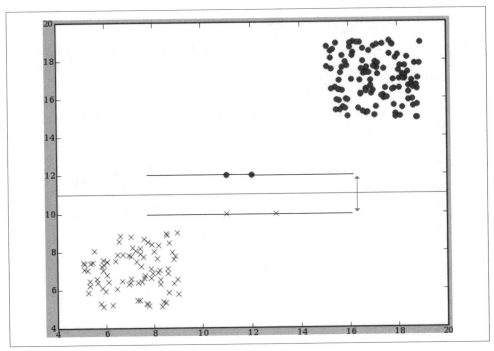

Figure 9-10. Finding the best dividing line

points near the line are called the *support vectors*. The algorithm that finds the support vectors and uses them to find the dividing line is the support-vector machine.

You have already seen how a linear classifier can be turned into a nonlinear classifier by using the kernel trick, as long as it uses dot-products for comparisons. Support-vector machines also use dot-products so they can be used with kernels to perform nonlinear classification.

Applications of Support-Vector Machines

Because support-vector machines work well with high-dimensional datasets, they are most often applied to data-intensive scientific problems and other problems that deal with very complex sets of data. Some examples include:

- Classifying facial expressions
- Detecting intruders using military datasets
- Predicting the structure of proteins from their sequences
- Handwriting recognition
- Determining the potential for damage during earthquakes

Using LIBSVM

The explanation in the previous section should help you understand how and why support-vector machines work, but the algorithm for training a support-vector machine involves mathematical concepts that are very computationally intensive and are beyond the scope of this chapter. For these reasons, this section will introduce an open-source library called *LIBSVM*, which can train an SVM model, make predictions, and test the predictions within a dataset. It even has built-in support for the radial-basis function and other kernel methods.

Getting LIBSVM

You can download LIBSVM from *http://www.csie.ntu.edu.tw/~cjlin/libsvm*.

LIBSVM is written in C++ and includes a version written in Java. The download package includes a Python wrapper called *svm.py*. In order to use *svm.py*, you need compiled versions of LIBSVM for your platform. If you're using Windows, a DLL called *svmc.dll* is included. (Python 2.5 requires that you rename this file to *svmc.pyd* because it can't import libraries with DLL extensions.) The documentation for LIBSVM explains how to compile the library for other platforms.

A Sample Session

Once you have a compiled version of LIBSVM, put it and *svm.py* in your Python path or working directory. You can now import the library in your Python session and try a simple problem:

```
>>> from svm import *
```

The first step is to create a simple dataset. LIBSVM reads the data from a tuple containing two lists. The first list contains the classes and the second list contains the input data. Try creating a simple dataset with two possible classes:

```
>>> prob = svm_problem([1,-1],[[1,0,1],[-1,0,-1]])
```

You also need to specify which kernel you want to use by creating svm_parameter:

```
>>> param = svm_parameter(kernel_type = LINEAR, C = 10)
```

Next, you can train the model:

```
>>> m = svm_model(prob, param)
*
optimization finished, #iter = 1
nu = 0.025000
obj = -0.250000, rho = 0.000000
nSV = 2, nBSV = 0
Total nSV = 2
```

And finally, use it to create predictions about new classes:

```
>>> m.predict([1, 1, 1])
1.0
```

This shows all the functionality of LIBSVM that you need to create a model from training data and use it to make predictions. LIBSVM includes another very nice feature, the ability to load and save the trained models you've built:

```
>>> m.save(test.model)
>>> m=svm_model(test.model)
```

Applying SVM to the Matchmaker Dataset

In order to use LIBSVM on the matchmaker dataset, you must convert it to the tuple of lists required by svm_model. This is a simple transformation from the scaledset; you can do it in one line in your Python session:

```
>>> answers,inputs=[r.match for r in scaledset],[r.data for r in scaledset]
```

Again, we're using the scaled data to prevent overweighting of variables, as this improves the performance of the algorithm. Use this new function to generate the new dataset and build a model using a radial-basis function as the kernel:

```
>>> param = svm_parameter(kernel_type = RBF)
>>> prob = svm_problem(answers,inputs)
>>> m=svm_model(prob,param)
*
optimization finished, #iter = 319
nu = 0.777538
obj = -289.477708, rho = -0.853058
nSV = 396, nBSV = 380
Total nSV = 396
```

Now you can make predictions about whether people with a given set of attributes will be a match or not. You'll need to use the scale function to scale the data you want predictions for, so that the variables are on the same scale as the ones with which you built the model:

```
>>> newrow=[28.0,-1,-1,26.0,-1,1,2,0.8] # Man doesn't want children, woman does
>>> m.predict(scalef(newrow))
0.0
>>> newrow=[28.0,-1,1,26.0,-1,1,2,0.8] # Both want children
>>> m.predict(scalef(newrow))
1.0
```

Although this appears to give good predictions, it would be nice to know how good they really are so that you can choose the best parameters for your basis function. LIBSVM also includes functionality for cross-validating the models. You saw how this works in Chapter 8—the dataset is automatically divided into training sets and test sets. The training sets are used to build the model, and the test sets are used to test the model to see how well it makes predictions.

You can test the quality of the model using the cross-validation function. This function takes a parameter, n, and divides the dataset into *n* subsets. It then uses each subset as a test set and trains the model with all the other subsets. It returns a list of answers that you can compare to the original list.

```
>>> guesses = cross_validation(prob, param, 4)
...
>>> guesses
[0.0, 0.0, 0.0, 0.0, 1.0, 0.0,...
 0.0, 0.0, 0.0, 0.0, 0.0, 0.0,...
 1.0, 1.0, 0.0, 0.0, 0.0, 0.0,...
...]
>>> sum([abs(answers[i]-guesses[i]) for i in range(len(guesses))])
116.0
```

The number of differences between the answers and the guesses is 116. Since there were 500 rows in the original dataset, this means that the algorithm got 384 matches correct. If you like, you can look at other kernels and parameters in the LIBSVM documentation and see if you can get any improvement by changing param.

Matching on Facebook

Facebook is a popular social networking site that was originally for college students but eventually opened up to a larger audience. Like other social networking sites, it allows users to make profiles, enter demographic information about themselves, and connect to their friends on the site. Facebook also includes an API that lets you query information about people and find out if two people are friends or not. By doing this, you can build a set similar to the matchmaker dataset using real people.

As of this writing, Facebook has remained very committed to privacy, so you can only view the profiles of people who are your friends. The API applies the same rules, requiring a user to log in and only allowing queries, so unfortunately, you'll only be able to work through this section if you have a Facebook account and have connected to at least 20 people.

Getting a Developer Key

If you have a Facebook account, you can sign up for a developer key on the Facebook developer site at *http://developers.facebook.com*.

You'll get two strings, an API key and a "secret" key. The API key is used to identify you, and the secret key is used to encrypt your requests in the hash function that you'll see later. To start, create a new file called *facebook.py*, import some modules you'll need, and set up some constants:

```
import urllib,md5,webbrowser,time
from xml.dom.minidom import parseString
```

```
apikey="Your API Key"
secret="Your Secret Key"
FacebookSecureURL = "https://api.facebook.com/restserver.php"
```

There are two convenience methods to add: getsinglevalue gets the next value from inside a named node, and callid returns a number based on the system time.

```
def getsinglevalue(node,tag):
  nl=node.getElementsByTagName(tag)
  if len(nl)>0:
    tagNode=nl[0]
    if tagNode.hasChildNodes():
      return tagNode.firstChild.nodeValue
  return ''

def callid():
  return str(int(time.time()*10))
```

Some of the Facebook calls require that you send a sequence number, which can be any number as long as it is higher than the last sequence number you used. Using the system time is an easy way to get consistently higher numbers.

Creating a Session

The procedure for creating a session on Facebook is actually intended for you to create an application for other people to use without ever learning their login information. This is accomplished in several steps:

1. Use the Facebook API to request a token.

2. Send the user a URL to the Facebook login page, with the token in the URL.

3. Wait until the user has logged in.

4. Request a session from the Facebook API using the token.

Because several variables are used by all the calls, it's better to wrap the Facebook functionality in a class. Create a new class in *facebook.py* called fbsession and add an __init__ method that carries out the steps listed above:

```
class fbsession:
  def __init__(self):
    self.session_secret=None
    self.session_key=None
    self.token=self.createtoken()
    webbrowser.open(self.getlogin())
    print "Press enter after logging in:",
    raw_input()
    self.getsession()
```

There are several methods used by __init__ that have to be added to the class for it to work. The first thing you'll need is a way to send requests to the Facebook API. The sendrequest method opens a connection to Facebook and posts the arguments.

An XML file is returned and parsed using the minidom parser. Add this method to your class:

```
def sendrequest(self, args):
    args['api_key'] = apikey
    args['sig'] = self.makehash(args)
    post_data = urllib.urlencode(args)
    url = FacebookURL + "?" + post_data
    data=urllib.urlopen(url).read()
    return parseString(data)
```

The line shown in bold generates the signature of the request. This is accomplished with the makehash method, which joins all the arguments together in a string and hashes them with the secret key. You'll see shortly that the secret key changes once you get a session, so the method checks to see if you already have a session secret key. Add makehash to your class:

```
def makehash(self,args):
    hasher = md5.new(''.join([x + '=' + args[x] for x in sorted(args.keys())]))
    if self.session_secret: hasher.update(self.session_secret)
    else: hasher.update(secret)
    return hasher.hexdigest()
```

Now you're ready to write some actual Facebook API calls. Begin with createtoken, which creates and stores a token to use in the login page:

```
def createtoken(self):
    res = self.sendrequest({'method':"facebook.auth.createToken"})
    self.token = getsinglevalue(res,'token')
```

Also add getlogin, which just returns the user login page URL:

```
def getlogin(self):
    return "http://api.facebook.com/login.php?api_key="+apikey+\
           "&auth_token=" + self.token
```

After the user has logged in, getsession should be called to get a session key and the session secret key that will be used to hash future requests. Add this method to your class:

```
def getsession(self):
    doc=self.sendrequest({'method':'facebook.auth.getSession',
                          'auth_token':self.token})
    self.session_key=getsinglevalue(doc,'session_key')
    self.session_secret=getsinglevalue(doc,'secret')
```

It's a lot of work to set up a Facebook session, but after going through the process, the future calls are pretty simple. This chapter only looks at getting information about people, but if you look at the documentation, you'll see that it's easy to call methods to download photos and events.

Download Friend Data

Now you can actually start creating some useful methods. The getfriends method downloads the list of friend IDs for the currently logged-in user and returns them as a list. Add this method to fbsession:

```
def getfriends(self):
    doc=self.sendrequest({'method':'facebook.friends.get',
                          'session_key':self.session_key,'call_id':callid()})
    results=[]
    for n in doc.getElementsByTagName('result_elt'):
      results.append(n.firstChild.nodeValue)
    return results
```

Since getfriends only returns IDs, you'll need another method to actually download information about the people. The getinfo method calls Facebook's getInfo with a list of user IDs. It requests a small number of selected fields, but you can extend this by adding more fields to fields and modifying the parsing code to extract the relevant information. A complete list of fields is in the Facebook developer documentation:

```
def getinfo(self,users):
    ulist=','.join(users)

    fields='gender,current_location,relationship_status,'+\
           'affiliations,hometown_location'

    doc=self.sendrequest({'method':'facebook.users.getInfo',
      'session_key':self.session_key,'call_id':callid(),
      'users':ulist,'fields':fields})

    results={}
    for n,id in zip(doc.getElementsByTagName('result_elt'),users):
      # Get the location
      locnode=n.getElementsByTagName('hometown_location')[0]
      loc=getsinglevalue(locnode,'city')+', '+getsinglevalue(locnode,'state')

      # Get school
      college=''
      gradyear='0'
      affiliations=n.getElementsByTagName('affiliations_elt')
      for aff in affiliations:
        # Type 1 is college
        if getsinglevalue(aff,'type')=='1':
          college=getsinglevalue(aff,'name')
          gradyear=getsinglevalue(aff,'year')

      results[id]={'gender':getsinglevalue(n,'gender'),
                   'status':getsinglevalue(n,'relationship_status'),
                   'location':loc,'college':college,'year':gradyear}
    return results
```

The results are in the form of a dictionary that maps the user IDs to a subset of the information. You can use this to create a new matchmaker dataset. If you like, you can try out your new Facebook class in your Python session:

```
>>> import facebook
>>> s=facebook.fbsession()
Press enter after logging in:
>>> friends=s.getfriends()
>>> friends[1]
u'iY5TTbS-Ofvs.'
>>> s.getinfo(friends[0:2])
{u'iA810MUfhfsw.': {'gender': u'Female', 'location': u'Atlanta, '},
 u'iY5TTbS-Ofvs.': {'gender': u'Male', 'location': u'Boston, '}}
```

Building a Match Dataset

The final Facebook API call required for our exercise is one that determines whether or not two people are friends. This will be used as the "answer" in our new dataset. The call allows you to pass two equal-length lists of IDs, and returns a list with a number for every pair—1 if the people are friends, and 0 if they are not. Add this method to your class:

```
def arefriends(self,idlist1,idlist2):
  id1=','.join(idlist1)
  id2=','.join(idlist2)
  doc=self.sendrequest({'method':'facebook.friends.areFriends',
                        'session_key':self.session_key,'call_id':callid(),
                        'id1':id1,'id2':id2})
  results=[]
  for n in doc.getElementsByTagName('result_elt'):
    results.append(n.firstChild.nodeValue)
  return results
```

And finally, you can put it all together to create a dataset that works with LIBSVM. This gets a list of all the friends of the logged-in user, downloads information about them, and creates a row for every pair of people. It then checks every pair to see if they are friends. Add makedataset to the class:

```
def makedataset(self):
  from advancedclassify import milesdistance
  # Get all the info for all my friends
  friends=self.getfriends()
  info=self.getinfo(friends)
  ids1,ids2=[],[]
  rows=[]

  # Nested loop to look at every pair of friends
  for i in range(len(friends)):
    f1=friends[i]
    data1=info[f1]
```

```
    # Start at i+1 so we don't double up
    for j in range(i+1,len(friends)):
      f2=friends[j]
      data2=info[f2]
      ids1.append(f1)
      ids2.append(f2)

      # Generate some numbers from the data
      if data1['college']==data2['college']: sameschool=1
      else: sameschool=0
      male1=(data1['gender']=='Male') and 1 or 0
      male2=(data2['gender']=='Male') and 1 or 0

      row=[male1,int(data1['year']),male2,int(data2['year']),sameschool]
      rows.append(row)
# Call arefriends in blocks for every pair of people
arefriends=[]
for i in range(0,len(ids1),30):
  j=min(i+20,len(ids1))
  pa=self.arefriends(ids1[i:j],ids2[i:j])
  arefriends+=pa
return arefriends,rows
```

This method changes gender and status to numbers so that the dataset can be used directly by LIBSVM. The final loop requests the friend status of every pair of people in blocks, since Facebook restricts how large a single request can be.

Creating an SVM Model

To try building an SVM on your data, reload the class, create a new session, and build the dataset:

```
>>> reload(facebook)
<module 'facebook' from 'facebook.pyc'>
>>> s=facebook.fbsession()
Press enter after logging in:
>>> answers,data=s.makedataset()
```

You should be able to run the svm methods on it directly:

```
>>> param = svm_parameter(kernel_type = RBF)
>>> prob = svm_problem(answers,data)
>>> m=svm_model(prob,param)
>>> m.predict([1,2003,1,2003,1]) # Two men, same year, same school
1.0
>>> m.predict([1,2003,1,1996,0]) # Different years, different schools
0.0
```

Of course, your results will vary, but typically the model will determine that people who went to the same college or had the same hometown are likely to be friends.

Exercises

1. *Bayesian classifier*. Can you think of ways that the Bayesian classifier you built in Chapter 6 could be used on the matchmaker dataset? What would be good examples of features?

2. *Optimizing a dividing line*. Do you think it's possible to choose a dividing line using the optimization methods you learned in Chapter 5, instead of just using the averages? What cost function would you use?

3. *Choosing the best kernel parameters*. Write a function that loops over different values for gamma and determines what the best value for a given dataset is.

4. *Hierarchy of interests*. Design a simple hierarchy of interests, along with a data structure to represent it. Alter the matchcount function to use the hierarchy to give partial points for matches.

5. *Other LIBSVM kernels*. Look through the LIBSVM documentation and see what other kernels are available. Try a polynomial kernel. Does the prediction quality improve?

6. *Other Facebook predictions*. Look at all the fields available through the Facebook API. What datasets can be built for individuals? Could you use an SVM model to predict if someone listed a movie as a favorite based on the school she went to? What other things could you make predictions about?

CHAPTER 10

Finding Independent Features

Most of the chapters so far have focused primarily on *supervised* classifiers, except Chapter 3, which was about *unsupervised* techniques called *clustering*. This chapter will look at ways to extract the important underlying features from sets of data that are not labeled with specific outcomes. Like clustering, these methods do not seek to make predictions as much as they try to characterize the data and tell you interesting things about it.

You'll recall from Chapter 3 that clustering assigns every row in a dataset to a group or point in a hierarchy—each item fits into exactly one group that represents the average of the members. *Feature extraction* is a more general form of this idea; it tries to find new data rows that can be used in combination to reconstruct rows of the original dataset. Rather than belonging to one cluster, each row is created from a combination of the features.

One of the classic problems illustrating the need to find independent features is known as the *cocktail party problem*, the problem of interpreting conversation when many people are talking. A remarkable feature of the human auditory system is our ability to focus on a single voice in a room full of people talking, despite the fact that a mixture of all the different voices is reaching our ears. The brain is quite adept at separating the independent sounds that create all the noise it's hearing. By using algorithms like the one described in this chapter, and getting the input from multiple microphones placed in a room, it's possible for a computer to do the same thing—take a cacophony of sounds and separate them without any prior knowledge of what they are.

Another interesting use of feature extraction is identifying recurring word-usage patterns in a corpus of documents, which can help identify themes that are independently present in various combinations. In this chapter, you'll build a system that downloads news articles from a variety of feeds and identifies the key themes that emerge from a set of articles. You may find that articles contain more than one theme, and you will certainly find that themes apply to more than one article.

The second example in this chapter concerns stock market data, which is presumed to have multiple underlying causes that combine to create results. The same algorithm can be applied to this data to search for these causes and their independent effects.

A Corpus of News

To begin, you'll need a set of news articles to work with. These should be from a variety of sources so that the themes being discussed in different places are easier to discern. Fortunately, most of the major news services and web sites provide RSS or Atom feeds, either for all the articles or for individual categories. You've used the *Universal Feed Parser* in previous chapters to parse RSS and Atom feeds for blogs, and you can use the same parser to download news. If you don't already have the parser, you can download it from *http://feedparser.org*.

Selecting Sources

There are thousands of sources of what can be considered "news," from major news wires and newspapers to political blogs. Some ideas include:

- Reuters
- The Associated Press
- *The New York Times*
- Google News
- Salon.com
- Fox News
- *Forbes* magazine
- CNN International

This is just a small sample of the possibilities. Combining sources from different points on the political spectrum and those that use different writing styles is a better test for the algorithm, since it should be able to find the important features and ignore irrelevant sections. It's also possible, given the right set of data, for a feature-extraction algorithm to identify a feature that is present in stories with a particular political slant and assign that feature to the story, in addition to the features that describe the subject of the story.

Create a new file called *newsfeatures.py* and add the following code to import some libraries and give a list of sources:

```
import feedparser
import re

feedlist=['http://today.reuters.com/rss/topNews',
          'http://today.reuters.com/rss/domesticNews',
```

```
                  'http://today.reuters.com/rss/worldNews',
                  'http://hosted.ap.org/lineups/TOPHEADS-rss_2.0.xml',
                  'http://hosted.ap.org/lineups/USHEADS-rss_2.0.xml',
                  'http://hosted.ap.org/lineups/WORLDHEADS-rss_2.0.xml',
                  'http://hosted.ap.org/lineups/POLITICSHEADS-rss_2.0.xml',
                  'http://www.nytimes.com/services/xml/rss/nyt/HomePage.xml',
                  'http://www.nytimes.com/services/xml/rss/nyt/International.xml',
                  'http://news.google.com/?output=rss',
                  'http://feeds.salon.com/salon/news',
                  'http://www.foxnews.com/xmlfeed/rss/0,4313,0,00.rss',
                  'http://www.foxnews.com/xmlfeed/rss/0,4313,80,00.rss',
                  'http://www.foxnews.com/xmlfeed/rss/0,4313,81,00.rss',
                  'http://rss.cnn.com/rss/edition.rss',
                  'http://rss.cnn.com/rss/edition_world.rss',
                  'http://rss.cnn.com/rss/edition_us.rss']
```

The feed list includes a variety of sources, drawing primarily from the Top News, World News, and U.S. News sections. You can modify the feed list to include whatever you like, but you should aim to have some overlapping themes. If none of the articles have anything in common, it will be very difficult for the algorithm to extract important features, and you'll end up with features that don't really mean anything.

Downloading Sources

The feature-extraction algorithm, like the clustering algorithm, takes a big matrix of numbers, with each row representing an item and each column representing a property. In this case, the different articles will be the rows, and words will be the columns. The numbers will represent the number of times a word appears in a given article. Thus, the following matrix tells you that article A contains the word "hurricane" three times, article B contains the word "democrats" twice, and so on.

```
articles = ['A','B','C',...
words = ['hurricane','democrats','world',...
matrix = [[3,0,1,...]
          [1,2,0,...]
          [0,0,2,...]
               ...]
```

To get from a feed to a matrix of this kind, you'll need a couple of methods similar to those used in previous chapters. The first method removes any images and markup from the articles. Add stripHTML to *newsfeatures.py*:

```
def stripHTML(h):
  p=''
  s=0
  for c in h:
    if c=='<': s=1
    elif c=='>':
      s=0
      p+=' '
    elif s==0: p+=c
  return p
```

You'll also need a way to separate the words in the text, as you've done in previous chapters. If you created a more sophisticated way to separate words than the simple alphanumeric regular expression, you can reuse that function here; otherwise, add this function to *newsfeatures.py*:

```
def separatewords(text):
  splitter=re.compile('\\W*')
  return [s.lower( ) for s in splitter.split(text) if len(s)>3]
```

The next function loops over all the feeds, parses them with the feedparser, strips out the HTML, and extracts the individual words using the previously defined functions. It keeps track of how many times each word is used overall, as well as how many times it is used in each individual article.

Add this function to *newsfeatures.py*:

```
def getarticlewords( ):
  allwords={}
  articlewords=[]
  articletitles=[]
  ec=0
  # Loop over every feed
  for feed in feedlist:
    f=feedparser.parse(feed)

    # Loop over every article
    for e in f.entries:
      # Ignore identical articles
      if e.title in articletitles: continue

      # Extract the words
      txt=e.title.encode('utf8')+stripHTML(e.description.encode('utf8'))
      words=separatewords(txt)
      articlewords.append({})
      articletitles.append(e.title)

      # Increase the counts for this word in allwords and in articlewords
      for word in words:
        allwords.setdefault(word,0)
        allwords[word]+=1
        articlewords[ec].setdefault(word,0)
        articlewords[ec][word]+=1
      ec+=1
  return allwords,articlewords,articletitles
```

The function has three variables:

- allwords keeps a count of word usage across all the different articles. This will be used to determine which words should be considered parts of features.
- articlewords are the counts of the words in each article.
- articletitles is a list of the titles of the articles.

Converting to a Matrix

Now you have dictionaries of counts for the words in all articles, as well as counts for each article, all of which have to be converted into the matrix that was described earlier. The first step is to create a list of words to be used as the columns of the matrix. To reduce the size of the matrix, you can eliminate words that appear in only a couple of articles (which probably won't be useful for finding features), and also those that appear in too many articles.

To start, try only including words that appear in more than three articles but fewer than 60 percent of the total. You can then use a nested list comprehension to create the matrix, which right now is just a list of lists. Each of the nested lists is created by looping over wordvec and looking up the word in the dictionary—if the word is absent, a 0 is added; otherwise, the word count for that article and word is added.

Add the makematrix function to *newsfeatures.py*:

```
def makematrix(allw,articlew):
  wordvec=[]

  # Only take words that are common but not too common
  for w,c in allw.items():
    if c>3 and c<len(articlew)*0.6:
      wordvec.append(w)

  # Create the word matrix
  l1=[[(word in f and f[word] or 0) for word in wordvec] for f in articlew]
  return l1,wordvec
```

Start a Python session and import newsfeatures. You can then try parsing the feeds and creating the matrix.

```
$ python
>>> import newsfeatures
>>> allw,artw,artt= newsfeatures.getarticlewords()
>>> wordmatrix,wordvec= newsfeatures.makematrix(allw,artw)
>>> wordvec[0:10]
['increase', 'under', 'regan', 'rise', 'announced', 'force',
 'street', 'new', 'men', 'reported']
>>> artt[1]
u'Fatah, Hamas men abducted freed: sources'
>>> wordmatrix[1][0:10]
[0, 0, 0, 0, 0, 0, 0, 0, 1, 0]
```

In this example, the first 10 words of the word vector are displayed. The second article's title is shown, followed by the first 10 values of its row in the word matrix. You can see that the article contains the word "men" once and none of the other words in the first 10 values.

Previous Approaches

In previous chapters, you've looked at different ways of dealing with word counts for textual data. For purposes of comparison, it's useful to try these first and see what sort of results you get, then compare them with the results of feature extraction. If you have the code that you wrote for those chapters, you can import those modules and try them here on your feeds. If not, don't worry—this section illustrates how these methods work on the sample data.

Bayesian Classification

Bayesian classification is, as you've seen, a supervised learning method. If you were to try to use the classifier built in Chapter 6, you would first be required to classify several examples of stories to train the classifier. The classifier would then be able to put later stories into your predefined categories. Besides the obvious downside of having to do the initial training, this approach also suffers from the limitation that the developer has to decide what all the different categories are. All the classifiers you've seen so far, such as decision trees and support-vector machines, will have this same limitation when applied to a dataset of this kind.

If you'd like to try the Bayesian classifier on this dataset, you'll need to place the module you built in Chapter 6 in your working directory. You can use the articlewords dictionary as is for the feature set of each article.

Try this in your Python session:

```
>>> def wordmatrixfeatures(x):
...     return [wordvec[w] for w in range(len(x)) if x[w]>0]
...
>>> wordmatrixfeatures(wordmatrix[0])
['forces', 'said', 'security', 'attacks', 'iraq', 'its', 'pentagon',...]
>>> import docclass
>>> classifier=docclass.naivebayes(wordmatrixfeatures)
>>> classifier.setdb('newstest.db')
>>> artt[0]
u'Attacks in Iraq at record high: Pentagon'
>>> # Train this as an 'iraq' story
>>> classifier.train(wordmatrix[0],'iraq')
>>> artt[1]
u'Bush signs U.S.-India nuclear deal'
>>> # Train this as an 'india' story
>>> classifier.train(wordmatrix[1],'india')
>>> artt[2]
u'Fatah, Hamas men abducted freed: sources'
>>> # How is this story classified?
>>> classifier.classify(wordmatrix[1])
u'iraq'
```

With the examples used, there are many possible themes and only a few stories in each one. The Bayesian classifier will eventually learn all the themes, but since it requires training on several examples per theme, this classifier is better suited to fewer categories with more examples in each category.

Clustering

The other unsupervised approach you've seen so far is clustering, which we covered in Chapter 3.

The data in Chapter 3 was arranged in a matrix identical to the one you've just created. If you still have the code from that chapter, you can import it into your Python session and run the clustering algorithm on the matrix:

```
>>> import clusters
>>> clust=clusters.hcluster(wordmatrix)
>>> clusters.drawdendrogram(clust,artt,jpeg='news.jpg')
```

Figure 10-1 shows a potential result of this clustering, which will now be saved in a file called *news.jpg*.

As expected, similar news stories are grouped together. This works even better than the blog example in Chapter 3 because various publications tend to report on exactly the same stories using similar language. However, a couple of examples in Figure 10-1 illustrate the point that you don't always get an accurate picture by putting news stories in "buckets." For instance, "The Nose Knows Better," a health article, is grouped with an article about the Suffolk Strangler. Sometimes news articles, like people, can't be pigeonholed and have to be considered unique.

If you like, you can rotate the matrix to see how the words in the stories cluster together. In this example, words like "station," "solar," and "astronauts" group closely together.

Non-Negative Matrix Factorization

The technique for extracting the important features of the data is called *non-negative matrix factorization* (NMF). This is one of the most sophisticated techniques covered in this book, and it requires a bit more explanation and a quick introduction to linear algebra. Everything you need to know will be covered in this section.

A Quick Introduction to Matrix Math

To understand what NMF is doing, you'll first need to understand a bit about matrix multiplication. If you're already familiar with linear algebra, you can safely skip this section.

An example of matrix multiplication is shown in Figure 10-2.

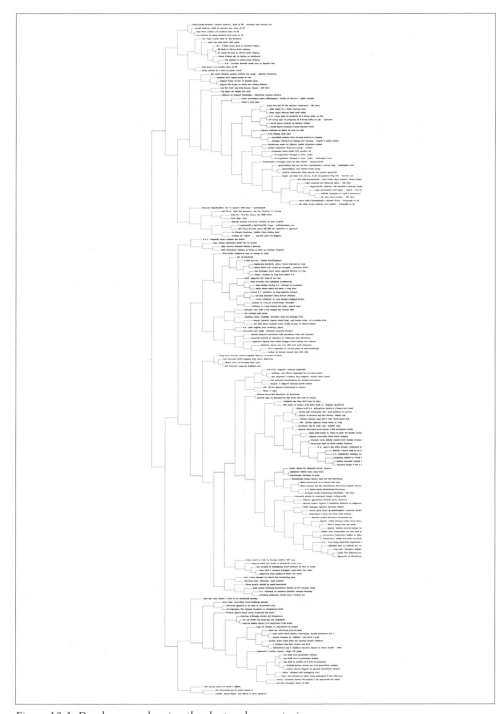

Figure 10-1. Dendrogram showing the clustered news stories

$$\begin{bmatrix} 1 & 4 \\ 0 & 3 \end{bmatrix} X \begin{bmatrix} 0 & 3 & 0 \\ 2 & 1 & 4 \end{bmatrix} = \begin{bmatrix} 1*0 + 4*2 & 1*3 + 4*1 & 1*0 + 4*4 \\ 0*0 + 3*2 & 0*3 + 3*1 & 0*0 + 3*4 \end{bmatrix} = \begin{bmatrix} 8 & 7 & 16 \\ 6 & 3 & 12 \end{bmatrix}$$

A   B

Figure 10-2. Example of matrix multiplication

This figure shows how two matrices are multiplied together. When multiplying matrices, the first matrix (Matrix A in the figure) must have the same number of columns as the second matrix (Matrix B) has rows. In this case, Matrix A has two columns and Matrix B has two rows. The resulting matrix (Matrix C) will have the same number of rows as Matrix A and the same number of columns as Matrix B.

The value for each cell in Matrix C is calculated by multiplying the values from the same row in Matrix A by the values from the same column in Matrix B and adding all the products together. Looking at the value in the top left corner of Matrix C, you can see that the values from the first row of Matrix A are multiplied by the corresponding values from the first column of Matrix B. These are added together to get the final value. The other cells in Matrix C are all calculated in the same way.

Another common matrix operation is *transposing*. This means that the columns become rows and the rows become columns. It's usually indicated with a "T," as shown in Figure 10-3.

$$\begin{pmatrix} a & d \\ b & e \\ c & f \end{pmatrix}^T = \begin{pmatrix} a & b & c \\ d & e & f \end{pmatrix}$$

Figure 10-3. Transposing a matrix

You'll be using the transpose and multiplication operations in the implementation of the NMF algorithm.

What Does This Have to Do with the Articles Matrix?

So far, what you have is a matrix of articles with word counts. The goal is to *factorize* this matrix, which means finding two smaller matrices that can be multiplied together to reconstruct this one. The two smaller matrices are:

The features matrix

This matrix has a row for each feature and a column for each word. The values indicate how important a word is to a feature. Each feature should represent a theme that emerged from a set of articles, so you might expect an article about a new TV show to have a high weight for the word "television."

The weights matrix

This matrix maps the features to the articles matrix. Each row is an article and each column is a feature. The values state how much each feature applies to each article.

The features matrix, like the articles matrix, has one column for every word. Each row of the matrix is a different feature, so a feature is a list of word weights. Figure 10-4 shows an example portion of a feature matrix.

	hurricane	democrats	florida	elections
feature 1	2	0	3	0
feature 2	0	2	0	1
feature 3	0	0	1	1

Figure 10-4. Portion of a features matrix

Since each row is a feature that consists of a combination of words, it should become clear that reconstructing the articles matrix is a matter of combining rows from the features matrix in different amounts. The weights matrix, an example of which is shown in Figure 10-5, maps the features to the articles. It has one column for every feature and one row for every article.

	feature 1	feature 2	feature 3
hurricane in Florida	10	0	0
Democrats sweep elections	0	8	1
Democrats dispute Florida ballots	0	5	6

Figure 10-5. Portion of weights matrix

Figure 10-6 shows how the articles matrix is reconstructed by multiplying the weights matrix by the features matrix.

	hurricane	democrats	florida	elections			feature 1	feature 2	feature 3			hurricane	democrats	florida	elections
F1	2	0	3	0	hurricane...	10	0	0	hurricane...					
F2	0	2	0	1	**X** ...sweep...	0	8	1	= ...sweep...					
F3	0	0	1	1	Florida ballots	0	5	6	Florida ballots					

Figure 10-6. Multiplying the weights matrix by the features matrix

If the number of features are the same as the number of articles, the best answer is to have one feature that perfectly matches each article. However, the purpose of using matrix factorization here is to reduce a large set of observations (the articles, in this case) to a smaller set that captures their common features. Ideally, this smaller set of features could be combined with different weights to perfectly reproduce the original dataset, but in practice this is very unlikely, so the algorithm aims to reproduce it as closely as possible.

The reason it's called *non-negative* matrix factorization is that it returns features and weights with no negative values. In practice, this means that all the features must have positive values, which is true for our example because an article cannot have negative occurrences of words. It also means that features cannot take away pieces of other features—NMF will not find results that explicitly exclude certain words. Although this restriction may prevent the algorithm from coming up with the best possible factorization, the results are often easier to interpret.

Using NumPy

Python does not come standard with functions for matrix operations. While it's possible to code them yourself, a better option is to install a package called *NumPy*, which not only provides a matrix object and all the necessary matrix operations, but is comparable in performance to commercial mathematical software. You can download NumPy from *http://numpy.scipy.org*.

For more information on installing NumPy, see Appendix A.

NumPy provides a matrix object that can be instantiated with nested lists and is very much like the one you created for the articles. To see this in action, you can import NumPy into your Python session and create a matrix:

```
>>> from numpy import *
>>> l1=[[1,2,3],[4,5,6]]
>>> l1
[[1, 2, 3], [4, 5, 6]]
>>> m1=matrix(l1)
>>> m1
matrix([[1, 2, 3],
        [4, 5, 6]])
```

The matrix objects support mathematical operations such as multiplication and addition using standard operators. Transposing the matrix is accomplished with the transpose function:

```
>>> m2=matrix([[1,2],[3,4],[5,6]])
>>> m2
matrix([[1, 2],
        [3, 4],
        [5, 6]])
>>> m1*m2
matrix([[22, 28],
        [49, 64]])
```

The shape function returns the number of rows and columns in the matrix, which is useful for looping over all the elements in a matrix:

```
>>> shape(m1)
(2, 3)
>>> shape(m2)
(3, 2)
```

Finally, NumPy also provides a fast array object, which, like a matrix, can be multi-dimensional. Matrices can be easily converted to arrays and vice versa. An array behaves differently from a matrix when doing multiplication; arrays can only be multiplied if they have exactly the same shape, and every value is multiplied by the corresponding value in the other array. Thus:

```
>>> a1=m1.A
>>> a1
array([[1, 2, 3],
       [4, 5, 6]])
>>> a2=array([[1,2,3],[1,2,3]])
>>> a1*a2
array([[ 1,  4,  9],
       [ 4, 10, 18]])
```

The fast performance of NumPy is necessary for the NMF algorithm you'll see next, which requires many matrix operations.

The Algorithm

The algorithm you'll be using to factorize the matrix was first published in the late 1990s, making it the newest algorithm covered by this book. It has been shown to perform very well on certain problems, such as automatically determining different facial features from a collection of photographs.

The algorithm tries to reconstruct the articles matrix as closely as possible by calculating the best features and weights matrices. It's useful in this case to have a way to measure just how close the result is. The difcost function loops over every value in two equal-sized matrices and sums the squares of the differences between them.

Create a new file called *nmf.py* and add the difcost function:

```
from numpy import *

def difcost(a,b):
  dif=0
  # Loop over every row and column in the matrix
  for i in range(shape(a)[0]):
    for j in range(shape(a)[1]):
      # Add together the differences
      dif+=pow(a[i,j]-b[i,j],2)
  return dif
```

Now you need a way to gradually update the matrices to reduce the cost function. If you've read Chapter 5, you'll notice that you have a cost function and can definitely use annealing or swarm optimization to search for a good solution. However, a more efficient way to search for good solutions is to use *multiplicative update rules*.

The derivation of these rules is beyond the scope of this chapter, but if you're interested in reading more about it, you can find the original paper at *http://hebb.mit.edu/people/seung/papers/nmfconverge.pdf*.

The rules generate four new update matrices. In these descriptions, the original articles matrix is referred to as the *data matrix*:

hn
> The transposed weight matrix multiplied by the data matrix

hd
> The transposed weights matrix multiplied by the weights matrix multiplied by the features matrix

wn
> The data matrix multiplied by the transposed features matrix

wd
> The weights matrix multiplied by the features matrix multiplied by the transposed features matrix

To update the features and weights matrices, all these matrices are converted to arrays. Every value in the features matrix is multiplied by the corresponding value in *hn* and divided by the corresponding value in *hd*. Likewise, every value in the weights matrix is multiplied by the value in *wn* and divided by the value in wd.

The factorize function performs these calculations. Add factorize to *nmf.py*:

```
def factorize(v,pc=10,iter=50):
  ic=shape(v)[0]
  fc=shape(v)[1]

  # Initialize the weight and feature matrices with random values
  w=matrix([[random.random() for j in range(pc)] for i in range(ic)])
  h=matrix([[random.random() for i in range(fc)] for i in range(pc)])

  # Perform operation a maximum of iter times
  for i in range(iter):
    wh=w*h

    # Calculate the current difference
    cost=difcost(v,wh)

    if i%10==0: print cost

    # Terminate if the matrix has been fully factorized
    if cost==0: break
```

```
# Update feature matrix
hn=(transpose(w)*v)
hd=(transpose(w)*w*h)

h=matrix(array(h)*array(hn)/array(hd))

# Update weights matrix
wn=(v*transpose(h))
wd=(w*h*transpose(h))

w=matrix(array(w)*array(wn)/array(wd))

return w,h
```

The function to factorize the matrix requires you to specify the number of features you want to find. In some cases, you'll know how many features you want to find (two voices in a recording or five major news themes of the day), and in other cases, you'll have no idea how many to specify. There's generally no way to automatically determine the correct number of components, but experimentation can help find the appropriate range.

You can try running this on the matrix m1*m2 from your session to see if the algorithm finds a solution similar to the original matrix:

```
>>> import nmf
>>> w,h= nmf.factorize(m1*m2,pc=3,iter=100)
7632.94395925
0.0364091326734
...
1.12810164789e-017
6.8747907867e-020
>>> w*h
matrix([[ 22.,   28.],
        [ 49.,   64.]])
>>> m1*m2
matrix([[22, 28],
        [49, 64]])
```

The algorithm manages to find a weights and features matrix that multiplies together perfectly to match the original. You can also try this on the articles matrix to see how well it can extract the important features (this may take some time):

```
>>> v=matrix(wordmatrix)
>>> weights,feat=nmf.factorize(v,pc=20,iter=50)
1712024.47944
2478.13274637
2265.75996871
2229.07352131
2211.42204622
```

The variable feat now holds the features of the news articles, and weights holds the values that indicate how much each feature applies to each article. Looking at the matrix won't do you much good, however, so you'll need a way to view and interpret the results.

Displaying the Results

Exactly how you view the results is a little complicated. Every feature in the features matrix has a weighting that indicates how strongly each word applies to that feature, so you can try displaying the top five or ten words in each feature to see what the most important words are in that feature. The equivalent column in the weights matrix tells you how much this particular feature applies to each of the articles, so it's also interesting to show the top three articles and see how strongly this feature applies to all of them.

Add a new function called showfeatures to *newsfeatures.py*:

```python
from numpy import *
def showfeatures(w,h,titles,wordvec,out='features.txt'):
  outfile=file(out,'w')
  pc,wc=shape(h)
  toppatterns=[[] for i in range(len(titles))]
  patternnames=[]

  # Loop over all the features
  for i in range(pc):
    slist=[]
    # Create a list of words and their weights
    for j in range(wc):
      slist.append((h[i,j],wordvec[j]))
    # Reverse sort the word list
    slist.sort()
    slist.reverse()

    # Print the first six elements
    n=[s[1] for s in slist[0:6]]
    outfile.write(str(n)+'\n')
    patternnames.append(n)

    # Create a list of articles for this feature
    flist=[]
    for j in range(len(titles)):
      # Add the article with its weight
      flist.append((w[j,i],titles[j]))
      toppatterns[j].append((w[j,i],i,titles[j]))

    # Reverse sort the list
    flist.sort()
    flist.reverse()

    # Show the top 3 articles
    for f in flist[0:3]:
      outfile.write(str(f)+'\n')
    outfile.write('\n')

  outfile.close()
  # Return the pattern names for later use
  return toppatterns,patternnames
```

This function loops over each of the features and creates a list of all the word weights and words from the word vector. It sorts the list so that the most heavily weighted words for the feature appear at the start of the list, and then it prints the first 10 of these words. This should give you a good idea of the theme represented by this particular feature. The function returns the top patterns and pattern names, so they only have to be calculated once and can be used again in the showarticles function below.

After displaying the feature, the function loops over the article titles and sorts them according to their value in the weights matrix for that article and feature. It then prints the three articles that are most strongly linked to the feature, along with the value from the weights matrix. You'll see that sometimes a feature is important for several related articles, and sometimes it only applies to one.

You can now call this function to view the features:

```
>>> reload(newsfeatures)
<module 'newsfeatures' from 'newsfeatures.py'>
>>> topp,pn= newsfeatures.showfeatures(weights,feat,artt,wordvec)
```

Because the results are quite long, the code will save them to a text file. The function was told to create 20 different features. There are obviously more than 20 themes among the hundreds of articles, but the most prominent ones have, we hope, been discovered. For example, consider:

```
[u'palestinian', u'elections', u'abbas', u'fatah', u'monday', u'new']
(14.189453058041485, u'US Backs Early Palestinian Elections - ABC News')
(12.748863898714507, u'Abbas Presses for New Palestinian Elections Despite Violence')
(11.286669969240645, u'Abbas Determined to Go Ahead With Vote')
```

This feature clearly shows a set of words pertaining to Palestinian elections and a nice set of related articles. Because the results are driven by a portion of the body of the article as well as the titles, you can see the first and third articles are both associated with this feature even though they share no title words. Also, since the most important terms are derived from words that are used in many articles, the words "palestinian" and "elections" appear first.

Some features do not have such a clear set of articles associated with them, but they still show interesting results. Consider this example:

```
[u'cancer', u'fat', u'low', u'breast', u'news', u'diet']
(29.808285029040864, u'Low-Fat Diet May Help Breast Cancer')
(2.3737882572527238, u'Big Apple no longer Fat City')
(2.3430261571622881, u'The Nose Knows Better')
```

Clearly, the feature is very strongly tied to an article about breast cancer. However, the weaker associations are also health-related articles that have some words in common with the first article.

Displaying by Article

An alternative way to display the data is to show each article and the top three features that apply to it. This allows you to see if an article consists of equal amounts of several themes or a single strong theme.

Add a new function, showarticles, to *newsfeatures.py*:

```
def showarticles(titles,toppatterns,patternnames,out='articles.txt'):
  outfile=file(out,'w')

  # Loop over all the articles
  for j in range(len(titles)):
    outfile.write(titles[j].encode('utf8')+'\n')

    # Get the top features for this article and
    # reverse sort them
    toppatterns[j].sort()
    toppatterns[j].reverse()

    # Print the top three patterns
    for i in range(3):
      outfile.write(str(toppatterns[j][i][0])+' '+
                    str(patternnames[toppatterns[j][i][1]])+'\n')
    outfile.write('\n')

  outfile.close()
```

Since the top features for each article were calculated by showfeatures, this function simply loops over all the article titles, prints them, and then displays the top patterns for each article.

To use this function, reload *newsfeatures.py* and call it with the titles and the results from showfeatures:

```
>>> reload(newsfeatures)
<module 'newsfeatures' from 'newsfeatures.py'>
>>> newsfeatures.showarticles(artt,topp,pn)
```

This will produce a file called *articles.txt*, which contains articles along with the most closely associated patterns. Here is a good example of an article that contains equal parts of two features:

```
Attacks in Iraq at record high: Pentagon
5.4890098003 [u'monday', u'said', u'oil', u'iraq', u'attacks', u'two']
5.33447632219 [u'gates', u'iraq', u'pentagon', u'washington', u'over', u'report']
0.618495842404 [u'its', u'iraqi', u'baghdad', u'red', u'crescent', u'monday']
```

Clearly, both of the features relate to Iraq, but not this article specifically, since it does not mention "oil" or "gates." By creating patterns that can be applied in combination, but that aren't specifically tailored to one article, the algorithm can cover many more articles with fewer patterns.

Here is an example of an article with a strong single feature that can't really be applied to anything else:

```
Yogi Bear Creator Joe Barbera Dies at 95
11.8474089735 [u'barbera', u'team', u'creator', u'hanna', u'dies', u'bear']
2.21373704749 [u'monday', u'said', u'oil', u'iraq', u'attacks', u'two']
0.421760994361 [u'man', u'was', u'year', u'his', u'old', u'kidnapping']
```

Since the number of patterns used is quite low, there will also likely be several *orphan* articles that are not similar to anything else and didn't get patterns of their own. Here is one example:

```
U.S. Files Charges in Fannie Mae Accounting Case
0.856087848533 [u'man', u'was', u'year', u'his', u'old', u'kidnapping']
0.784659717694 [u'climbers', u'hood', u'have', u'their', u'may', u'deaths']
0.562439763693 [u'will', u'smith', u'news', u'office', u'box', u'all']
```

You can see that the top features for this example are unrelated and appear to be almost random. Fortunately, the weights here are very small, so it's easy to see that the features don't really apply to this article.

Using Stock Market Data

As well as dealing with somewhat nominal data like word counts, NMF is suited for problems involving true numerical data. This section will show how the same algorithm can be applied to *trading volume* in the United States stock market using data downloaded from Yahoo! Finance. This data may show patterns of important trading days or the ways that underlying factors can drive the volume of multiple stocks.

Financial markets are considered a quintessential example of collective intelligence because they have a great number of participants acting independently based on different information and biases and producing a small set of outputs, such as price and volume. It has proven extremely difficult for individuals to do a better job than the collective in predicting future prices. There is a large body of academic research on the ways that groups of people are more successful at setting prices in a financial market than any individual could possibly be.

What Is Trading Volume?

The trading volume for a specific stock is the number of shares that are bought and sold within a given period, usually one day. Figure 10-8 shows a chart of Yahoo! stock, which has the ticker symbol *YHOO*. The line at the top is the *closing price*, the price of the last transaction of the day. The bar chart below shows the trading volume.

You'll notice that the volume tends to be much higher on days when there is a big change in the stock price. This often happens when a company makes a major announcement or releases financial results. Spikes can also occur due to news about the company or the industry. In the absence of external events, trading volume is usually, but not always, constant for a given stock.

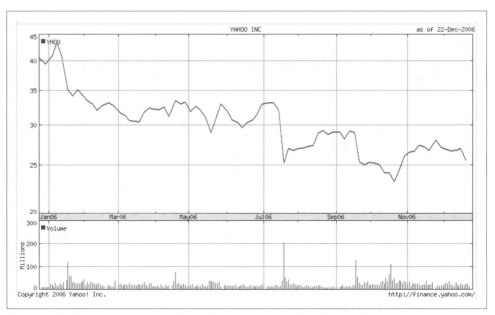

Figure 10-7. Stock chart showing price and trading volume

In this section, you'll be looking at volume for a set of stocks in a time series. This will let you search for patterns of changes in volume that affect multiple stocks at once, or for events that are so influential they become their own features. Volume is used instead of closing price because NMF tries to find positive features that can be added together; prices often move down in response to events, and NMF will not find negative features. Volume, however, is more easily modeled as having a basal level that can increase in response to outside influence, making it suitable for positive matrices.

Downloading Data from Yahoo! Finance

Yahoo! Finance is an excellent resource for all kinds of financial data, including stock prices, options, currency exchange rates, and bond interest rates. It also conveniently allows the downloading of historical stock volume and price data in an easy-to-process CSV format. By accessing a URL such as *http://ichart.finance.yahoo.com/table.csv?s=YHOO&d=11&e=26&f=2006&g=d&a=3&b=12&c=1996&ignore=.csv*, you can download a list of daily data for the stock in a comma-separated file, the first few lines of which look like this:

```
Date,Open,High,Low,Close,Volume,Adj. Close*
22-Dec-06,25.67,25.88,25.45,25.55,14666100,25.55
21-Dec-06,25.71,25.75,25.13,25.48,27050600,25.48
20-Dec-06,26.24,26.31,25.54,25.59,24905600,25.59
19-Dec-06,26.05,26.50,25.91,26.41,18973800,26.41
18-Dec-06,26.89,26.97,26.07,26.30,19431200,26.30
```

Each line contains the date, open and close prices, high and low prices, volume, and adjusted close. The adjusted close takes into account that the stock may have split or paid dividends, and it can be used to calculate exactly how much money you would have made if you owned the stock between two different dates.

For this example, you'll get the volume data for a set of stocks. Create a new file called *stockvolume.py* and add the following code, which downloads the comma-separated files for a list of ticker symbols and puts them in a dictionary. It also tracks which of them has the smallest number of days recorded, which will be used as the vertical size of the observations matrix:

```
import nmf
import urllib2
from numpy import *

tickers=['YHOO','AVP','BIIB','BP','CL','CVX',
         'DNA','EXPE','GOOG','PG','XOM','AMGN']

shortest=300
prices={}
dates=None

for t in tickers:
  # Open the URL
  rows=urllib2.urlopen('http://ichart.finance.yahoo.com/table.csv?'+\
                       's=%s&d=11&e=26&f=2006&g=d&a=3&b=12&c=1996'%t +\
                       '&ignore=.csv').readlines()

  # Extract the volume field from every line
  prices[t]=[float(r.split(',')[5]) for r in rows[1:] if r.strip()!='']
  if len(prices[t])<shortest: shortest=len(prices[t])

  if not dates:
    dates=[r.split(',')[0] for r in rows[1:] if r.strip()!='']
```

This code opens the URL for each ticker symbol and downloads the data. It then creates a list by splitting each line on commas and taking the float value of the fifth element, which is the trading volume for that stock.

Preparing a Matrix

The next step is to turn this into a matrix of observations that can be fed to the NMF function. This is simply a matter of creating a nested list in which each interior list represents the total volume over a set of stocks for each day. For example, consider the following:

```
[[4453500.0, 842400.0, 1396100.0, 1883100.0, 1281900.0,...]
 [5000100.0, 1486900.0, 3317500.0, 2966700.0, 1941200.0,...
 [5222500.0, 1383100.0, 3421500.0, 2885300.0, 1994900.0,...
 [6028700.0, 1477000.0, 8178200.0, 2919600.0, 2061000.0,...]
 ...]
```

This list indicates that on the most recent day, 4,453,500 shares of AMGN were traded, 842,400 shares of AVP were traded, and so on. On the previous day, the numbers were 5,000,100 and 1,486,900, respectively. Compare this with the news stories example; the articles are now days, the words are now shares, and the word counts are trading volumes.

The matrix can be easily created with a list comprehension. The inner loop is over the list of tickers, and the outer loop is over the list of observations (days). Add this code to end of *stockvolume.py*:

```
l1=[[prices[tickers[i]][j]
     for i in range(len(tickers))]
     for j in range(shortest)]
```

Running NMF

Now all you have to do is call the `factorize` function from the `nmf` module. You'll need to specify the number of different features to search for; with a small set of stocks, four or five is probably good.

Add this code to end of *stockvolume.py*:

```
w,h= nmf.factorize(matrix(l1),pc=5)

print h
print w
```

You can now run this from the command line to see if it works:

```
$ python stockvolume.py
```

The matrices you see represent the weights and features. Each row in the features matrix is a feature, which is a set of trading volumes for the stocks that can be added to other features to recreate the trading volume data for that day. Each row in the weights matrix represents a specific day, and the values indicate how much each of the features applies to that day.

Displaying the Results

It's obviously difficult to interpret the matrices directly, so you'll need some code to display the features in a better way. What you'd like to see are the volume contributions of each feature to each stock, as well as the dates most strongly associated with those features.

Add this code to the end of *stockvolume.py*:

```
# Loop over all the features
for i in range(shape(h)[0]):
  print "Feature %d" %i
```

```
# Get the top stocks for this feature
ol=[(h[i,j],tickers[j]) for j in range(shape(h)[1])]
ol.sort()
ol.reverse()
for j in range(12):
  print ol[j]
print

# Show the top dates for this feature
porder=[(w[d,i],d) for d in range(300)]
porder.sort()
porder.reverse()
print [(p[0],dates[p[1]]) for p in porder[0:3]]
print
```

Because there will be a lot of text, it's probably best to redirect the output to a file. On the command line, enter:

```
$ python stockvolume.py > stockfeatures.txt
```

The *stockfeatures.txt* file now has a list of features, including which stocks they apply to most strongly and on which dates they appear most strongly. Here's one example, selected from the file because it shows a very high weight for a particular stock on a single date:

```
Feature 4
(74524113.213559602, 'YHOO')
(6165711.6749675209, 'GOOG')
(5539688.0538382991, 'XOM')
(2537144.3952459987, 'CVX')
(1283794.0604679288, 'PG')
(1160743.3352889531, 'BP')
(1040776.8531969623, 'AVP')
(811575.28223116993, 'BIIB')
(679243.76923785623, 'DNA')
(377356.4897763988, 'CL')
(353682.37800343882, 'EXPE')
(0.31345784102699459, 'AMGN')

[(7.950090052903934, '19-Jul-06'),
 (4.7278341805021329, '19-Sep-06'),
 (4.6049947721971245, '18-Jan-06')]
```

You can see that this feature applies almost exclusively to YHOO, and applies very strongly on July 19, 2006. As it happens, that was the day of a massive spike in trading volume for Yahoo!, which issued earnings guidance on that day.

Another feature that applies more evenly to a couple of companies is this one:

```
Feature 2
(46151801.813632453, 'GOOG')
(24298994.720555616, 'YHOO')
(10606419.91092159, 'PG')
(7711296.6887903402, 'CVX')
(4711899.0067871698, 'BIIB')
```

```
(4423180.7694432881, 'XOM')
(3430492.5096612777, 'DNA')
(2882726.8877627672, 'EXPE')
(2232928.7181202639, 'CL')
(2043732.4392455407, 'AVP')
(1934010.2697886101, 'BP')
(1801256.8664912341, 'AMGN')

[(2.9757765047938824, '20-Jan-06'),
 (2.8627791325829448, '28-Feb-06'),
 (2.356157903021133, '31-Mar-06'),
```

This feature represents large spikes in Google's trading volume, which in the top three cases were due to news events. The strongest day, January 20th, was the day that Google announced it would not give information about its search engine usage to the government. What's really interesting about this feature is that events that affect Google's trading volume also seem to contribute heavily to Yahoo!'s trading volume, even if they have little to do with Yahoo!. The second date on the list is a volume spike that occurred when Google's Chief Financial Officer announced that growth was slowing; the chart shows that Yahoo! also had increased trading that day, possibly as people considered how the information might affect Yahoo!.

It's important to recognize the difference between what is being shown here and simply finding the correlations between stock volumes. The two features above show that there are times when Google and Yahoo! have similar volume patterns and other times when they move completely distinctly. Looking only at correlations would average all these relationships and would not compensate for the fact that there were simply a few days when Yahoo! made announcements that had a big impact.

This example uses a small selection of stocks to illustrate a simple point, but using a larger selection of stocks and searching for more patterns would reveal even more complex interactions.

Exercises

1. *Varying news sources.* The example in this chapter used mostly pure news sources. Try adding some top political blogs. (*http://technorati.com* is a good place to find blogs.) How does this affect the results? Are there features that apply strongly to political commentary? Are news stories with related commentary grouped easily?

2. *K-means clustering.* Hierarchical clustering was used on the articles matrix, but what happens if you use K-means clustering? How many clusters do you need to get good separation of different stories? How does this compare to the number of features you need to use to extract all the themes?

3. *Optimizing for factorization.* Can you use the optimization code that you built in Chapter 5 to factorize the matrix? Is this a lot faster or slower? How do the results compare?

4. *Stopping criteria.* The NMF algorithm in this chapter stops when the cost has dropped to 0 or when it reaches the maximum number of iterations. Sometimes improvement will almost entirely stop once a very good though not perfect solution has been reached. Modify the code so it stops when the cost is not improving by more than one percent per iteration.

5. *Alternative display methods.* The functions given in this chapter for displaying results are simple and show important features, but they lose a lot of context. Can you think of other ways of displaying results? Try writing a function that displays the articles in their original text with key words from each feature highlighted, or perhaps a trading volume chart with important dates clearly shown.

CHAPTER 11

Evolving Intelligence

Throughout this book you've seen a number of different problems, and in each case you used an algorithm that was suited to solve that particular problem. In some of the examples, you had to tweak the parameters or use optimization to search for a good set of parameters. This chapter will look at a different way to approach problems. Instead of choosing an algorithm to apply to a problem, you'll make a program that attempts to automatically build the best program to solve a problem. Essentially, you'll be creating an algorithm that creates algorithms.

To do this, you will use a technique called *genetic programming*. Since this is the last chapter in which you'll learn a completely new type of algorithm, I've picked a topic that is new, exciting, and being actively researched. This chapter is a little different from the others because it doesn't use any open APIs or public datasets, and because programs that can modify themselves based on their interactions with many people are an interesting and different kind of collective intelligence. Genetic programming is a very large topic about which many books have been written, so you'll only get an introduction here, but I hope it's enough to get you excited about the possibilities and perhaps to research and experiment on your own.

The two problems in this chapter are recreating a mathematical function given a dataset, and automatically creating an AI (artificial intelligence) player for a simple board game. This is just a very small sampling of the possibilities of genetic programming—computational power is really the only constraint on the types of problems it can be used to solve.

What Is Genetic Programming?

Genetic programming is a machine-learning technique inspired by the theory of biological evolution. It generally works by starting with a large set of programs (referred to as the *population*), which are either randomly generated or hand-designed and are known to be somewhat good solutions. The programs are then made to compete in some user-defined task. This may be a game in which the programs compete against each other directly, or it may be an individual test to see which program performs better. After the competition, a ranked list of the programs from best to worst can be determined.

Next—and here's where evolution comes in—the best programs are replicated and modified in two different ways. The simpler way is *mutation*, in which certain parts of the program are altered very slightly in a random manner in the hope that this will make a good solution even better. The other way to modify a program is through *crossover* (sometimes referred to as *breeding*), which involves taking a portion of one of the best programs and replacing it with a portion of one of the other best programs. This replication and modification procedure creates many new programs that are based on, but different from, the best programs.

At each stage, the quality of the programs is calculated using a *fitness function*. Since the size of the population is kept constant, many of the *worst* programs are eliminated from the population to make room for the new programs. The new population is referred to as "the next generation," and the whole procedure is then repeated. Because the best programs are being kept and modified, it is expected that with each generation they will get better and better, in much the same way that teenagers can be smarter than their parents.

New generations are created until a termination condition is reached, which, depending on the problem, can be that:

- The perfect solution has been found.
- A good enough solution has been found.
- The solution has not improved for several generations.
- The number of generations has reached a specified limit.

For some problems, such as determining a mathematical function that correctly maps a set of inputs to an output, a perfect solution is possible. For others, such as a board game, there may not be a perfect solution, since the quality of a solution depends on the strategy of the program's adversary.

An overview of the genetic programming process is shown as a flowchart in Figure 11-1.

Genetic Programming Versus Genetic Algorithms

Chapter 5 introduced a related set of algorithms known as *genetic algorithms*. Genetic algorithms are an optimization technique that use the idea of evolutionary pressure to choose the best result. With any form of optimization, you have already selected an algorithm or metric and you're simply trying to find the best parameters for it.

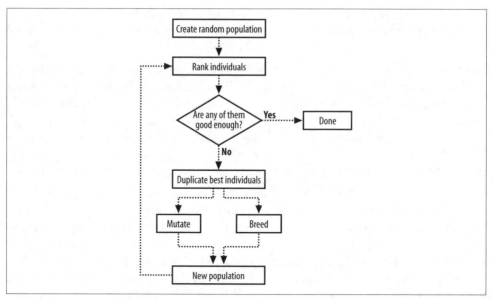

Figure 11-1. Genetic programming overview

Successes of Genetic Programming

Genetic programming has been around since the 1980s, but it is very computationally intensive, and with the computing power that was available at the time, it couldn't be used for anything more than simple problems. As computers have gotten faster, however, people have been able to apply genetic programming to sophisticated problems. Many previously patented inventions have been rediscovered or improved using genetic programming, and recently several new patentable inventions have been designed by computers.

The genetic programming technique has been applied in designing antennas for NASA, and in photonic crystals, optics, quantum computing systems, and other scientific inventions. It has also been used to develop programs for playing many games, such as chess and backgammon. In 1998, researchers from Carnegie Mellon University entered a robot team that was programmed entirely using genetic programming into the Robo-Cup soccer contest, and placed in the middle of the pack.

Like optimization, genetic programming requires a way to measure how good a solution is; but unlike optimization, the solutions are not just a set of parameters being applied to a given algorithm. Instead, the algorithm itself and all its parameters are designed automatically by means of evolutionary pressure.

Programs As Trees

In order to create programs that can be tested, mutated, and bred, you'll need a way to represent and run them from within your Python code. The representation has to lend itself to easy modification and, more importantly, has to be guaranteed to be an actual program—which means generating random strings and trying to treat them as Python code won't work. Researchers have come up with a few different ways to represent programs for genetic programming, and the most commonly used is a tree representation.

Most programming languages, when compiled or interpreted, are first turned into a *parse tree*, which is very similar to what you'll be working with here. (The programming language Lisp and its variants are essentially ways of entering a parse tree directly.) An example of a parse tree is shown in Figure 11-2.

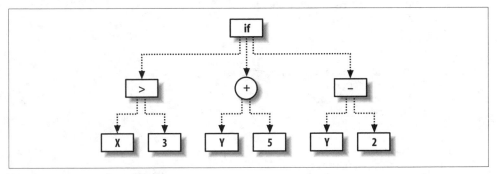

Figure 11-2. Example program tree

Each node represents either an operation on its child nodes or an endpoint, such as a parameter with a constant value. For example, the circular node is a sum operation on its two branches, in this case, the values Y and 5. Once this point is evaluated, it is given to the node above it, which in turn applies its own operation to its branches. You'll also notice that one of the nodes has the operation "if," which specifies that if its leftmost branch evaluates to true, return its center branch; if it doesn't, return its rightmost branch.

Traversing the complete tree, you can see that it corresponds to the Python function:

```
def func(x,y)
  if x>3:
    return y + 5
  else:
    return y - 2
```

At first, it might appear that these trees can only be used to build very simple functions. There are two things to consider here—first, the nodes that compose the tree can potentially be very complex functions, such as distance measures or

Gaussians. The second thing is that trees can be made recursive by referring to nodes higher up in the tree. Creating trees like this allows for loops and other more complicated control structures.

Representing Trees in Python

You're now ready to construct tree programs in Python. The trees are made up of nodes, which, depending on the functions associated with them, have some number of child nodes. Some of the nodes will return parameters passed to the program, others will return constants, and the most interesting ones will return operations on their child nodes.

Create a new file called *gp.py* and create four new classes called fwrapper, node, paramnode, and constnode:

```
from random import random,randint,choice
from copy import deepcopy
from math import log

class fwrapper:
  def __init__(self,function,childcount,name):
    self.function=function
    self.childcount=childcount
    self.name=name

class node:
  def __init__(self,fw,children):
    self.function=fw.function
    self.name=fw.name
    self.children=children

  def evaluate(self,inp):
    results=[n.evaluate(inp) for n in self.children]
    return self.function(results)

class paramnode:
  def __init__(self,idx):
    self.idx=idx

  def evaluate(self,inp):
    return inp[self.idx]

class constnode:
  def __init__(self,v):
    self.v=v
  def evaluate(self,inp):
    return self.v
```

The classes here are:

fwrapper

A wrapper for the functions that will be used on function nodes. Its member variables are the name of the function, the function itself, and the number of parameters it takes.

node

The class for function nodes (nodes with children). This is initialized with an fwrapper. When evaluate is called, it evaluates the child nodes and then applies the function to their results.

paramnode

The class for nodes that only return one of the parameters passed to the program. Its evaluate method returns the parameter specified by idx.

constnode

Nodes that return a constant value. The evaluate method simply returns the value with which it was initialized.

You'll also want some functions for the nodes to apply. To do this, you have to create functions and then give them names and parameter counts using fwrapper. Add this list of functions to *gp.py*:

```
addw=fwrapper(lambda l:l[0]+l[1],2,'add')
subw=fwrapper(lambda l:l[0]-l[1],2,'subtract')
mulw=fwrapper(lambda l:l[0]*l[1],2,'multiply')

def iffunc(l):
  if l[0]>0: return l[1]
  else: return l[2]
ifw=fwrapper(iffunc,3,'if')

def isgreater(l):
  if l[0]>l[1]: return 1
  else: return 0
gtw=fwrapper(isgreater,2,'isgreater')

flist=[addw,mulw,ifw,gtw,subw]
```

Some of the simpler functions such as add and subtract can be defined inline using lambda, while others require you to define the function in a separate block. In each case, they have been wrapped in an fwrapper with their names and the number of parameters required. The last line creates a list of all the functions so that later they can easily be chosen at random.

Building and Evaluating Trees

You can now construct the program tree shown in Figure 11-2 using the node class you just created. Add the exampletree function to *gp.py* to create the tree:

```
def exampletree( ):
  return node(ifw,[
                node(gtw,[paramnode(0),constnode(3)]),
                node(addw,[paramnode(1),constnode(5)]),
                node(subw,[paramnode(1),constnode(2)]),
                ]
             )
```

Start up a Python session to test your program:

```
>>> import gp
>>> exampletree=gp.exampletree( )
>>> exampletree.evaluate([2,3])
1
>>> exampletree.evaluate([5,3])
8
```

The program successfully performs the same function as the equivalent code block, so you've managed to build a mini tree-based language and interpreter within Python. This language can be easily extended with more node types, and it will serve as the basis for understanding genetic programming in this chapter. Try building a few other simple program trees to make sure you understand how they work.

Displaying the Program

Because you'll be creating program trees automatically and won't know what their structure looks like, it's important to have a way to display them so that you can easily interpret them. Fortunately the design of the node class means every node has a string representing the name of its function, so a display function simply has to return that string and the display strings of the child nodes. To make it easier to read, the display should also indent the child nodes so you can visually identify the parent-child relationships in the tree.

Create a new method in the node class called display, which shows a string representation of the tree:

```
def display(self,indent=0):
  print (' '*indent)+self.name
  for c in self.children:
    c.display(indent+1)
```

You'll also need to create a display method for the paramnode class, which simply prints the index of the parameter it returns:

```
def display(self,indent=0):
  print '%sp%d' % (' '*indent,self.idx)
```

And finally, one for the constnode class:

```
def display(self,indent=0):
  print '%s%d' % (' '*indent,self.v)
```

Use these methods to print out the tree:

```
>>> reload(gp)
<module 'gp' from 'gp.py'>
>>> exampletree=gp.exampletree()
>>> exampletree.display()
if
 isgreater
  p0
  3
 add
  p1
  5
 subtract
  p1
  2
```

If you've read Chapter 7, you'll notice that this is similar to the way in which decision trees were displayed in that chapter. Chapter 7 also shows how to display those trees graphically for a cleaner, easier-to-read output. If you feel so inclined, you can use the same idea to build a graphical display of your tree programs.

Creating the Initial Population

Although it's possible to hand-create programs for genetic programming, most of the time the initial population consists of a set of random programs. This makes the process easier to start, since it's not necessary to design several programs that almost solve a problem. It also creates much more *diversity* in the initial population—a set of programs designed by a single programmer to solve a problem are likely to be very similar, and although they may give answers that are almost correct, the ideal solution make look quite different. You'll learn more about the importance of diversity shortly.

Creating a random program consists of creating a root node with a random associated function and then creating as many random child nodes as necessary, which in turn may have their own associated random child nodes. Like most functions that work with trees, this is most easily defined recursively. Add a new function, makerandomtree, to *gp.py*:

```
def makerandomtree(pc,maxdepth=4,fpr=0.5,ppr=0.6):
  if random()<fpr and maxdepth>0:
    f=choice(flist)
    children=[makerandomtree(pc,maxdepth-1,fpr,ppr)
              for i in range(f.childcount)]
    return node(f,children)
  elif random()<ppr:
    return paramnode(randint(0,pc-1))
  else:
    return constnode(randint(0,10))
```

This function creates a node with a random function and then looks to see how many child nodes this function requires. For every child node required, the function calls itself to create a new node. In this way an entire tree is constructed, with branches ending only if the function requires no more child nodes (that is, if the function returns a constant or an input variable). The parameter pc, used throughout this chapter, is the number of parameters that the tree will take as input. The parameter fpr gives the probability that the new node created will be a function node, and ppr gives that probability that it will be a paramnode if it is not a function node.

Try out this function in your Python session to build a few programs, and see what sort of results you get with different variables:

```
>>> random1=gp.makerandomtree(2)
>>> random1.evaluate([7,1])
7
>>> random1.evaluate([2,4])
2
>>> random2=gp.makerandomtree(2)
>>> random2.evaluate([5,3])
1
>>> random2.evaluate([5,20])
0
```

If all of a program's terminating nodes are constants, the program will not actually reference the input parameters at all, so the result will be the same no matter what input you pass to it. You can use the function defined in the previous section to display the randomly generated trees:

```
>>> random1.display()
p0
>>> random2.display()
subtract
 7
 multiply
  isgreater
   p0
   p1
  if
   multiply
    p1
    p1
   p0
   2
```

You'll see that some of the trees get quite deep, since each branch will keep growing until it hits a zero-child node. This is why it's important that you include a maximum depth constraint; otherwise, the trees can get very large and potentially overflow the stack.

Testing a Solution

You would now have everything you'd need to build programs automatically, if you could just generate random programs until one is correct. Obviously, this would be ridiculously impractical because there are infinite possible programs and it's highly unlikely that you would stumble across a correct one in any reasonable time frame. However, at this point it is worth looking at ways to test a solution to see if it's correct, and if it's not, to determine how close it is.

A Simple Mathematical Test

One of the easiest tests for genetic programming is to reconstruct a simple mathematical function. Imagine you were given a table of inputs and an output that looked like Table 11-1.

Table 11-1. Data and result for an unknown function

X	Y	Result
26	35	829
8	24	141
20	1	467
33	11	1215
37	16	1517

There is some function that maps X and Y to the result, but you're not told what it is. A statistician might see this and try to do a regression analysis, but that requires guessing the structure of the formula first. Another option is to build a predictive model using k-nearest neighbors as you did in Chapter 8, but that requires keeping all the data. In some cases, you just need a formula, perhaps to codify in another much simpler program or to describe to other people what's going on.

I'm sure you're in suspense, so I'll tell you what the function is. Add `hiddenfunction` to *gp.py*:

```
def hiddenfunction(x,y):
    return x**2+2*y+3*x+5
```

You're going to use this function to build a dataset against which you can test your generated programs. Add a new function, `buildhiddenset`, which creates the dataset:

```
def buildhiddenset():
  rows=[]
  for i in range(200):
    x=randint(0,40)
    y=randint(0,40)
    rows.append([x,y,hiddenfunction(x,y)])
  return rows
```

And use this to create a dataset in your Python session:

```
>>> reload(gp)
<module 'gp' from 'gp.py'>
>>> hiddenset=gp.buildhiddenset()
```

Of course, you know what the function used to generate the dataset looks like, but the real test is whether genetic programming can reproduce it without being told.

Measuring Success

As with optimization, it's necessary to come up with a way to measure how good a solution is. In this case, you're testing a program against a numerical outcome, so an easy way to test a program is to see how close it gets to the correct answers for the dataset. Add scorefunction to *gp.py*:

```
def scorefunction(tree,s):
  dif=0
  for data in s:
    v=tree.evaluate([data[0],data[1]])
    dif+=abs(v-data[2])
  return dif
```

This function checks every row in the dataset, calculating the output from the function and comparing it to the real result. It adds up all the differences, giving lower values for better programs—a return value of 0 indicates that the program got every result correct. You can now test some of your generated programs in your Python session to see how they stack up:

```
>>> reload(gp)
<module 'gp' from 'gp.py'>
>>> gp.scorefunction(random2,hiddenset)
137646
>>> gp.scorefunction(random1,hiddenset)
125489
```

Since you only generated a few programs and they were generated completely randomly, the chance that one of them is actually the correct function is vanishingly small. (If one of your programs is the correct function, I suggest that you put the book down and go buy yourself a lottery ticket.) However, you now have a way to test how well a program performs on predicting a mathematical function, which is important for deciding which programs make it to the next generation.

Mutating Programs

After the best programs are chosen, they are replicated and modified for the next generation. As mentioned earlier, mutation takes a single program and alters it slightly. The tree programs can be altered in a number of ways—by changing the function on a node or by altering its branches. A function that changes the number of required child nodes either deletes or adds new branches, as shown in Figure 11-3.

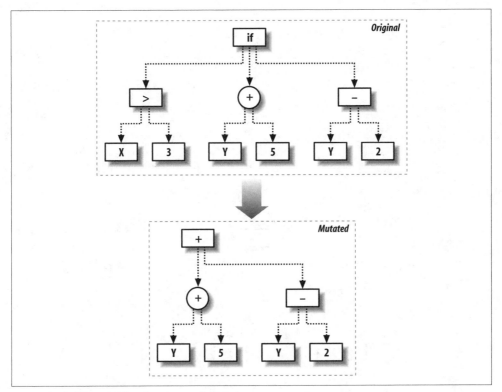

Figure 11-3. Mutation by changing node functions

The other way to mutate is by replacing a subtree with an entirely new one, as shown in Figure 11-4.

Mutation is not something that should be done too much. You would not, for instance, mutate the majority of nodes in a tree. Instead, you can assign a relatively small probability that any node will be modified. Beginning at the top of the tree, if a random number is lower than that probability, the node is mutated in one of the ways described above; otherwise, the test is performed again on its child nodes.

To keep things simple, the code given here only performs the second kind of mutation. Create a new function called mutate to perform this operation:

```
def mutate(t,pc,probchange=0.1):
  if random( )<probchange:
    return makerandomtree(pc)
  else:
    result=deepcopy(t)
    if isinstance(t,node):
      result.children=[mutate(c,pc,probchange) for c in t.children]
    return result
```

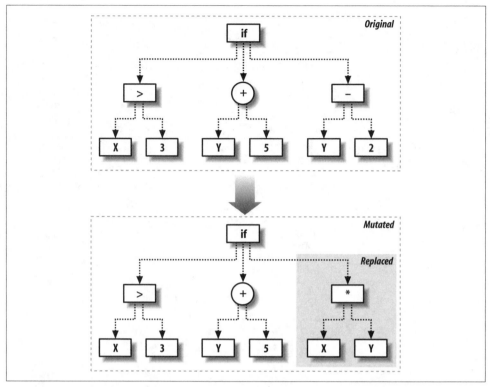

Figure 11-4. Mutation by replacing subtrees

This function begins at the top of the tree and decides whether the node should be altered. If not, it calls mutate on the child nodes of the tree. It's possible that the entire tree will be mutated, and it's also possible to traverse the entire tree without changing it.

Try running mutate a few times on the randomly generated programs you built earlier, and see how it modifies the trees:

```
>>> random2.display( )
subtract
 7
 multiply
  isgreater
   p0
   p1
  if
   multiply
    p1
    p1
   p0
   2
```

```
>>> muttree=gp.mutate(random2,2)
>>> muttree.display()
subtract
 7
 multiply
  isgreater
   p0
   p1
  if
   multiply
    p1
    p1
   p0
   p1
```

See if the result of scorefunction has changed significantly, for better or worse, after the tree has been mutated:

```
>>> gp.scorefunction(random2,hiddenset)
125489
>>> gp.scorefunction(muttree,hiddenset)
125479
```

Remember that the mutations are random, and they aren't necessarily directed toward improving the solution. The hope is simply that some will improve the result. These changes will be used to continue, and over several generations the best solution will eventually be found.

Crossover

The other type of program modification is crossover or breeding. This involves taking two successful programs and combining them to create a new program, usually by replacing a branch from one with a branch from another. Figure 11-5 shows an example of how this works.

The function for performing a crossover takes two trees as inputs and traverses down both of them. If a randomly selected threshold is reached, the function returns a copy of the first tree with one of its branches replaced by a branch in the second tree. By traversing both trees at once, the crossover happens at approximately the same level on each tree. Add the crossover function to *gp.py*:

```
def crossover(t1,t2,probswap=0.7,top=1):
  if random()<probswap and not top:
    return deepcopy(t2)
  else:
    result=deepcopy(t1)
    if isinstance(t1,node) and isinstance(t2,node):
      result.children=[crossover(c,choice(t2.children),probswap,0)
                        for c in t1.children]
    return result
```

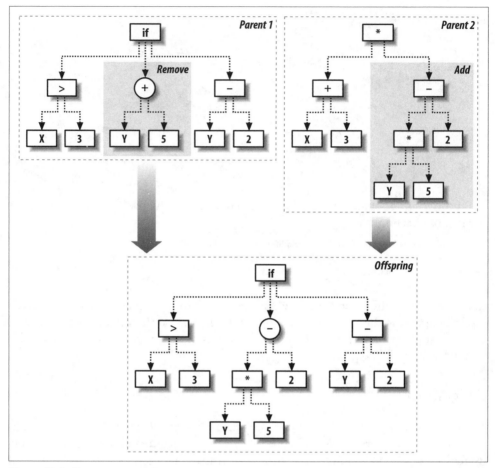

Figure 11-5. Crossover operation

Try crossover on a few of the randomly generated programs. See what they look like after the crossover, and see if crossing over two of the best programs occasionally leads to a better program:

```
>>> random1=gp.makerandomtree(2)
>>> random1.display( )
multiply
 subtract
  p0
  8
 isgreater
  p0
  isgreater
   p1
   5
```

```
>>> random2=gp.makerandomtree(2)
>>> random2.display( )
if
 8
 p1
 2
>>> cross=gp.crossover(random1,random2)
>>> cross.display( )
multiply
 subtract
  p0
  8
  2
```

You'll probably notice that swapping out branches can radically change what the program does. You may also notice that programs may be close to being correct for completely different reasons, so merging them produces a result that's very different from either of its predecessors. Again, the hope is that some crossovers will improve the solution and be kept around for the next generation.

Building the Environment

Armed with a measure of success and two methods of modifying the best programs, you're now ready to set up a competitive environment in which programs can evolve. The steps are shown in the flowchart in Figure 11-1. Essentially, you create a set of random programs and select the best ones for replication and modification, repeating this process until some stopping criteria is reached.

Create a new function called evolve to carry out this procedure:

```
def evolve(pc,popsize,rankfunction,maxgen=500,
           mutationrate=0.1,breedingrate=0.4,pexp=0.7,pnew=0.05):
  # Returns a random number, tending towards lower numbers. The lower pexp
  # is, more lower numbers you will get
  def selectindex( ):
    return int(log(random( ))/log(pexp))

  # Create a random initial population
  population=[makerandomtree(pc) for i in range(popsize)]
  for i in range(maxgen):
    scores=rankfunction(population)
    print scores[0][0]
    if scores[0][0]==0: break

    # The two best always make it
    newpop=[scores[0][1],scores[1][1]]
```

```
      # Build the next generation
      while len(newpop)<popsize:
        if random( )>pnew:
          newpop.append(mutate(
                        crossover(scores[selectindex( )][1],
                                  scores[selectindex( )][1],
                                  probswap=breedingrate),
                              pc,probchange=mutationrate))
        else:
        # Add a random node to mix things up
          newpop.append(makerandomtree(pc))

     population=newpop
   scores[0][1].display( )
   return scores[0][1]
```

This function creates an initial random population. It then loops up to maxgen times, each time calling rankfunction to rank the programs from best to worst. The best program is automatically passed through to the next generation unaltered, which is sometimes referred to as *elitism*. The rest of the next generation is constructed by randomly choosing programs that are near the top of the ranking, and then breeding and mutating them. This process repeats until either a program has a perfect score of 0 or maxgen is reached.

The function has several parameters, which are used to control various aspects of the environment. They are:

rankfunction
> The function used on the list of programs to rank them from best to worst.

mutationrate
> The probability of a mutation, passed on to mutate.

breedingrate
> The probability of crossover, passed on to crossover.

popsize
> The size of the initial population.

probexp
> The rate of decline in the probability of selecting lower-ranked programs. A higher value makes the selection process more stringent, choosing only programs with the best ranks to replicate.

probnew
> The probability when building the new population that a completely new, random program is introduced. probexp and probnew will be discussed further in the upcoming section "The Importance of Diversity."

The final thing you'll need before beginning the evolution of your programs is a way to rank programs based on the result of scorefunction. In *gp.py*, create a new function called getrankfunction, which returns a ranking function for a given dataset:

```
def getrankfunction(dataset):
  def rankfunction(population):
    scores=[(scorefunction(t,dataset),t) for t in population]
    scores.sort()
    return scores
  return rankfunction
```

You're ready to automatically create a program that represents the formula for your mathematical dataset. Try this in your Python session:

```
>>> reload(gp)
>>> rf=gp.getrankfunction(gp.buildhiddenset())
>>> gp.evolve(2,500,rf,mutationrate=0.2,breedingrate=0.1,pexp=0.7,pnew=0.1)
16749
10674
5429
3090
491
151
151
0
add
 multiply
  p0
  add
   2
   p0
 add
  add
   p0
   4
  add
   p1
   add
    p1
    isgreater
     10
     5
```

The numbers change slowly, but they should decrease until they finally reach 0. Interestingly, the solution shown here gets everything correct, but it's quite a bit more complicated than the function used to create the dataset. (It's very likely that the solution you generated will also seem more complicated than it has to be.) However, a little algebra shows us that these functions are actually the same—remember that p0 is X and p1 is Y. The first line is the function represented by this tree:

```
(X*(2+X))+X+4+Y+Y+(10>5)
= 2*X+X*X+X+4+Y+Y+1
= X**2 + 3*X + 2*Y + 5
```

This demonstrates an important property of genetic programming: the solutions it finds may well be correct or very good, but because of the way they are constructed, they will often be far more complicated than anything a human programmer would design. There will often be large sections of a program that don't do anything or that represent a complicated formula that returns the same value every time. Notice in the above example that the node (10>5) is just an odd way of saying 1.

It is possible to force the programs to remain simple, but in many cases this will make it more difficult to find a good solution. A better way to deal with this issue is to allow the programs to evolve to a good solution and then remove and simplify unnecessary portions of the tree. You can do this manually, and in some cases you can do it automatically using a pruning algorithm.

The Importance of Diversity

Part of the evolve function ranks the programs from best to worst, so it's tempting to just take two or three of the programs at the top and replicate and modify them to become the new population. After all, why would you bother allowing anything less than the best to continue?

The problem is that choosing only a couple of the top solutions quickly makes the population extremely homogeneous (or inbred, if you like), containing solutions that are all pretty good but that won't change much because crossover operations between them lead to more of the same. This problem is called reaching a *local maxima*, a state that is good but not quite good enough, and one in which small changes don't improve the result.

It turns out that having the very best solutions combined with a large number of moderately good solutions tends to lead to better results. For this reason, the evolve function has a couple of extra parameters that allow you to tune that amount of diversity in the selection process. By lowering the probexp value, you allow weaker solutions into the final result, turning the process from "survival of the fittest" to "survival of the fittest and luckiest." By increasing the probnew value, you allow completely new programs to be added to the mix occasionally. Both of these values increase the amount of diversity in the evolution process but won't disrupt it too much, since the very worst programs will always be eliminated eventually.

A Simple Game

A more interesting problem for genetic programming is building an AI for a game. You can force the programs to evolve by having them compete against each other and against real people, and giving the ones that win the most a higher chance of making it to the next generation. In this section, you'll create a simulator for a very simple game called Grid War, which is depicted in Figure 11-6.

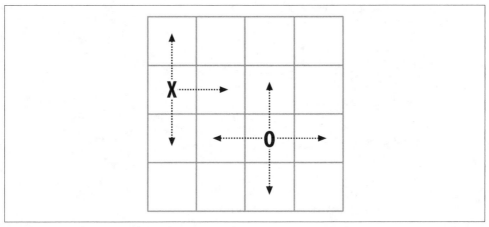

Figure 11-6. Grid War example

The game has two players who take turns moving around on a small grid. Each player can move in one of four directions, and the board is limited so if a player attempts to move off one side, he forfeits his turn. The object of the game is to capture the other player by moving onto the same square as his on your turn. The only additional constraint is that you automatically lose if you try to move in the same direction twice in a row. This game is very basic but since it pits two players against each other, it will let you explore more competitive aspects of evolution.

The first step is to create a function that uses two players and simulates a game between them. The function passes the location of the player and the opponent to each program in turn, along with the last move made by the player, and takes the return value as the move.

The move should be a number from 0 to 3, indicating one of four possible directions, but since these are random programs that can return any integer, the function has to handle values outside this range. To do this, it uses *modulo 4* on the result. Random programs are also liable to do things like create a player that moves in a circle, so the number of moves is limited to 50 before a tie is declared.

Add gridgame to *gp.py*:

```
def gridgame(p):
  # Board size
  max=(3,3)

  # Remember the last move for each player
  lastmove=[-1,-1]

  # Remember the player's locations
  location=[[randint(0,max[0]),randint(0,max[1])]]

  # Put the second player a sufficient distance from the first
  location.append([(location[0][0]+2)%4,(location[0][1]+2)%4])
```

```
# Maximum of 50 moves before a tie
for o in range(50):

    # For each player
    for i in range(2):
      locs=location[i][:]+location[1-i][:]
      locs.append(lastmove[i])
      move=p[i].evaluate(locs)%4

      # You lose if you move the same direction twice in a row
      if lastmove[i]==move: return 1-i
      lastmove[i]=move
      if move==0:
        location[i][0]-=1
        # Board limits
        if location[i][0]<0: location[i][0]=0
      if move==1:
        location[i][0]+=1
        if location[i][0]>max[0]: location[i][0]=max[0]
      if move==2:
        location[i][1]-=1
        if location[i][1]<0: location[i][1]=0
      if move==3:
        location[i][1]+=1
        if location[i][1]>max[1]: location[i][1]=max[1]

      # If you have captured the other player, you win
      if location[i]==location[1-i]: return i
  return -1
```

The program will return 0 if player 1 is the winner, 1 if player 2 is the winner, and −1 in the event of a tie. You can try building a couple of random programs and having them compete:

```
>>> reload(gp)
<module 'gp' from 'gp.py'>
>>> p1=gp.makerandomtree(5)
>>> p2=gp.makerandomtree(5)
>>> gp.gridgame([p1,p2])
1
```

These programs are totally unevolved, so they probably lose by moving in the same direction twice in a row. Ideally, an evolved program will learn not to do this.

A Round-Robin Tournament

In keeping with collective intelligence, you would want the programs to test their fitness by playing against real people, and force their evolution that way. This would be a great way to capture the behavior of thousands of people and use it to develop a more intelligent program. However, with a large population and many generations, this could quickly add up to tens of thousands of games, and most of them would be against very poor opponents. That's impractical for our purposes, so you can first have the programs evolve by competing against each other in a tournament.

The tournament function takes a list of players as its input and pits each one against every other one, tracking how many times each program loses its game. Programs get two points if they lose and one point if they tie. Add tournament to *gp.py*:

```python
def tournament(pl):
  # Count losses
  losses=[0 for p in pl]

  # Every player plays every other player
  for i in range(len(pl)):
    for j in range(len(pl)):
      if i==j: continue

      # Who is the winner?
      winner=gridgame([pl[i],pl[j]])

      # Two points for a loss, one point for a tie
      if winner==0:
        losses[j]+=2
      elif winner==1:
        losses[i]+=2
      elif winner==-1:
        losses[i]+=1
        losses[i]+=1
        pass

  # Sort and return the results
  z=zip(losses,pl)
  z.sort()
  return z
```

At the end of the function, the results are sorted and returned with the programs that have the fewest losses at the top. This is the return type needed by evolve to evaluate programs, which means that tournament can be used as an argument to evolve and that you're now ready to evolve a program to play the game. Try it in your Python session (this may take some time):

```python
>>> reload(gp)
<module 'gp' from 'gp.py'>
>>> winner=gp.evolve(5,100,gp.tournament,maxgen=50)
```

As the programs evolve, notice that the loss numbers don't strictly decrease like they did with the mathematical function. Take a minute to think about why this is—after all, the best player is always allowed into the next generation, right? As it turns out, since the next generation consists entirely of newly evolved programs, the best program in one generation might fare a lot worse in the next.

Playing Against Real People

Once you've evolved a program that performs well against its robotic competitors, it's time to battle against it yourself. To do this, you can create another class that also has an evaluate method that displays the board to the user and asks what move they want to make. Add the humanplayer class to *gp.py*:

```python
class humanplayer:
  def evaluate(self,board):

    # Get my location and the location of other players
    me=tuple(board[0:2])
    others=[tuple(board[x:x+2]) for x in range(2,len(board)-1,2)]

    # Display the board
    for i in range(4):
      for j in range(4):
        if (i,j)==me:
          print 'O',
        elif (i,j) in others:
          print 'X',
        else:
          print '.',
      print

    # Show moves, for reference
    print 'Your last move was %d' % board[len(board)-1]
    print ' 0'
    print '2 3'
    print ' 1'
    print 'Enter move: ',

    # Return whatever the user enters
    move=int(raw_input())
    return move
```

In your Python session, you can take on your creation:

```
>>> reload(gp)
<module 'gp' from 'gp.py'>
>>> gp.gridgame([winner,gp.humanplayer()])
. O . .
. . . .
. . . .
. . . X
Your last move was -1
 0
2 3
 1
Enter move:
```

Depending on how well your program evolved, you may find it easy or difficult to beat. Your program will almost certainly have learned that it can't make the same move twice in a row, since that leads to instant death, but the extent to which it has mastered other strategies will vary with each run of evolve.

Further Possibilities

This chapter is just an introduction to genetic programming, which is a huge and rapidly advancing field. You've used it so far to approach simple problems in which programs are built in minutes rather than days, but the principles can be extended to much more complex problems. The number of programs in the populations here have been very small compared to those used in more complex problems—a population of thousands or tens of thousands is more typical. You are encouraged to come up with more difficult problems and try larger population sizes, but you may have to wait hours or days while the programs run.

The following section outlines a few ways in which the simple genetic programming model can be extended for different applications.

More Numerical Functions

We have used a very small set of functions to construct the programs so far. This limits the scope of what a simple program can do—for more complicated problems, it's necessary to greatly increase the number of functions available to build a tree. Here are some possible functions to add:

- Trigonometric functions like sine, cosine, and tangent
- Other mathematical functions like power, square root, and absolute value
- Statistical distributions, such as a Gaussian
- Distance metrics, like Euclidean and Tanimoto distances
- A three-parameter function that returns 1 if the first parameter is between the second and third
- A three-parameter function that returns 1 if the difference between the first two parameters is less than the third

These can get as complicated as you like, and they are often tailored to specific problems. Trigonometric functions may be a necessity when working in a field like signal processing, but they are not much use in a game like the one you built in this chapter.

Memory

The programs in this chapter are almost entirely reactive; they give a result based solely on their inputs. This is the right approach for solving mathematical functions, but it doesn't allow the programs to work from a longer-term strategy. The chasing game passes the programs the last move they made—mostly so the programs learn they can't make the same move twice in a row—but this is simply the output of the program, not something they set themselves.

For a program to develop a longer-term strategy, it needs a way to store information for use in the next round. One simple way to do this is to create new kinds of nodes that can store and retrieve values from predefined slots. A *store* node has a single child and an index of a memory slot; it gets the result from its child and stores it in the memory slot and then passes this along to its parent. A *recall* node has no children and simply returns the value in the appropriate slot. If a store node is at the top of the tree, the final result is available to any part of the tree that has the appropriate recall node.

In addition to individual memory, it's also possible to set up shared memory that can be read and written to by all the different programs. This is similar to individual memory, except that there are a set of slots that all the programs can read from and write to, creating the potential for higher levels of cooperation and competition.

Different Datatypes

The framework described in this chapter is for programs that take integer parameters and return integers as results. It can easily be altered to work with float values, since the operations are the same. To do this, simply alter makerandomtree to create the constant nodes with a random float value instead of a random integer.

Building programs that handle other kinds of data will require more extensive modification, mostly changing the functions on the nodes. The basic framework can be altered to handle types such as:

Strings
These would have operations like concatenate, split, indexing, and substrings.

Lists
These would have operations similar to strings.

Dictionaries
These would include operations like replacement and addition.

Objects
Any custom object could be used as an input to a tree, with the functions on the nodes being method calls to the object.

An important point that arises from these examples is that, in many cases, you'll require the nodes in the tree to process more than one type of return value. A substring operation, for example, requires a string and two integers, which means that one of its children would have to return a string and the other two would have to return integers.

The naïve approach to this would be to randomly generate, mutate, and breed trees, simply discarding the ones in which there is a mismatch in datatypes. However, this would be computationally wasteful, and you've already seen how you can put a constraint on the way trees are constructed—every function in the integer trees knows how many children it needs, and this can be easily extended to constrain the types of children and their return types. For example, you might redefine the fwrapper class like the following, where params is a list of strings specifying datatypes that can be used for each parameter:

```
class fwrapper:
  def __init__(self,function,params,name):
    self.function=function
    self.childcount=param
    self.name=name
```

You'd also probably want to set up flist as a dictionary with return types. For example:

```
flist={'str':[substringw,concatw],'int':[indexw,addw,subw]}
```

Then you could change the start of makerandomtree to something like:

```
def makerandomtree(pc,datatype,maxdepth=4,fpr=0.5,ppr=0.5):
  if random()<fpr and maxdepth>0:
    f=choice(flist[datatype])
    # Call makerandomtree with all the parameter types for f
    children=[makerandomtree(pc,type,maxdepth-1,fpr,ppr)
              for type in f.params]
    return node(f,children)
  etc...
```

The crossover function would also have to be altered to ensure that swapped nodes have the same return type.

Ideally, this section has given you some ideas about how genetic programming can be extended from the simple model described here, and has inspired you to improve it and to try automatically generating programs for more complex problems. Although they may take a very long time to generate, once you find a good program, you can use it again and again.

Exercises

1. *More function types.* We started with a very short list of functions. What other functions can you think of? Implement a Euclidean distance node with four parameters.

2. *Replacement mutation.* Implement a mutation procedure that chooses a random node on the tree and changes it. Make sure it deals with function, constant, and parameter nodes. How is evolution affected by using this function instead of the branch replacement?

3. *Random crossover.* The current crossover function chooses branches from two trees at the same level. Write a different crossover function that crosses any two random branches. How does this affect evolution?

4. *Stopping evolution.* Add an additional criteria to evolve that stops the process and returns the best result if the best score hasn't improved within X generations.

5. *Hidden functions.* Try creating other mathematical functions for the programs to guess. What sort of functions can be found easily, and which are more difficult?

6. *Grid War player.* Try to hand-design your own tree program that does well at Grid War. If you find this easy, try to write another completely different one. Instead of having a completely random initial population, make it *mostly* random, with your hand-designed programs included. How do they compare to random programs, and can they be improved with evolution?

7. *Tic-tac-toe.* Build a tic-tac-toe simulator for your programs to play. Set up a tournament similar to the Grid War tournament. How well do the programs do? Can they ever learn to play perfectly?

8. *Nodes with datatypes.* Some ideas were provided in this chapter about implementing nodes with mixed datatypes. Implement this and see if you can evolve a program that learns to return the second, third, sixth, and seventh characters of a string (e.g., "genetic" becomes "enic").

## CHAPTER 12

Algorithm Summary

This book has introduced a number of different algorithms, and if you've been working through the examples, you now have Python code that implements many of them. The earlier chapters are structured around working through an example problem with algorithms and variations introduced throughout the chapter. This chapter will be a reference for the algorithms covered, so when you want to do some data mining or machine learning on a new dataset, you can look at the algorithms here, decide which one is appropriate, and use the code you've already written to analyze your data.

To save you from going back through the book to find the details of an algorithm, I'll provide a description of each one, a high-level overview of how it works, what sort of datasets you can apply it to, and how you would use the code you've previously written to run it. I'll also mention some of the strengths and weaknesses of each algorithm (or, if you like, how to sell the idea to your boss). In some cases, I'll use examples to help explain the properties of the algorithm. These examples are greatly simplified—most are so simple you can solve them just by looking at the data yourself—but they are useful for illustration.

Supervised learning methods, which guess a classification or a value based on training examples, will be covered first.

Bayesian Classifier

Bayesian classifiers were covered in Chapter 6. In that chapter, you saw how to create a document classification system, such as those used for spam filtering or dividing up a set of documents based on an ambiguous keyword search.

Although all the examples dealt with documents, the Bayesian classifier described in Chapter 6 will work on any dataset that can be turned into lists of *features*. A feature is simply something that is either present or absent for a given item. In the case of documents, the features are the words in the document, but they could also be characteristics of an unidentified object, symptoms of a disease, or anything else that can be said to be present of absent.

Training

Like all supervised methods, a Bayesian classifier is trained with examples. Each example is a list of an item's features and the classification for that item. Suppose you're trying to train a classifier to recognize if a document containing the word "python" is about the programming language or the snake. A sample training set might look like Table 12-1.

Table 12-1. Features and classifications for a set of documents

Features	Classification
Pythons are constrictors that feed on birds and mammals	Snake
Python was originally developed as a scripting language	Language
A 49-ft.-long python was found in Indonesia	Snake
Python has a dynamic type system	Language
Python with vivid scales	Snake
Open source project	Language

The classifier keeps track of all the features it has seen so far, along with numerical probabilities that the features are associated with a particular classification. The classifier is trained by receiving examples one by one. After each example, the classifier updates the probabilities for the features and classifier in that example, generating the probability that a document about a certain category will contain a given word. For example, trained on a set of documents like those in Table 12-1, you might end up with a set of probabilities like those in Table 12-2.

Table 12-2. Probabilities of words for a given category

Feature	Language	Snake
dynamic	0.6	0.1
constrictor	0.0	0.6
long	0.1	0.2
source	0.3	0.1
and	0.95	0.95

This table shows that after training, features become more strongly associated with the different categories. The word "constrictor" has a higher probability for snake, and the word "dynamic" has a higher probability for the programming language.

Features that are ambiguous like the word "and" have similar probabilities for both categories (the word "and" appears in almost every document, regardless of its category). A trained classifier is nothing more than a list of features along with their associated probabilities. Unlike some other classification methods, there is no need to store the original data after it has been used for training.

Classifying

After a Bayesian classifier has been trained, it can be used to automatically classify new items. Suppose you have a new document with the features "long," "dynamic," and "source." Table 12-2 shows a probability value for each of these, but this is just for the individual words. If all of the words had a higher probability in one category, then the answer would be clear. However, in this case "dynamic" is higher for the language category, and "long" is higher for the snake category. To actually classify a document, you need a way to combine the feature probabilities into a single probability for the entire item.

One method of doing this, described in Chapter 6, is with a naïve Bayes classifier. It combines probabilities with the following formula:

$$Pr(Category \mid Document) = Pr(Document \mid Category) * Pr(Category)$$

Where:

$$Pr(Document \mid Category) = Pr(Word1 \mid Category) * Pr(Word2 \mid Category) * \ldots$$

The numbers for $Pr(Word \mid Category)$ are the values from the table, for example, $Pr(dynamic \mid Language) = 0.6$. The value of $Pr(Category)$ is the overall frequency of the category. Since "language" appears half the time, the value of $Pr(Language)$ is 0.5. Whichever category gets a higher score for $Pr(Category \mid Document)$ is the predicted category.

Using Your Code

To use the Bayesian classifier built in Chapter 6 on any dataset, all you need is a feature-extraction function that turns the data you're using for training or classification into a list of features. That chapter worked with documents, so the function split a string into words, but you can use any function that takes an object and returns a list:

```
>>> docclass.getwords('python is a dynamic language')
{'python': 1, 'dynamic': 1, 'language': 1}
```

This function can be used to create a new classifier, which can then be trained on strings:

```
>>> cl=docclass.naivebayes(docclass.getwords)
>>> cl.setdb('test.db')
>>> cl.train('pythons are constrictors','snake')
```

```
>>> cl.train('python has dynamic types','language')
>>> cl.train('python was developed as a scripting language','language')
```

and classification:

```
>>> cl.classify('dynamic programming')
u'language'
>>> cl.classify('boa constrictors')
u'snake'
```

There is no limit to the number of different categories you can use, but for the classifier to work well, you need to have plenty of examples for each category.

Strengths and Weaknesses

Perhaps the biggest advantage of naïve Bayesian classifiers over other methods is the speed at which they can be trained and queried with large datasets. Even with a huge training set, there are usually a relatively small number of features for each item, and training and classifying items is just a mathematical manipulation of the probabilities of these features.

This is particularly true when training is incremental—each new piece of training data can be used to update the probabilities without using any of the old training data. (You'll notice that the code lets you train the Bayesian classifier with one item at a time, while other methods like decision trees and support-vector machines need the whole dataset at once.) This support for incremental training is very important for an application like a spam filter, which is constantly trained on new email messages that come in, has to be updated quickly, and may not even have access to all the email messages that have been received.

Another big advantage of naïve Bayesian classifiers is the relative simplicity of interpreting what the classifier has actually learned. Because the probabilities of each feature are stored, you can look at your database at any time and see which features are best at dividing spam and nonspam, or programming languages and snakes. This information is interesting to look at, and it can potentially be used for other applications or as a starting point for other applications.

The biggest downside to naïve Bayesian classifiers is their inability to deal with outcomes that change based on combinations of features. Imagine the following scenario in which you are trying to distinguish spam from nonspam email: let's say your job is building web applications, so the word "online" frequently appears in your work-related email. Your best friend works at a pharmacy and likes sending you funny stories about things that happen to him at work. Also, like most people who haven't closely guarded their email addresses, you occasionally receive spam containing the words "online pharmacy."

You can probably see the dilemma here already—the classifier is constantly being told that "online" and "pharmacy" exist in nonspam email messages, so their probabilities become higher for nonspam. When you tell the classifier that a certain email message with the words "online pharmacy" is spam, those words are adjusted slightly more toward spam, creating a constant battle. Since features are all given probabilities separately, the classifier can never learn about combinations. In document classification this is usually not a big deal, since an email message with the words "online pharmacy" probably contains other spam indicators, but in other problems, understanding feature combinations can be much more important.

Decision Tree Classifier

Decision trees were introduced in Chapter 7 to show you how to build a model of user behavior from server logs. Decision trees are notable for being extremely easy to understand and interpret. An example of a decision tree is shown in Figure 12-1.

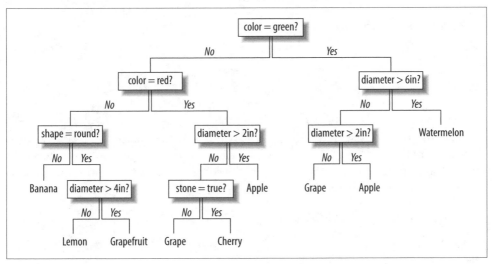

Figure 12-1. Example decision tree

It should be clear from the figure what a decision tree does when faced with the task of classifying a new item. Beginning at the node at the top of the tree, it checks the item against the node's criteria—if the item matches the criteria, it follows the Yes branch; otherwise, it follows the No branch. This process is repeated until an endpoint is reached, which is the predicted category.

Training

Classifying in a decision tree is quite simple; training it is trickier. The algorithm described in Chapter 7 built the tree from the top, choosing an attribute at each step that would divide the data in the best possible manner. To illustrate this, consider the fruit dataset shown in Table 12-3. This will be referred to as the original set.

Table 12-3. Fruit data

Diameter	Color	Fruit
4	Red	Apple
4	Green	Apple
1	Red	Cherry
1	Green	Grape
5	Red	Apple

There are two possible variables on which this data can be divided, either Diameter or Color, to create the top node of the tree. The first step is to try each of them in order to decide which of these variables divides the data best. Dividing the set on Color gives the results shown in Table 12-4.

Table 12-4. Fruit data divided by Color

Red	Green
Apple	Apple
Cherry	Grape
Apple	

The data is still pretty mixed. However, if you divide the dataset by Diameter (less than four inches and greater than or equal to four inches), the results divide much more cleanly (referred to as Subset 1 on the left and Subset 2 on the right). This division is shown in Table 12-5.

Table 12-5. Fruit data divided by Diameter

Diameter < 4in	Diameter ≥ 4in
Cherry	Apple
Grape	Apple

This is obviously a much better result, since Subset 1 contains all the Apple entries from the original set. Although the better variable is clear in this example, larger datasets will not always have such clean divisions. Chapter 7 introduced the concept of entropy (the amount of disorder in a set) to measure how good a division is:

- $p(i) = frequency(outcome) = count(outcome) / count(total rows)$
- $Entropy = sum of p(i) * log(p(i))$ for all outcomes

A low entropy within a set tells you that the set is mostly homogeneous, and a value of 0 means that it consists of entirely one type of item. Subset 1 (diameter ≥ 4) in Table 12-5 has an entropy of 0. The entropy for each set is used to calculate the *information gain*, which is defined as:

- *weight1 = size of subset1 / size of original set*
- *weight2 = size of subset2 / size of original set*
- *gain = entropy(original) − weight1*entropy(set1) − weight2*entropy(set2)*

So for each possible division, the information gain is calculated and used to determine the dividing variable. Once the dividing variable has been chosen, the first node can be created, as shown in Figure 12-2.

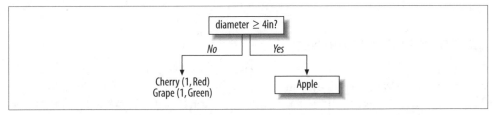

Figure 12-2. Root node of the fruit decision tree

The criteria is shown on the node, the data that doesn't pass the criteria gets pushed down the No branch, and the data that meets or passes the criteria is pushed down the Yes branch. Since the Yes branch now has just one possible outcome, it becomes an endpoint. The No branch still has a mixture, so it can be divided further using exactly the same method that was used to choose the top node. In this case, color is the best variable on which to divide the data. This process repeats until there is no information gain from dividing up the data on a given branch.

Using Your Decision Tree Classifier

The code for the decision trees built in Chapter 7 was trained on a list of lists. Each internal list has a set of values, with the final value in the list being the category. You can create the simple fruit dataset above like this:

```
>>> fruit=[[4,'red','apple'],
... [4,'green','apple'],
... [1,'red','cherry'],
... [1,'green','grape'],
... [5,'red','apple']]
```

Now you can train the decision tree and use it to classify new examples:

```
>>> import treepredict
>>> tree=treepredict.buildtree(fruit)
>>> treepredict.classify([2,'red'],tree)
{'cherry': 1}
>>> treepredict.classify([5,'red'],tree)
{'apple': 3}
>>> treepredict.classify([1,'green'],tree)
{'grape': 1}
>>> treepredict.classify([120,'red'],tree)
{'apple': 3}
```

Obviously, something ten feet across and purple is not an apple, but the decision tree is limited by what it has already seen. Finally, you can print or graph the tree to understand its decision-making process:

```
>>> treepredict.printtree(tree)
0:4?
T-> {'apple': 3}
F-> 1:green?
  T-> {'grape': 1}
  F-> {'cherry': 1}
```

Strengths and Weaknesses

The most striking advantage of decision trees is how easy it is to interpret a trained model and how well the algorithm brings important factors to the top of the tree. This means that a decision tree is useful not just for classification, but also for interpretation. Like the Bayesian classifier, you can look under the hood and understand why it works the way it does, and this can help you make decisions outside the classification process. For example, the model in Chapter 7 predicted which users would become paying customers, and having a decision tree that shows which variables are best at cleanly dividing the data could be useful for planning an advertising strategy or deciding what other data should be collected.

Decision trees also work with numerical data as inputs, since they find the dividing line that maximizes information gain. The ability to mix categorical and numerical data is useful for many classes of problems—something that traditional statistical methods like regression have trouble doing. On the other hand, decision trees are not as good at making predictions for numerical results. A regression tree can divide the data into mean values with the lowest variance, but if the data is complex, the tree will have to get very large before it is able to make accurate decisions.

The main advantage that decision trees have over the Bayesian classifier is that they can easily cope with interactions of variables. A spam filter built using a decision tree would easily determine that "online" and "pharmacy" are fine in isolation but that when they're together they indicate spam.

Unfortunately, using the algorithm from Chapter 7 is not practical for a spam filter for the simple reason that it does not support incremental training. (Alternative algorithms for decision trees that support incremental training are an active area of research.) You can take a big set of documents and build a decision tree for spam filtering, but you can't train it on individual new email messages as they come in—you would have to start from scratch each time. Since many people have tens of thousands of email messages, this would be impractical to do each time. Also, since the number of possible nodes is very large (each feature is present or absent), the trees can become extremely large and complex and would be slow to make classifications.

Neural Networks

Chapter 4 showed how to build a simple neural network for altering the ranking of search results based on what links users have clicked in the past. That neural network was able to learn which words in which combinations were important, and also which words were unimportant to a particular query. Neural networks can be applied to both classification and numerical prediction problems.

The neural network in Chapter 4 was used as a classifier—it gave a number for every link, predicting that the link with the highest number would be the one that the user would click. Because it gave numbers for every link, you could use all the numbers to change the rankings of the search results.

There are many different kinds of neural networks. The one covered in this book is known as a multilayer perceptron network, so named because it has a layer of input neurons that feed into one or more layers of hidden neurons. The basic structure is shown in Figure 12-3.

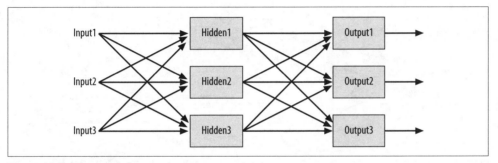

Figure 12-3. Basic neural network structure

This network has two layers of neurons. The layers of neurons are connected to each other by *synapses*, which each have an associated weight. The outputs from one set of neurons are fed to the next layer through the synapses. The higher the weight of a synapse leading from one neuron to the next, the more influence it will have on the output of that neuron.

As a simple example, consider again the problem of spam filtering that was described in the earlier section "Bayesian Classifier." In our simplified email world, an email message can contain the word "online," the word "pharmacy," or both. To determine which of these messages is spam, you might use a neural network that looks like Figure 12-4.

In this figure, the weights on the synapses are already set to solve the problem. (You'll see how they are set in the next section.) The neurons in the first layer respond to the words that are used as input—if a word is present in the email message, then the neurons that are strongly connected to that word become active. The second layer is fed by the first layer, so it responds to combinations of words.

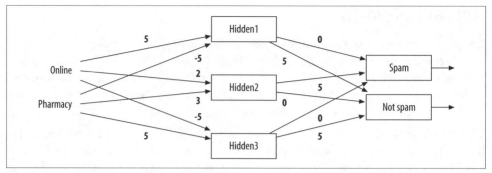

Figure 12-4. Neural network for spam classification

Finally, these neurons feed their results to the outputs, and particular combinations may be strongly or weakly associated with the possible results. In the end, the final decision is whichever output is strongest. Figure 12-5 shows how the network reacts to the word "online" when it is *not* accompanied by the word "pharmacy."

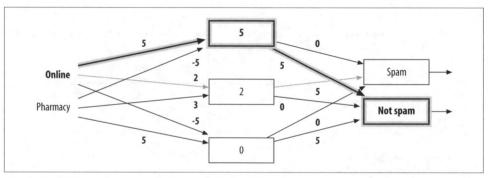

Figure 12-5. Network response to the word "online"

One of the neurons in the first layer responds to "online" and feeds its output to the second layer, where one of the neurons has learned to recognize messages that contain only the word "online" by itself. This neuron has a much stronger synapse leading to Not Spam than to Spam, so the message is classified as Not Spam. Figure 12-6 shows what happens when the words "online" and "pharmacy" are fed to the network together.

Since the neurons in the first layer react to the individual words, they both become active. In the second layer, things get a bit more interesting. The presence of "pharmacy" negatively affects the "online"-only neuron, and both of the first layer neurons work together to activate the middle neuron, which has been trained to respond to "online" and "pharmacy" together. This neuron feeds very strongly into the Spam category, so the document is classified as spam. This example demonstrates how multilayer neural networks can easily deal with features that mean different things in different combinations.

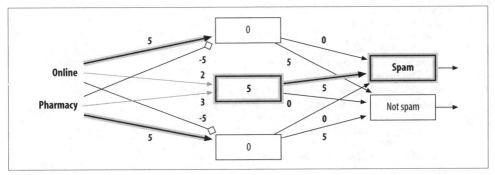

Figure 12-6. Neural network response to "online pharmacy"

Training a Neural Network

In the example above, the neural network already has the appropriate weights for all the synapses. The real power of neural networks is that they can start with random weights and then learn from examples through training. The most common method of training a multilayer perceptron network, and the method described in Chapter 4, is called backpropagation.

To train a network with backpropagation, you start with an example, such as the word "online" by itself and the correct answer, which in this case is Not Spam. You then feed the example into the neural network to see what its current guess looks like.

Initially, the network might give a slightly higher result for Spam than Not Spam, which is incorrect. To correct this, the network is told that Spam should be closer to 0 and Not Spam should be closer to 1. The synapse weights leading to Spam are adjusted slightly downward in proportion to how much each is contributing, and the weights leading to Not Spam are adjusted slightly upward. The synapse weights between the input and hidden layers are also adjusted according to how much they contribute to the important nodes in the output layer.

The actual formulae for these adjustments are given in Chapter 4. To stop the network from overcompensating when it is trained with noisy or uncertain data, it is trained slowly so the more times it sees a particular example, the better it will get at classifying it.

Using Your Neural Network Code

The code in Chapter 4 is easy to apply to this problem. The only trick is that it doesn't take the words directly, but uses number IDs for everything, so you'll need to assign numbers to the possible inputs. It uses a database to store training data, so just open with the name of a file and start training:

```
>>> import nn
>>> online,pharmacy=1,2
>>> spam,notspam=1,2
>>> possible=[spam,notspam]
>>> neuralnet=nn.searchnet('nntest.db')
>>> neuralnet.maketables()
>>> neuralnet.trainquery([online],possible,notspam)
>>> neuralnet.trainquery([online,pharmacy],possible,spam)
>>> neuralnet.trainquery([pharmacy],possible,notspam)
>>> neuralnet.getresult([online,pharmacy],possible)
[0.7763, 0.2890]
>>> neuralnet.getresult([online],possible)
[0.4351, 0.1826]
>>> neuralnet.trainquery([online],possible,notspam)
>>> neuralnet.getresult([online],possible)
[0.3219, 0.5329]
>>> neuralnet.trainquery([online],possible,notspam)
>>> neuralnet.getresult([online],possible)
[0.2206, 0.6453]
```

You can see that the network gives more certain results the more it is trained. It can also handle the occasional incorrect example and still retain good predictive power.

Strengths and Weaknesses

The main strength of neural networks is that they can handle complex nonlinear functions and discover dependencies between different inputs. Although the example only showed numerical inputs of 1 or 0 (present or absent), any number can be used as an input, and the network can also estimate numbers as outputs.

Neural networks also allow for incremental training and generally don't require a lot of space to store the trained models, since they are just a list of numbers representing the synapse weights. There is no need to keep the original data following training, which means that neural networks can be used for applications in which there is a continuous stream of training data.

The major downside of neural networks is that they are a black box method. The example network shown here was contrived to be extremely simple to follow, but in reality, a network might have hundreds of nodes and thousands of synapses, making it impossible to determine how the network came up with the answer that it did. Not being able to understand the reasoning process may be a deal breaker for some applications.

Another downside is that there are no definitive rules for choosing the training rate and network size for a particular problem. This decision usually requires a good amount of experimentation. Choosing a training rate that's too high means that the network might overgeneralize on noisy data, and choosing one that's too low means it might never learn, given the data you have.

Support-Vector Machines

Support-vector machines (SVMs) were introduced in Chapter 9, and are probably the most sophisticated classification method covered by this book. SVMs take datasets with numerical inputs and try to predict which category they fall into. You might, for example, want to decide positions for a basketball team from a list of people's heights and running speeds. To simplify, consider just two possibilities—front-court positions in which tall players are required, and back-court positions where you need the faster movers.

An SVM builds a predictive model by finding the dividing line between the two categories. If you plot a set of values for height versus speed and the best position for each person, you get a graph like the one shown in Figure 12-7. Front-court players are shown as Xs and back-court players are shown as Os. Also shown on the graph are a few lines that separate the data into the two categories.

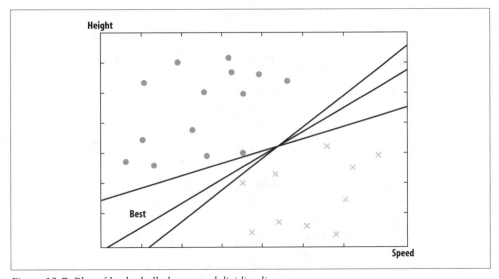

Figure 12-7. Plot of basketball players and dividing lines

A support-vector machine finds the line that separates the data most cleanly, which means that it is the greatest possible distance from points near the dividing line. In Figure 12-7, although all the different lines separate the data, the one that does this best is the one labeled "Best." The only points necessary to determine where the line should be are the points closest to it, and these are known as the *support vectors*.

After the dividing line has been found, classifying new items is just a matter of plotting them on the graph and seeing on which side of the line they fall. There's no need to go through the training data to classify new points once the line has been found, so classification is very fast.

The Kernel Trick

Support-vector machines, along with other linear classifiers that use vector *dot-products*, often take advantage of a technique called the *kernel trick*. To understand this, consider how the problem would change if the classification you were trying to predict was not position, but rather, whether the players would be appropriate for an amateur team in which the positions are often switched around. This is more interesting because the division is not linear. You don't want players who are too tall or too fast because they would make the game too difficult for others, but you don't want them to be too short or too slow either. Figure 12-8 shows what this might look like, where an O indicates that a player is appropriate for the team and an X indicates that he isn't.

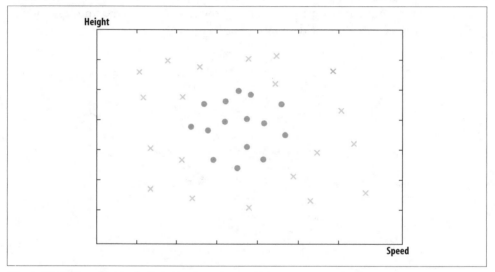

Figure 12-8. Plot of basketball players for amateur team

There is no straight dividing line here that will work, so you can't use a linear classifier to find the division without first altering the data in some way. One way to do this would be to transform the data into a different space—perhaps a space with more than two dimensions—by applying different functions to the axis variables. In this case, we might create a new space by subtracting the average values for height and speed and squaring the height and speed values. This would look like Figure 12-9.

This is called a *polynomial transformation*, and it transforms data on different axes. It's now easy to see that there is a dividing line between the members that are appropriate and inappropriate for the team, which can be found with a linear classifier. Classifying new points would be a matter of transforming them into this space and seeing on which side of the line they fall.

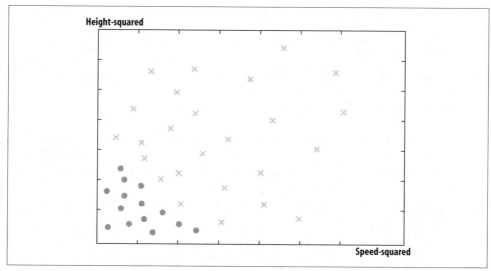

Figure 12-9. Basketball players in polynomial space

The transformation works in this case, but in many examples, finding the dividing line will require transformation into much more complex spaces. Some of these spaces have thousands or even infinite dimensions, so it's not always practical to actually do this transformation. This is where the kernel trick comes in—rather than transforming the space, you replace the dot-product function with a function that returns what the dot-product *would* be if the data was transformed into a different space. For example, instead of doing the polynomial transformation above, you would change:

```
dotproduct(A,B)
```

to:

```
dotproduct(A,B)**2
```

In Chapter 9, you built a simple linear classifier that used group averages. You saw how this could be altered by replacing the dot-product function with other functions for combining vectors, which allowed it to solve nonlinear problems.

Using LIBSVM

Chapter 9 introduced a library called LIBSVM. You can use it to train on a dataset (to find the dividing line in a transformed space) and then to classify new observations:

```
>>> from random import randint
>>> # Create 200 random points
>>> d1=[[randint(-20,20),randint(-20,20)] for i in range(200)]
>>> # Classify them as 1 if they are in the circle and 0 if not
>>> result=[(x**2+y**2)<144 and 1 or 0 for (x,y) in d1]
>>> from svm import *
```

```
>>> prob=svm_problem(result,d1)
>>> param=svm_parameter(kernel_type=RBF)
>>> m=svm_model(prob,param)
>>> m.predict([2,2])
1.0
>>> m.predict([14,13])
0.0
>>> m.predict([-18,0])
0.0
```

LIBSVM supports many different kernel functions, and it's easy to try them all out with different parameters to see what works best for a given dataset. To test how well a model works, you can try the cross_validation function, which takes a parameter, n, and divides the dataset into *n* subsets. It then uses each subset as a test set and trains the model with all the other subsets. It returns a list of answers that you can compare to the original list:

```
>>> guesses=cross_validation(prob,param,4)
>>> sum([abs(guesses[i]-result[i]) for i in range(len(guesses))])
28.0
```

When approaching a new problem, you can try the different kernel functions with different parameters to see which gives the best results. This will vary depending on the dataset, and after you've decided, you can use those parameters to create the model that will be used to classify new observations. In practice, you might create some nested loops to try different values and track which ones gave the best result.

Strengths and Weaknesses

Support-vector machines are a very powerful classifier; once you get the parameters correct, they will likely work as well as or better than any other classification method that this book has covered. Further, after training they are very fast to classify new observations, since classification is simply done by determining on which side of a dividing line a point is. By transforming categorical inputs to numbers, you can make them work with a mixture of categorical and numerical data.

One disadvantage is that the best kernel transformation function and the parameters for that function will be slightly different for every dataset, and you'll have to find them each time. Looping through possible values helps to alleviate this problem, but it does require that you have a big enough dataset to do reliable cross-validation. Generally, SVMs are much more suited to problems in which there is a lot of data available, while other methods such as decision trees can still give interesting information with very small datasets.

Like neural networks, SVMs are a black box technique—it's actually even more difficult to interpret how an SVM is doing classification because of the transformation into high-dimensional spaces. An SVM may give great answers, but you'll never really know why.

k-Nearest Neighbors

Chapter 8 covered the topic of numerical prediction using an algorithm called k-nearest neighbors (kNN), and used it to show how you could build models for predicting prices given a set of examples. The recommendation algorithm in Chapter 2 for predicting how much someone would like a movie or a link was also a simple version of kNN.

kNN works by taking a new item for which you want a numerical prediction and comparing it to a set of items for which it already has values. It finds the ones most similar to the item in question and averages their values to get a predicted value. Table 12-6 shows a list of digital cameras, along with their megapixel rating, zoom power, and sale price.

Table 12-6. Digital cameras and prices

Camera	Megapixels	Zoom	Price
C1	7.1	3.8x	$399
C2	5.0	2.4x	$299
C3	6.0	4.0x	$349
C4	6.0	12.0x	$399
C5	10.0	3x	$449

Suppose you want to guess the price for a new camera with a six megapixels and a 6x zoom lens. The first thing you'll need is a way to measure how similar two items are. Chapter 8 used Euclidean distance, and you've seen many other distance metrics throughout this book, such as Pearson correlation and Tanimoto score. Using Euclidean distance in this example reveals that the closest item in the table is C3. To visualize this, imagine plotting the items on a chart with megapixels as the x-axis and zoom as the y-axis. The items themselves are identified by their prices in Figure 12-10.

You could just take the price of $349 as the answer (it is the closest match, after all), but you'd never know if its price was just an anomaly. For this reason, it's better to take more than one of the best matches and average them. The *k* in k-nearest neighbors refers to how many of the top matches you use for averaging. For example, if you took the best three matches and averaged them, this would be kNN with k=3.

An extension to the basic averaging is to use a weighted average based on how far away the neighbors are. A very close neighbor would count for more than an item that was further away. The weights would be in proportion to the total distance. Chapter 8 covered different functions for determining the weights. In the example, you might use the price of $349 weighted most heavily, with the two $399 prices weighted less. For example:

```
price = 0.5 * 349 + 0.25 * 399 + 0.25 * 399 = 374
```

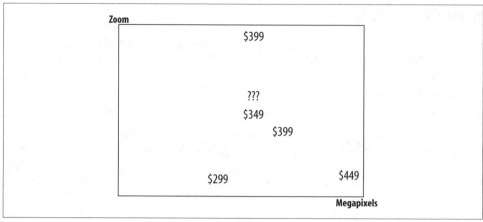

Figure 12-10. Camera prices in zoom-megapixel space

Scaling and Superfluous Variables

A big problem with the kNN algorithm described so far is that it calculates distance across all the variables. This means that if the variables measure different things and one of the variables tends to be much larger than the others, it will exert a much stronger influence on what is "close." Imagine if the dataset above gave resolution in pixels instead of in megapixels—a zoom difference of 10x is much more important than a resolution difference of 10 extra pixels, but they will be treated the same. In other cases, the dataset will contain some variables that are completely useless for making predictions, but these will still affect the distances.

This problem can be solved by scaling the data before calculating the distances. In Chapter 8, you created a method for scaling, which meant increasing the magnitudes of some variables and decreasing the magnitudes of others. Entirely useless variables could all be multiplied by 0 so that they no longer affect the outcome. Variables that were valuable but in vastly different ranges could be scaled to be more comparable—you might determine that a difference of 2,000 pixels is the equivalent of a zoom difference of 1x.

Because the appropriate amount to scale the data depends on the application, you can test how good a certain set of scaling factors is by cross-validating the prediction algorithm. Cross-validation removes items from the dataset and then tries to see how well it can guess them using the rest of the data. Figure 12-11 shows how this works.

By using cross-validation with many different scaling factors, you can get an error rate for each item and use it to determine which scaling factors should be used for making predictions about new items.

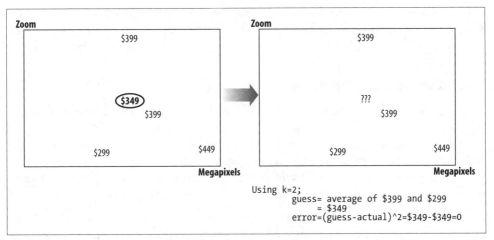

Figure 12-11. *Cross-validation of a single item*

Using Your kNN Code

In Chapter 8, you built functions for kNN and weighted kNN. These are easy to run on the sample dataset given in Table 12-6.

```
>>> cameras=[{'input':(7.1,3.8),'result':399},
... {'input':(5.0,2.4),'result':299},
... {'input':(6.0,4.0),'result':349},
... {'input':(6.0,12.0),'result':399},
... {'input':(10.0,3.0),'result':449}]
>>> import numpredict
>>> numpredict(cameras,(6.0,6.0),k=2)
374.0
>>> numpredict.weightedknn(cameras,(6.0,6.0),k=3)
351.52666892719458
```

It's possible that these can be improved by scaling the data. The rescale function will do this:

```
>>> scc=numpredict.rescale(cameras,(1,2))
>>> scc
[{'input': [7.1, 7.6], 'result': 399}, {'input': [5.0, 4.8], 'result': 299},
{'input': [6.0, 8.0], 'result': 349}, {'input': [6.0, 24.0], 'result': 399},
{'input': [10.0, 6.0], 'result': 449}]
```

And by using crossvalidate, you can figure out which scaling factor works best:

```
>>> numpredict.crossvalidate(knn1,cameras,test=0.3,trials=2)
3750.0
>>> numpredict.crossvalidate(knn1,scc,test=0.3,trials=2)
2500.0
```

With a dataset with more variables, it will become tedious to guess the possible scaling factors, so you can loop through all the different values looking for the best result or, as shown in Chapter 8, you can use one of the optimization algorithms.

Strengths and Weaknesses

k-nearest neighbors is one of the few algorithms that will make numerical predictions in complex functions and still remain easy to interpret. The reasoning process is easy to understand, and a simple change to the code will allow you to see exactly which neighbors are being used in the calculation. Neural networks can also make numerical predictions in complex functions, but they will certainly not be able to show you similar examples to help you understand the reasoning process.

Furthermore, the process of determining the correct amounts to scale the data not only improves predictions, but also tells you which variables are important in making predictions. Any variable that gets scaled down to 0 can be thrown out. In some cases, that data may have been difficult or expensive to collect, so knowing that it's not useful may save you some time and money in the future.

KNN is an *online technique*, meaning that new data can be added at any time, unlike techniques such as support-vector machines that require retraining if the data changes. Moreover, adding new data does not require any computation at all; the data is simply added to the set.

The major weakness of KNN is that it requires all the training data to be present in order to make predictions. In a dataset with millions of examples, this is not just a space issue but also a time issue—every item for which you're trying to make a prediction has to be compared with every other item to determine which are the closest. This process may be too slow for some applications.

Another disadvantage is that finding the correct scaling factors can be tedious. Although there are ways to make this process more automatic, cross-validation and scoring thousands of possible scaling factors can be very computationally intensive with a large dataset. If there are many different variables to try, it might be necessary to try millions of different scaling factors before finding the right one.

Clustering

Hierarchical clustering and K-means clustering are unsupervised learning techniques, meaning they don't require examples for training data because they don't attempt to make predictions. Chapter 3 looked at how to take a list of top bloggers and automatically cluster them so you could see which ones naturally fell into groups that write about similar subjects or use similar words.

Hierarchical Clustering

Clustering works on any set of items that have one or more numerical properties. The example in Chapter 3 used word counts for the different blogs, but any set of numbers can be used for clustering. To demonstrate how the hierarchical clustering algorithm works, consider a simple table of items (some letters of the alphabet) and some numerical properties (Table 12-7).

Table 12-7. Simple table for clustering

Item	P1	P2
A	1	8
B	3	8
C	2	6
D	1.5	1
E	4	2

Figure 12-12 shows the process of clustering these items. In the first pane, the items have been plotted in two dimensions, with P1 on the x-axis and P2 on the y-axis. Hierarchical clustering works by finding the two items that are closest together and merging them into a cluster. In the second pane, you can see that the closest items, A and B, have been grouped together. The "location" of this cluster is the average of the two items in it. In the next pane, it turns out that the closest items are C and the new A-B cluster. This process continues until the final pane in which everything is contained in one big cluster.

This process creates a hierarchy, which can be illustrated as a *dendrogram*, a tree-like structure that shows which items and groups are closest together. The dendrogram for the example dataset is shown in Figure 12-13.

The two closest items, A and B, are connected together at the end. C is connected to the combination of A and B. From the dendrogram you can pick any branch point and decide if it is a group of interest. In Chapter 3, you saw branches consisting almost entirely of political blogs and other branches of technology blogs and so on.

K-Means Clustering

Another method of clustering data is called K-means clustering. While hierarchical clustering creates a tree of the items, K-means clustering actually separates the data into distinct groups. It also requires you to decide how many groups you want before the algorithm starts running. Figure 12-14 shows an example of K-means clustering in action, trying to find two clusters with a slightly different dataset than was used with the hierarchical clustering example.

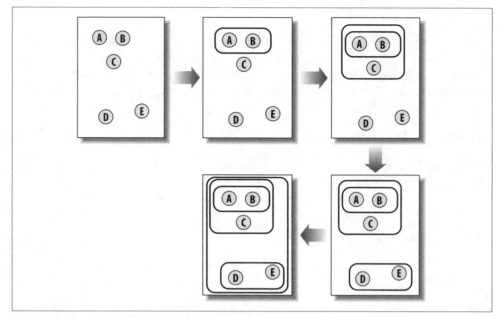

Figure 12-12. Process of hierarchical clustering

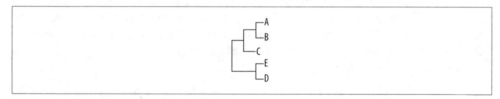

Figure 12-13. Dendrogram of clustered letters

In the first frame, the two centroids (shown as dark circles) are placed randomly. Frame 2 shows that each of the items is assigned to the nearest one—in this case, A and B are assigned to the top centroid, and C, D, and E are assigned to the bottom centroid. In the third frame, the centroids have been moved to the average location of the items that were assigned to them. When the assignments are calculated again, it turns out that C is now closer to the top centroid, while D and E remain closest to the bottom one. Thus, the final result is reached with A, B, and C in one cluster, and D and E in the other.

Using Your Clustering Code

In order to do clustering, you'll need a dataset and a distance metric. The dataset consists of lists of numbers, with each number representing a variable. In Chapter 3, both Pearson correlation and Tanimoto score were used as distance metrics, but it's easy to use other metrics such as Euclidean distance:

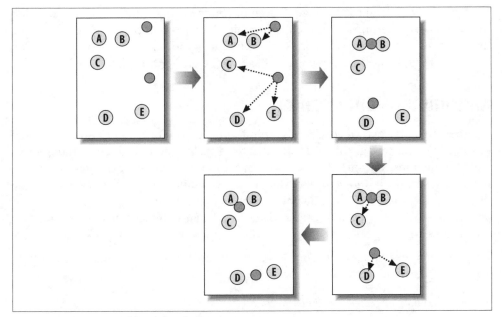

Figure 12-14. Process of K-means clustering

```
>>> data=[[1.0,8.0],[3.0,8.0],[2.0,7.0],[1.5,1.0],[4.0,2.0]]
>>> labels=['A','B','C','D','E']
>>> def euclidean(v1,v2): return sum([(v1[i]-v2[i])**2 for i in range(len(v1))])
>>> import clusters
>>> hcl=clusters.hcluster(data,distance=euclidean)
>>> kcl=clusters.kcluster(data,distance=euclidean,k=2)
Iteration 0
Iteration 1
```

For K-means clustering, you can easily print the results of which items were placed in each of your two clusters:

```
>>> kcl
[[0, 1, 2], [3, 4]]
>>> for c in kcl: print [labels[1] for l in c]
...
['A', 'B', 'C']
['D', 'E']
```

Hierarchical clustering doesn't lend itself well to printing, but the code built in Chapter 3 included a function to draw the dendrogram of the hierarchical clusters:

```
>>> clusters.drawdendrogram(hcl,labels,jpeg='hcl.jpg')
```

The choice of which algorithm to use really depends on what you're trying to do. It's often useful to have the data divided into distinct groups, such as the ones you get from K-means clustering, since it's much easier to display and to characterize the groups. On the other hand, with a completely new dataset you may have no idea how many groups you want, and you may also want to see which groups are most similar to each other. In this case, hierarchical clustering would be a better choice.

It's also possible to take advantage of both methods by first using K-means clustering to create a set of groups, and then hierarchically clustering these groups using the distances between their centroids. This would give you distinct groups at one level that are arranged into a tree so you can see how the groups are related.

Multidimensional Scaling

Another method covered in Chapter 3 and applied to blogs was multidimensional scaling. Like clustering, this is an unsupervised technique that does not attempt to make predictions, but instead makes it easier to understand how different items are related. It creates a lower-dimensional representation of a dataset where the distances are as close to the original dataset as possible. For display on a screen or paper, this usually means scaling data from many dimensions down to two dimensions.

Imagine, for example, that you have the four-dimensional dataset shown in Table 12-8 (every item has four associated values).

Table 12-8. Simple four-dimensional table for scaling

A	0.5	0.0	0.3	0.1
B	0.4	0.15	0.2	0.1
C	0.2	0.4	0.7	0.8
D	1.0	0.3	0.6	0.0

Using the Euclidean distance formula, you can get a distance value for every pair of items. For example, the distance between A and B is $sqrt(0.1^2+0.15^2+0.1^2+0.0^2) = 0.2$. The full matrix of all the pairwise distances is given in Table 12-9.

Table 12-9. Sample distance matrix

	A	B	C	D
A	0.0	0.2	0.9	0.8
B	0.2	0.0	0.9	0.7
C	0.9	0.9	0.0	1.1
D	0.8	0.7	1.1	0.0

The goal here is to draw all the items in a two-dimensional chart so that the distances in two dimensions are as close as possible to their distances in four dimensions. All the items are placed randomly on the chart, and the current distances between all the items are calculated, as shown in Figure 12-15.

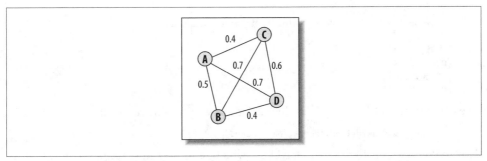

Figure 12-15. Distances between items

For every pair of items, the target distance is compared to the current distance and an error term is calculated. Every item is moved a small amount closer or farther away in proportion to the error between the two items. Figure 12-16 shows the forces acting on item A. The distance between A and B in the chart is 0.5, but the target distance is only 0.2, so A has to be moved closer to B. At the same time, A is also being pushed away by C and D because it is too close.

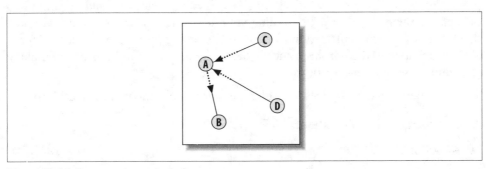

Figure 12-16. Forces acting on item A

Every node is moved according the combination of all the other nodes pushing and pulling on it. Each time this is done, the difference between the current distances and the target distances should get a little smaller. This procedure is repeated many times until the total amount of error cannot be reduced by moving the items any more.

Using Your Multidimensional Scaling Code

In Chapter 3, you built two functions for multidimensional scaling, one to actually run the algorithm and the other to display the results. The first function, scaledown, takes the list of item values in multiple dimensions and returns the list in the same order, scaled down to two dimensions:

```
>>> labels=['A','B','C','D']
>>> scaleset=[[0.5,0.0,0.3,0.1],
... [0.4,0.15,0.2,0.1],
... [0.2,0.4,0.7,0.8],
```

```
... [1.0,0.3,0.6,0.0]]
>>> twod=clusters.scaledown(scaleset,distance=euclidean)
>>> twod
[[0.45, 0.54],
 [0.40, 0.54],
 [-0.30, 1.02],
 [0.92, 0.59]]
```

The other function, draw2d, takes this scaled-down list and creates an image:

```
>>> clusters.draw2d(twod,labels,jpeg='abcd.jpg')
```

This will create a file called *abcd.jpg*, which contains the result. You can also visualize the results in different ways by taking the list generated by scaledown and using it with another program, such as a spreadsheet.

Non-Negative Matrix Factorization

Chapter 10 covered an advanced technique called non-negative matrix factorization (NMF), which is a way to break down a set of numerical observations into their component parts. This method was used to show how news stories could be composed of separate themes and how the trading volume of various stocks could be broken down into events that affected individual stocks or multiple stocks at once. This is also an unsupervised algorithm, since it helps characterize data rather than making predictions about categories or values.

To understand what NMF does, consider the set of values shown in Table 12-10:

Table 12-10. Simple table for NMF

Observation Number	A	B
1	29	29
2	43	33
3	15	25
4	40	28
5	24	11
6	29	29
7	37	23
8	21	6

Assume that observations A and B are composed of some combination of two pairs of numbers (the features), but you don't know what those pairs are or how much of each pair (the weights) is used to create each observation. NMF can find possible values for both the features and the weights. When working with news stories in Chapter 10, the observations were the stories and the columns were the words in the stories. With stock trading volumes, the observations were the days and the columns were various stock tickers. In each case, the algorithm attempted to find a smaller number of parts that could be added together in different amounts to get these observations.

One possible answer for the data in the table is that the two pairs are (3, 5) and (7, 2).

Using these parts, you can see that the observations can be recreated by combining the pairs in different amounts, such as the following:

$5*(3, 5) + 2*(7, 2) = (29, 29)$
$5*(3, 5) + 4*(7, 2) = (43, 33)$

This can also be viewed as a matrix multiplication, as shown in Figure 12-17.

$$
\begin{pmatrix} 5 & 2 \\ 5 & 4 \\ 5 & 0 \\ 4 & 4 \\ 1 & 3 \\ 5 & 2 \\ 3 & 4 \\ 0 & 3 \end{pmatrix}
X
\begin{pmatrix} 3 & 5 \\ 7 & 2 \end{pmatrix}
=
\begin{pmatrix} 29 & 29 \\ 43 & 33 \\ 15 & 25 \\ 40 & 28 \\ 24 & 11 \\ 29 & 29 \\ 37 & 23 \\ 21 & 6 \end{pmatrix}
$$

Weights   Features   Dataset

Figure 12-17. Factorizing a dataset into weights and features

The goal of NMF is to automatically find the features matrix and the weights matrix. To do this, it starts with random matrices for each and updates them according to the *update rules*. The rules generate four new update matrices. In these descriptions, the original matrix is referred to as the data matrix:

hn

> The transposed weights matrix multiplied by the data matrix

hd

> The transposed weights matrix multiplied by the weights matrix multiplied by the features matrix

wn

> The data matrix multiplied by the transposed features matrix

wd

> The weights matrix multiplied by the features matrix multiplied by the transposed features matrix

To update the features and weights matrices, all these matrices are converted to arrays. Every value in the features matrix is multiplied by the corresponding value in *hn* and divided by the corresponding value in *hd*. Likewise, every value in the weights matrix is multiplied by the value in *wn* and divided by the value in *wd*.

This is repeated until the product of the features and weights matrix is close enough to the data matrix. The features matrix can tell you the underlying causes that work in combination to create your dataset, such as news themes or stock market events.

Using Your NMF Code

Using the NMF code simply requires you to call the factorize function with a list of observations and the number of underlying features you want to find:

```
>>> from numpy import *
>>> import nmf
>>> data=matrix([[ 29.,   29.],
... [ 43.,   33.],
... [ 15.,   25.],
... [ 40.,   28.],
... [ 24.,   11.],
... [ 29.,   29.],
... [ 37.,   23.],
... [ 21.,    6.]])
>>> weights,features=nmf.factorize(data,pc=2)
>>> weights
matrix([[ 0.64897525,  0.75470755],
        [ 0.98192453,  0.80792914],
        [ 0.31602596,  0.70148596],
        [ 0.91871934,  0.66763194],
        [ 0.56262912,  0.22012957],
        [ 0.64897525,  0.75470755],
        [ 0.85551414,  0.52733475],
        [ 0.49942392,  0.07983238]])
>>> features
matrix([[ 41.62815416,   6.80725866],
        [  2.62930778,  32.57189835]])
```

The weights and the features are returned. They may not be the same every time, since there might be multiple valid feature sets for a small set of observations. The larger the set of observations, the more likely it is that the results will be consistent, although the features may be returned in a different order.

Optimization

Optimization, covered in Chapter 5, is a little different from the other methods; instead of working with a dataset, it attempts to select values that minimize the output of a cost function. Chapter 5 showed several examples of cost functions, such as planning group travel using a combination of price and waiting time at the airport, assigning students to the most appropriate dorm, and optimizing the layout of a simple graph. Once the cost function was designed, the same algorithms could be used to solve these three different problems. Two algorithms were covered: simulated annealing and genetic algorithms.

The Cost Function

A cost function is any function that takes a guess at a solution and returns a value that is higher for worse solutions and lower for better solutions. Optimization algorithms use this function to test solutions and to search possible solutions for the best one. The cost functions you use with optimization often have many variables to consider, and it's not always clear which is the best one to change in order to improve the result. However, for illustration, consider a function with only one variable, defined as:

```
y = 1/x * sin(x)
```

Figure 12-18 shows the graph of this function.

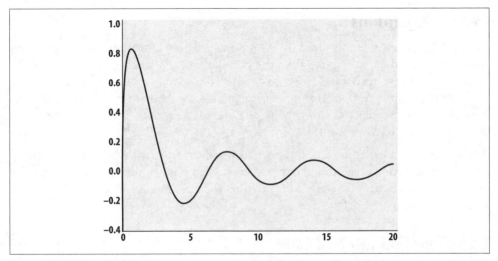

*Figure 12-18. Graph of 1/x * sin x*

Because the function has only one variable, it's easy to see from the graph where the lowest point is. We're using this for illustration so you can see how the optimization works; in reality, you wouldn't be able to simply graph complicated functions with many variables in order to find the lowest point.

What is interesting about this function is that it has several local minima. These are points that are lower than all the surrounding points but are not necessarily the lowest point overall. This means the problem can't necessarily be solved by trying a random solution and moving down the slope, because it can lead to getting stuck in a local minimum and never finding the global minimum.

Simulated Annealing

Simulated annealing, which was inspired by alloy cooling in physics, starts with a random guess at a solution. It tries to improve the solution by determining the cost for a similar solution that's a small distance away and in a random direction from the solution in question. If the cost is lower, this becomes the new solution. If the cost is higher, it becomes the new solution with a certain probability, depending on the current *temperature*. The temperature starts high and decreases slowly so that early on the algorithm is much more likely to accept worse solutions in order to avoid getting stuck in a local minimum.

When the temperature has reached 0, the algorithm returns the current solution.

Genetic Algorithms

Genetic algorithms were inspired by evolutionary theory. A genetic algorithm starts with several random solutions called the population. The strongest members of the population—those with the lowest cost—are chosen and modified either through slight changes (mutation) or through trait combination (crossover or breeding). This creates a new population, known as the next generation, and over successive generations the solutions improve.

The process stops when a certain threshold has been reached, when the population has not improved over several generations, or when a maximum number of generations has been reached. The algorithm returns the best solution that has been found in any generation.

Using Your Optimization Code

For both algorithms, you need to define a cost function and determine the domain of the solution. The domain is the possible ranges for each variable. In this simple example, you can use [(0,20)], meaning that there is one variable that can be between 0 and 5. Either of the optimization methods can then be called with the cost function and the domain as parameters:

```
>>> import math
>>> def costf(x): return (1.0/(x[0]+0.1))*math.sin(x[0])
>>> domain=[(0,20)]
>>> optimization.annealingoptimize(domain,costf)
[5]
```

For any problem, it may be necessary to run the optimization a few times to tweak the parameters, and to get the right balance of running time and quality of the solution. When building an optimizer for a related set of problems—such as travel planning, in which the goal remains the same but the underlying details (flight times and prices) change—you can experiment with the parameters once, decide on settings that work well for that set of problems, and leave them fixed from then on.

There are many possibilities for combining machine learning, open APIs, and open participation, and there will continue to be more in the future as algorithms are refined, as APIs are opened up, and as a greater number of people become active online participants. I hope that this book has given you the tools and the inspiration to find many new opportunities!

Third-Party Libraries

This book has introduced a number of third-party libraries that we used to collect, store, and analyze data. This appendix covers download and installation instructions, along with some examples of usage.

Universal Feed Parser

The Universal Feed Parser is a Python library written by Mark Pilgrim for parsing RSS and Atom feeds. This library is used throughout the book for easily downloading blog posts and articles from online news sources. The home page of the library is *http://feedparser.org*.

Installation for All Platforms

The download page for the library is *http://code.google.com/p/feedparser/downloads/list*. Download the latest version of the file named *feedparser-X.Y.zip*.

Extract the contents of the zip file into an empty directory. At a command prompt, enter:

```
c:\download\feedparser>python setup.py install
```

This will locate your Python installation and install the library there. After it is installed, you can enter **import feedparser** at your Python prompt to begin using it.

Example usage of the library is provided at *http://feedparser.org/*.

Python Imaging Library

The Python Imaging Library (PIL) is an open-source library that adds image creation and processing capabilities to Python. It supports a wide variety of drawing operations and file formats. The home page for this library is *http://www.pythonware.com/products/pil*.

Installation on Windows

PIL has a Windows installer available for download. On the library home page, scroll to the Downloads section and download the latest Windows executable for your version of Python. Run this file and follow the on-screen instructions.

Installation on Other Platforms

For platforms other than Windows, you'll need to build the library from the sources. The sources are available for download on the library's home page and will work with any recent version of Python.

To install, download the sources for the latest version and enter the following at the command prompt, replacing 1.1.6 with the version you have downloaded:

```
$ gunzip Imaging-1.1.6.tar.gz
$ tar xvf Imaging-1.1.6.tar
$ cd Imaging-1.1.6
$ python setup.py install
```

This will compile the extensions and install the library in your Python directory.

Simple Usage Example

This example creates a small image, draws some lines, and writes a message. It then saves the image as a JPEG file.

```
>>> from PIL import Image,ImageDraw
>>> img=Image.new('RGB',(200,200),(255,255,255))   # 200x200 white background
>>> draw=ImageDraw.Draw(img)
>>> draw.line((20,50,150,80),fill=(255,0,0))        # Red line
>>> draw.line((150,150,20,200),fill=(0,255,0))      # Green line
>>> draw.text((40,80),'Hello!',(0,0,0))             # Black text
>>> img.save('test.jpg','JPEG')                     # Save to test.jpg
```

A more extensive set of examples is available at *http://www.pythonware.com/library/pil/handbook/introduction.htm*.

Beautiful Soup

Beautiful Soup is a Python parser for HTML and XML documents. It is designed to work with poorly written web pages. It is used in this book to create datasets from web sites that do not have APIs, and to find all the text on pages for indexing. The home page for this library is *http://www.crummy.com/software/BeautifulSoup*.

Installation on All Platforms

Beautiful Soup is available as a single file source download. Near the bottom of the home page, there is a link to download *BeautifulSoup.py*. Simply download this and put it in either your working directory or your *Python/Lib* directory.

Simple Usage Example

This example parses the HTML of the Google home page, and shows how to extract elements from the DOM and search for links.

```
>>> from BeautifulSoup import BeautifulSoup
>>> from urllib import urlopen
>>> soup=BeautifulSoup(urlopen('http://google.com'))
>>> soup.head.title
<title>Google</title>
>>> links=soup('a')
>>> len(links)
21
>>> links[0]
<a href="http://www.google.com/ig?hl=en">iGoogle</a>
>>> links[0].contents[0]
u'iGoogle'
```

A more extensive set of examples is available at *http://www.crummy.com/software/BeautifulSoup/documentation.html*.

pysqlite

pysqlite is a Python interface to the SQLite embedded database. Unlike traditional databases, an embedded database does not run in a separate server process, so there's much less to install and set up. SQLite also stores the entire database in a single file. This book uses pysqlite to illustrate how to persist some of the data being collected.

The home page for pysqlite is *http://www.initd.org/tracker/pysqlite/wiki/pysqlite*.

Installation on Windows

The home page has links to download a binary installer for Windows. Simply download this file and run it. It will ask you where your installation of Python is and will install itself there.

Installation on Other Platforms

For platforms other than Windows, you'll need to install pysqlite from the source. The sources are available as a tarball on the pysqlite home page. Download the latest version and enter the following at the command prompt, replacing 2.3.3 with the version you have downloaded:

```
$ gunzip pysqlite-2.3.3.tar.gz
$ tar xvf pysqlite-2.3.3.tar.gz
$ cd pysqlite-2.3.3
$ python setup.py build
$ python setup.py install
```

Simple Usage Example

This example creates a new table, adds a row to it, and commits the change. The table is then queried for the new row:

```
>>> from pysqlite2 import dbapi2 as sqlite
>>> con=sqlite.connect('test1.db')
>>> con.execute('create table people (name,phone,city)')
<pysqlite2.dbapi2.Cursor object at 0x00ABE770>
>>> con.execute('insert into people values ("toby","555-1212","Boston")')
<pysqlite2.dbapi2.Cursor object at 0x00AC8A10>
>>> con.commit()
>>> cur=con.execute('select * from people')
>>> cur.next()
(u'toby', u'555-1212', u'Boston')
```

Notice that field types are optional with SQLite. To make this work with a more traditional database, you might have to add field types to your declarations when creating tables.

NumPy

NumPy is a mathematical library for Python that provides an array object, linear algebra functions, and Fourier transforms. It is a very popular way to do scientific computing in Python and it's gaining popularity, in some cases replacing more purpose-built tools like MATLAB. NumPy is used in Chapter 10 to implement the NMF algorithm. The home page for NumPy is *http://numpy.scipy.org*.

Installation on Windows

There is a Windows binary installer available for NumPy at *http://sourceforge.net/ project/showfiles.php?group_id=1369&package_id=175103*.

Download the *.exe* file that matches your version of Python and run it. It will ask you for the directory where Python is installed and will install itself there.

Installation on Other Platforms

On other platforms, NumPy can be installed from the sources, which can also be downloaded at *http://sourceforge.net/project/showfiles.php?group_id=1369&package_id=175103*.

Download the *tar.gz* file appropriate for your version of Python. To install from the source, use the following, replacing 1.0.2 with the version you have downloaded:

```
$ gunzip numpy-1.0.2.tar.gz
$ tar xvf numpy-1.0.2.tar.gz
$ cd numpy-1.0.2
$ python setup.py install
```

Simple Usage Example

This example shows you how to create matrices, multiply them together, and then transpose and flatten operations:

```
>>> from numpy import *
>>> a=matrix([[1,2,3],[4,5,6]])
>>> b=matrix([[1,2],[3,4],[5,6]])
>>> a*b
matrix([[22, 28],
        [49, 64]])
>>> a.transpose()
matrix([[1, 4],
        [2, 5],
        [3, 6]])
>>> a.flatten()
matrix([[1, 2, 3, 4, 5, 6]])
```

matplotlib

matplotlib is a 2D graphics library for Python that is much better for creating mathematical graphs than the Python Imaging Library. The figures it produces are intended to be of high enough quality to be used in publications.

Installation

Before installing matplotlib, you'll need to install NumPy, as described in the previous section. matplotlib has binary builds for all major platforms, including Windows, Mac OS X, RPM-based Linux distributions, and Debian-based distributions. You can find detailed instructions for installing matplotlib on any of the platforms at *http://matplotlib.sourceforge.net/installing.html*.

Simple Usage Example

This example will use orange circles to plot four points at (1,1), (2,4), (3,9), and (4,16). It will then save the output to a file and display it in a window on the screen.

```
>>> from pylab import *
>>> plot([1,2,3,4], [1,4,9,16], 'ro')
[<matplotlib.lines.Line2D instance at 0x01878990>]
>>> savefig('test1.png')
>>> show()
```

A great collection of usage examples is available at *http://matplotlib.sourceforge.net/tutorial.html*.

pydelicious

pydelicious is a library for retrieving data from the del.icio.us social bookmarking site. del.icio.us has an official API that is used for some calls, but pydelicious adds some extra features that we used in Chapter 2 to build the recommendation engine. Pydelicious is now hosted at Google code; you can find it at *http://code.google.com/p/pydelicious/source*.

Installation for All Platforms

Getting the latest version of pydelicious is easiest if you have the *Subversion* version control software installed. If you do, you can just enter the following at a command prompt:

```
svn checkout http://pydelicious.googlecode.com/svn/trunk/pydelicious.py
```

If you don't have Subversion, the files can be downloaded at *http://pydelicious.googlecode.com/svn/trunk*.

After you have the files, just run **python setup.py install** from the directory where you downloaded them. This will install pydelicious in your Python directory.

Simple Usage Example

pydelicious has a number of calls to get popular bookmarks or bookmarks for a specific user. It also allows you to add new bookmarks to your own account:

```
>> import pydelicious
>> pydelicious.get_popular(tag='programming')
[{'count': '', 'extended': '', 'hash': '',
  'description': u'How To Write Unmaintainable Code',
  'tags': '', 'href': u'http://thc.segfault.net/root/phun/unmaintain.html',
  'user': u'dorsia', 'dt': u'2006-08-19T09:48:56Z'},
```

```
 {'count': '', 'extended': '', 'hash': '',
  'description': u'Threading in C#', 'tags': '',
  'href':u'http://www.albahari.com/threading/', etc...
>> pydelicious.get_userposts('dorsia')
[{'count': '', 'extended': '', 'hash': '',
  'description': u'How To Write Unmaintainable Code',
  'tags': '', 'href': u'http://thc.segfault.net/root/phun/unmaintain.html',
  'user': u'dorsia', 'dt': u'2006-08-19T09:48:56Z'}, etc...
>>> a = pydelicious.apiNew(user, passwd)
>>> a.posts_add(url="http://my.com/", desciption="my.com",
                extended="the url is my.moc", tags="my com")
True
```

APPENDIX B

Mathematical Formulas

Throughout the book I have introduced a number of mathematical concepts. This appendix covers selected concepts and gives a description, relevant formulas, and code for each of them.

Euclidean Distance

Euclidean distance finds the distance between two points in multidimensional space, which is the kind of distance you measure with a ruler. If the points are written as $(p_1, p_2, p_3, p_4, ...)$ and $(q_1, q_2, q_3, q_4, ...)$, then the formula for Euclidean distance can be expressed as shown in Equation B-1.

$$\sqrt{(p_1 - q_1)^2 + (p_2 - q_2)^2 + ... + (p_n - q_n)^2} = \sqrt{\sum_{i=1}^{n} (p_i - q_i)^2}$$

Equation B-1. Euclidean distance

A clear implementation of this formula is shown here:

```
def euclidean(p,q):
  sumSq=0.0

  # add up the squared differences
  for i in range(len(p)):
    sumSq+=(p[i]-q[i])**2

  # take the square root
  return (sumSq**0.5)
```

Euclidean distance is used in several places in this book to determine how similar two items are.

Pearson Correlation Coefficient

The *Pearson correlation coefficient* is a measure of how highly correlated two variables are. It is a value between 1 and –1, where 1 indicates that the variables are perfectly correlated, 0 indicates no correlation, and –1 means they are perfectly inversely correlated.

Equation B-2 shows the Pearson correlation coefficient.

$$r = \frac{\sum XY - \frac{\sum X \sum Y}{N}}{\sqrt{\left(\sum X^2 - \frac{(\sum X)^2}{N}\right)\left(\sum Y^2 - \frac{(\sum Y)^2}{N}\right)}}$$

Equation B-2. Pearson correlation coefficient

This can be implemented with the following code:

```
def pearson(x,y):
  n=len(x)
  vals=range(n)

  # Simple sums
  sumx=sum([float(x[i]) for i in vals])
  sumy=sum([float(y[i]) for i in vals])

  # Sum up the squares
  sumxSq=sum([x[i]**2.0 for i in vals])
  sumySq=sum([y[i]**2.0 for i in vals])

  # Sum up the products
  pSum=sum([x[i]*y[i] for i in vals])

  # Calculate Pearson score
  num=pSum-(sumx*sumy/n)
  den=((sumxSq-pow(sumx,2)/n)*(sumySq-pow(sumy,2)/n))**.5
  if den==0: return 0

  r=num/den

  return r
```

We used the Pearson correlation in Chapter 2 to calculate the level of similarity between people's preferences.

Weighted Mean

The *weighted mean* is a type of average that has a weight for every observation being averaged. It is used in this book to make numerical predictions based on similarity scores. The weighted mean has the formula shown in Equation B-3, where $x_1...x_n$ are the observations and $w_1...w_n$ are the weights.

$$\bar{x} = \frac{w_1 x_1 + w_2 x_2 + ... + w_n x_n}{w_1 + w_2 + ... + w_n}$$

Equation B-3. Weighted mean

A simple implementation of this formula that takes a list of values and weights is given here:

```
def weightedmean(x,w):
  num=sum([x[i]*w[i] for i in range(len(w))])
  den=sum([w[i] for i in range(len(w))])

  return num/den
```

In Chapter 2, weighted means are used to predict how much you'll enjoy a movie. This is done by calculating an average rating from other people, weighted by how similar their tastes are to yours. In Chapter 8, weighted means are used to predict prices.

Tanimoto Coefficient

The *Tanimoto coefficient* is a measure of the similarity of two sets. It is used in this book to calculate how similar two items are based on lists of properties. If you have two sets, A and B, where:

A = [shirt, shoes, pants, socks]
B = [shirt, skirt, shoes]

Then the intersection (overlapping) set, which I'll call C, is [shirt, shoes]. The Tanimoto coefficient is shown in Equation B-4, where N_a is the number of items in A, N_b is the number of items in B, and N_c is the number of items in C, the intersection. In this case the Tanimoto coefficient is $2/(4+3-2) = 2/5 = 0.4$.

$$T = \frac{N_c}{(N_a + N_b - N_c)}$$

Equation B-4. Tanimoto coefficient

Here is a simple function that takes two lists and calculates the Tanimoto coefficient:

```
def tanimoto(a,b):
  c=[v for v in a if v in b]
  return float(len(c))/(len(a)+len(b)-len(c))
```

The Tanimoto coefficient is used in Chapter 3 to calculate similarities between people for clustering.

Conditional Probability

Probability is a way of measuring how likely something is to occur. It is usually written as $Pr(A) = x$, where A is an event. For example, we might say that there's a 20 percent chance of rain today, which would be written as $Pr(rain) = 0.2$.

If we were to note that it's already cloudy right now, then we might conclude there's a higher chance of rain later today. This is called *conditional probability*, which is the chance of A given that we know B. This is written as $Pr(A \mid B)$, so in this case, it's $Pr(rain \mid cloudy)$.

The formula for conditional probability is the probability of both events happening divided by the chance of the given condition, as shown in Equation B-5.

$$Pr(A|B) = \frac{Pr(A \cap B)}{Pr(B)}$$

Equation B-5. Conditional probability

So if 10 percent of the time it's cloudy in the morning and rains later, and 25 percent of the time it's cloudy in the morning, then $Pr(rain \mid cloudy) = 0.1/0.25 = 0.4$.

Since this is just a simple division, no function is given here. Conditional probability is used in Chapter 6 for document filtering.

Gini Impurity

Gini impurity is a measure of how impure a set is. If you have a set of items, such as [A, A, B, B, B, C], then Gini impurity tells you the probability that you would be wrong if you picked one item and randomly guessed its label. If the set were all As, you would always guess A and never be wrong, so the set would be totally pure.

Equation B-6 shows the formula for Gini impurity.

$$I_G(i) = 1 - \sum_{j=1}^{m} f(i,j)^2 = \sum_{j \neq k} f(i,j)f(i,k)$$

Equation B-6. Gini impurity

This function takes a list of items and calculates the Gini impurity:

```
def giniimpurity(l):
  total=len(l)
  counts={}
  for item in l:
    counts.setdefault(item,0)
    counts[item]+=1

  imp=0
  for j in l:
    f1=float(counts[j])/total
    for k in l:
      if j==k: continue
      f2=float(counts[k])/total
      imp+=f1*f2
  return imp
```

In Chapter 7, Gini impurity is used in decision tree modeling to determine if dividing a set makes it more pure.

Entropy

Entropy is another way to see how mixed a set is. It comes from information theory, and it measures the amount of disorder in a set. Loosely defined, entropy is how surprising a randomly selected item from the set is. If the entire set were As, you would never be surprised to see an A, so the entropy would be 0. The formula is shown in Equation B-7.

$$H(X) = \sum_{i=1}^{n} p(x_i) \log_2 \left(\frac{1}{p(x_i)} \right) = - \sum_{i=1}^{n} p(x_i) \log_2 p(x_i)$$

Equation B-7. Entropy

This function takes a list of items and calculates the entropy:

```
def entropy(l):
  from math import log
  log2=lambda x:log(x)/log(2)

  total=len(l)
  counts={}
  for item in l:
    counts.setdefault(item,0)
    counts[item]+=1

  ent=0
  for i in counts:
    p=float(counts[i])/total
    ent-=p*log2(p)
  return ent
```

In Chapter 7, Entropy is used in decision tree modeling to determine if dividing a set reduces the amount of disorder.

Variance

Variance measures how much a list of numbers varies from the mean (average) value. It is frequently used in statistics to measure how large the differences are in a set of numbers. It is calculated by averaging the squared difference of every number from the mean, as shown by the formula in Equation B-8.

$$\sigma^2 = \frac{1}{N} \sum_{i=1}^{N} (x_i - \bar{x})^2$$

Equation B-8. Variance

This is a simple function to implement:

```
def variance(vals):
  mean=float(sum(vals))/len(vals)
  s=sum([(v-mean)**2 for v in vals])
  return s/len(vals)
```

In Chapter 7, variance is used in regression tree modeling to determine how to best divide a set to make the subsets more tightly distributed.

Gaussian Function

The *Gaussian function* is the probability density function of the normal curve. It is used in this book as a weighting function for weighted k-nearest neighbors, since it starts high and falls off quickly but never reaches 0.

The formula for a Gaussian with a variance of σ is shown in Equation B-9.

$$\frac{1}{\sigma\sqrt{2\pi}} \exp\left(-\frac{(x-\mu)^2}{2\sigma^2}\right)$$

Equation B-9. Gaussian function

This can be implemented as a two-line function directly translating the formula:

```
import math
def gaussian(dist,sigma=10.0):
  exp=math.e**(-dist**2/(2*sigma**2))
  return (1/(sigma*(2*math.pi)**.5))*exp
```

In Chapter 8, the Gaussian function is given as a possible weighting function for building a numerical predictor.

Dot-Products

The *dot-product* is a method of multiplying two vectors. If you have two vectors, a = $(a_1, a_2, a_3, ...)$ and b = $(b_1, b_2, b_3, ...)$, then the dot-product is defined as shown in Equation B-10.

$$\mathbf{a} \bullet \mathbf{b} = \sum_{i=1}^{n} a_i b_i = a_1 b_1 + a_2 b_2 + ... + a_n b_n$$

Equation B-10. Dot-product with components

Dot-product is easily implemented with this function:

```
def dotproduct(a,b):
  return sum([a[i]*b[i] for i in range(len(a))])
```

If θ is the angle between the two vectors, then the dot-product can also be defined as shown in Equation B-11.

$$\mathbf{a} \bullet \mathbf{b} = |\mathbf{a}||\mathbf{b}|\cos\theta$$

Equation B-11. Dot-product with angle

This means that you can use the dot-product to calculate the angle between two vectors:

```
from math import acos

# Calculates the size of a vector
def veclength(a):
  return sum([a[i] for i in range(len(a))])**.5

# Calculates the angle between two vectors
def angle(a,b):
  dp=dotproduct(a,b)
  la=veclength(a)
  lb=veclength(b)
  costheta=dp/(la*lb)
  return acos(costheta)
```

Dot-products are used in Chapter 9 to calculate vector angles from classifying items.

Index

We'd like to hear your suggestions for improving our indexes. Send email to *index@oreilly.com*.

U

uneven distributions, 183–188
    graphing probabilities, 185
    probability density, estimating, 184
Universal Feed Parser, 31, 134, 309
unsupervised learning, 30
unsupervised learning techniques, 296–302
unsupervised techniques, 226
update rules, 303
urllib2, 56, 102
Usenet, 117
user-based collaborative filtering, 23
user-based efficiency, 28
user-based filtering
    versus item-based filtering, 27

V

variance, 321
    code, 321
varying assumed probabilities, 140
vector angles, calculating, 322
vectors, 203
vertical search engine, 101
virtual features, 141

W

weighted average, 175, 293
weighted mean, 318
    code, 318
weighted neighbors, 172–176
    bell curve, 174
    Gaussian function, 174
    inverse function, 172
    subtraction function, 173
    weighted kNN, 175

weighted scores, 15
weights matrix, 235
Wikipedia, 2, 56
word distance, 65, 68
word frequency, 64, 66
    bias, 84
word separation, 84
word usage patterns, 226
word vectors, 30–33
    clustering blogs based on word
        frequencies, 30
    counting words in feed, 31–33
wordlocation table, 63, 64
words commonly used together, 40

X

XML documents, parser, 310
xml.dom, 102

Y

Yahoo! application key, 207
Yahoo! Finance, 53, 244
Yahoo! Groups, 117
Yahoo! Maps, 207
yes/no questions, 206

Z

Zebo, 44
    scraping results, 45
    web site, 45
Zillow API, 159–161
zillow.py
    getaddressdata function, 159
    getpricelist function, 160

About the Author

Toby Segaran is a director of software development at Genstruct, a computational biology company, where he designs algorithms and applies data-mining techniques to help understand drug mechanisms. He also works with other companies and open source projects to help them analyze and find value in their collected datasets. In addition, he has built several free web applications including the popular tasktoy and Lazybase. He enjoys snowboarding and wine tasting. His blog is located at *blog.kiwitobes.com*. He lives in San Francisco.

Colophon

The animals on the cover of *Programming Collective Intelligence* are King penguins (*Aptenodytes patagonicus*). Although named for the Patagonia region, King Penguins no longer breed in South America; the last colony there was wiped out by 19th-century sealers. Today, these penguins are found on sub-Antarctic islands such as Prince Edward, Crozet, Macquarie, and Falkland Islands. They live on beaches and flat glacial lands near the sea. King penguins are extremely social birds; they breed in colonies of as many as 10,000 and raise their young in crèches.

Standing 30 inches tall and weighing up to 30 pounds, the King is one of the largest types of penguin—second only to its close relative the Emperor penguin. Apart from size, the major identifying feature of the King penguin is the bright orange patches on its head that extend down to its silvery breast plumage. These penguins have a sleek body frame and can run on land, instead of hopping like Emperor penguins. They are well adapted to the sea, eating a diet of fish and squid, and can dive down 700 feet, far deeper than most other penguins go. Because males and females are similar in size and appearance, they are distinguished by behavioral clues such as mating rituals.

King penguins do not build nests; instead, they tuck their single egg under their bellies and rest it on their feet. No other bird has a longer breeding cycle than these penguins, who breed twice every three years and fledge a single chick. The chicks are round, brown, and so fluffy that early explorers thought they were an entirely different species of penguin, calling them "woolly penguins." With a world population of two million breeding pairs, King penguins are not a threatened species, and the World Conservation Union has assigned them to the Least Concern category.

The cover image is from J. G. Wood's *Animate Creation*. The cover font is Adobe ITC Garamond. The text font is Linotype Birka; the heading font is Adobe Myriad Condensed; and the code font is LucasFont's TheSans Mono Condensed.

Related Titles from O'Reilly

Web Authoring and Design

ActionScript 3.0 Cookbook

Ajax Hacks

Ambient Findability

Creating Web Sites: The Missing Manual

CSS Cookbook, *2nd Edition*

CSS Pocket Reference, *2nd Edition*

CSS: The Definitive Guide, *3rd Edition*

CSS: The Missing Manual

Dreamweaver 8: Design and Construction

Dreamweaver 8: The Missing Manual

Dynamic HTML: The Definitive Reference, *3rd Edition*

Essential ActionScript 2.0

Flash 8: Projects for Learning Animation and Interactivity

Flash 8: The Missing Manual

Flash Hacks

Head First HTML with CSS & XHTML

Head Rush Ajax

HTML & XHTML: The Definitive Guide, *6th Edition*

HTML & XHTML Pocket Reference, *3rd Edition*

Information Architecture for the World Wide Web, *3rd Edition*

Information Dashboard Design

JavaScript: The Definitive Guide, *5th Edition*

Learning JavaScript

Learning Web Design, *2nd Edition*

PHP Hacks

Programming Flash Communication Server

Web Design in a Nutshell, *3rd Edition*

Web Site Measurement Hacks

O'REILLY®

The O'Reilly Advantage

Stay Current and Save Money